Victor Chevalley de Rivaz

Round the Table

Notes on Cookery and plain Recipes, With a Selection of Bills of Fare for Every Month

Victor Chevalley de Rivaz

Round the Table

Notes on Cookery and plain Recipes, With a Selection of Bills of Fare for Every Month

ISBN/EAN: 9783744789530

Printed in Europe, USA, Canada, Australia, Japan

Cover: Foto ©Andreas Hilbeck / pixelio.de

More available books at **www.hansebooks.com**

NOTES ON COOKERY

AND

PLAIN RECIPES,

WITH A

SELECTION OF BILLS OF FARE FOR EVERY MONTH.

BY

"THE G. G."

PHILADELPHIA:
J. B. LIPPINCOTT AND CO.
1876.

PREFACE.

WITHOUT claiming for this little book the merit of being a complete treatise on Cookery, I yet hope that in it the cardinal principles of the art are plainly set forth. All the recipes are derived from experience, and will be found on trial to be practical: they are in daily use in my own kitchen: and the Bills of Fare appended have also borne the test of actual experiment at my table.

Some of these papers have appeared during the last few years in the form of articles in the *Queen* newspaper, and the favour accorded to them by the readers of that journal has induced me to publish them in a collected form, with such emendations and additions as later experience has suggested to

THE G. C.

CONTENTS.

1. TABLE TALK . . . . *page* 1
2. STEPS IN COOKERY 17
3. GARNISHING 21
4. STOCK 25
5. ON SOME ANCIENT AND MODERN SOUPS . . . 30
6. BROTHS FOR THE SICK 45
7. ON A PINCH OF FLOUR 49
8. ON NAMES 53
9. ON SOME ANCIENT FOOD 62
10. FRYING 72
11. BATTER 78
12. BOILING MEAT 90
13. ON A TIN OF BEEF 95
14. MUTTON CUTLETS 99
15. EPIGRAMS 104
16. COLD MUTTON 107
17. ON PAPER CASES 116
18. STEAKS AND A PIE 121
19. HOW TO TRUSS FOWLS 126

20. How to Bone Fowls . . . . *page*	133
21. How to Cut up Fowls	136
22. Turkey	142
23. Roasting	147
24. Aspic Jelly	155
25. Vegetables	161
26. Dried Beans	205
27. Salads	210
28. Farinaceous Food	230
29. Eggs	244
30. Cooking Cheese	254
31. Simple Sweets	258
32. On a Scottish Custom	271
Bills of Fare	275
Index	289

ROUND THE TABLE.

TABLE TALK.

"He who asks his friends to dine, and gives no personal attention to the arrangements of the dinner, is unworthy of having any friends."

"If you ask a man to dinner you are responsible for his happiness during the whole time that he remains under your roof."

These wise words of the author of "La Physiologie du Goût" ought to be ever present to the mind of every dinner-giver who has any pretension to good taste; and although matters of taste may be an open question, there are some main principles applicable to every action of life, and these may not be disregarded with impunity.

The laws of taste are frequently outraged in the matter of dinner-giving. People, who on four days out of the seven dine off a joint and potatoes—when they have friends to dinner—with the help of the confectioner and the traditional greengrocer—will produce a meretricious burlesque of the dinner which his Grace the Duke of Daintyshire—who keeps a French cook and a *maître d'hôtel*—has every day set before him. They hire some huge and vulgar piece of electro-plate, stuff it with flowers—often artificial—and place it in the middle of the table, where it effectually prevents one half of the guests from seeing the other half; then they place before each guest an array of wine-glasses, and as many knives, forks, and spoons, as can be crammed on the table. It is also, unhappily, the custom to invite at one time as many friends as is possible, and the consequence generally is that—as at a certain entertainment—

> Où chacun, malgré soi, l'un sur l'autre porté,
> Faisait un tour à gauche, et mangeait de côté—

the unfortunate guest, if he eat at all, must do so sideways, and in such an uncomfortable position that the best of food cannot compensate him for the trouble he endures to get at it.

Dr. Johnson used to say, that there were many things worth seeing in the world, but very few worth going to see. So do I believe, that numerous as may be the things good to eat, there are none worth the sacrifice of going to the conventional dinner party.

In a general way, in London, hosts and guests, men and women, old and young, are, I think, agreed that a dinner party is a terrible bore. It is a kind of duty imposed upon people, to ask their friends to dinner two or three times a-year, and to attend similar entertainments themselves; but pleasure is a thing totally unconnected with a party of this description. This is a great evil, for, as Savarin has it, "I pray you remember that the pleasures of a well-ordered table are, of all the enjoyments of this life, the most durable, for they recur every day, and are, in fact, life itself, for we cannot keep alive without eating."

Admitting that we are capable of the feelings of friendship and love to our neighbours, what greater mark can we give our friends of our regard for them than by asking them to come and eat with us; and is it not our duty, when they do come, to procure for them the greatest amount of enjoyment in our power? That this is not done is from no other reason than from want of taste.

Shams are the bane of everything; avoid them, and you will have made a great stride towards good taste. Be content to be what you are, and do not attempt to appear otherwise. Dine well yourself, according to your means, and do not, because you are alone or *en famille*, dispense with any of the little ceremonies of the dinner table. Nothing spoils servants so much: for if you are well served every day, when you have friends to dinner, the servants waiting at table have not to step out of their everyday groove. Except on such occasions as a dance or the like do not hire waiters; it is a slight to your own servants, and effectually prevents them from ever improving in their business, for they know that if you have half a dozen people to dine you will hire a waiter. Ten is the very largest number of *friends* that should assemble at dinner, and two women, or one man or boy with a woman, are quite enough to wait, if they know their business.

Official dinners, or *diners de cérémonie*, are another thing, and of these I do not wish to speak.

The ornamentation or decoration of the dinner table is a matter of the last importance, which can seldom be left to the servants; it should be the special business of the lady of the house. The best ornament for the centre of the table is one of those glass stands or baskets, in which flowers and foliage are disposed on a foundation of clay and sand; or you may have a group of plants in a basket, the mould being neatly covered with moss; the latter method will be found cheaper, for the plants, if well attended to, will last a long time. In the disposition of this centre piece care must be taken that it does not occupy too much space, nor should it be too high, and flowers having a very strong perfume should not be used. If the size of the table will allow, a couple of smaller baskets may be added. Very beautiful designs and charming patterns can be produced, at little expense, by anyone having a garden, or even a small town conservatory, if the right flowers are cultivated in it. Flowers are not always a necessity, however, for very pretty effects can be produced with leaves alone. I once saw a stand of this sort set out entirely with leaves of vegetables, and very pretty it looked.

Where there is neither garden nor conservatory to get flowers from, a few shillings, judiciously expended upon some of the commonest flowers and leaves in Coventgarden, will enable those who choose to take the trouble, to produce a very creditable ornament; but, in any case, do not send to a florist to have your flower-stand decked out: you will spend a great deal more money, and have a thing not half so tasteful as if you had done it yourself, besides losing the pleasure of arranging the flowers, which is at all times a most agreeable occupation.

The next thing to be attended to is to give each guest ample space to sit at the table and eat his dinner in comfort. Everything put on the table should be scrupulously clean, and nothing should be placed upon it which is not wanted. Have no more glasses than will be required placed before each guest. It is now the fashion to have a salt cellar to each person, and a very good fashion it is; for at a well-appointed table every one should have within his reach—or be supplied with—everything that may be required, without having to ask or to wait for it. In France they have usually a water bottle, and a bottle or decanter of vin ordinaire, to every guest, or every second guest.

In what are called dinners *à la Russe* the dessert is placed on the table *ab initio*. This is not a good feature of that system—there should be on the table ornaments only, but no other eatables than those under discussion. I question the pleasure of eating salmon with a dish of candied fruit staring you in the face. Then, the cloth is not removed for dessert; and no dessert can look so well as one which is put on a well-kept mahogany table, in which it is reflected almost as a landscape on a calm river—the white tablecloth is too cold looking, and the operation of shaving it with a silver trowel, to remove stray bits of bread which have not been kept off by the side cloths or slips, is absurd. It is much better to remove the cloth bodily, the flowers, &c., can then be put back on the table quickly enough. It is the fashion, nevertheless, not to remove the tablecloth—a fashion no doubt invented by someone who had a deal top to his dining table.

At a dinner served à la Russe the dessert must invariably be spoilt before it is eaten. Delicate fruit, such as grapes, strawberries, &c., cannot stand being exposed to the heat of the dining-room and the fumes of soups, fish, entrées, and roast meats, without being materially deteriorated.

The temperature of the dining-room is one of the most important things to be attended to. In winter, unless the room be very large indeed, there should be no fire in the dining-room if more than two or three people are going to dine. Let the room be thoroughly warmed beforehand, and then let the fire go out. If you have a fire burning during dinner, some of your guests must of necessity be too hot, firescreens notwithstanding; and nothing is more uncomfortable and unwholesome than being too warm during dinner. Of course, if your dining-room is so large that the dinner-table can be set well away from the fire, or if the weather is particularly cold, have a fire by all means. Nevertheless, I think a fire is out of place: it is a cheerful thing to behold in a sitting-room, but at dinner people have more cheerful things to look at. The best way for those who do not mind the expense, is to have the dining-room warmed with hot-water pipes; and while they are about it, they should have ventilators so placed as to carry away the vitiated air, and keep the room, as much as possible, at the same temperature. At a certain season of the year, it is impossible in this country, not to dine by daylight; unless at the excessively late hour affected by ultra-fashionables. This is a great misfortune, for a dinner-table never looks so well as by candlelight; and it is therefore better, so long as the dinner cannot be concluded by daylight, to close the shutters and light up the dining-room beforehand, instead of doing so in the middle of dinner.

The very best way of lighting a dining-room is to have the apparatus called a sunlight fitted in the ceiling, and this has also the advantage of being a most efficient ventilator. In any other form—ventilate how you will—gas is very unpleasant in a room.

If the sunlight is not practicable, the next best thing is a chandelier, so constructed as to hold three or four moderator lamps; or a chandelier with wax candles may be used; but on no account should any lamp or candles be put upon the dinner-table itself. If you have handsome plate, or if the size of the room requires more light, candles or lamps may be placed upon the sideboard. Some people object to moderator lamps as being liable to get out of order, and "come to grief" in various ways at inconvenient times; but these shortcomings are not, in the majority of cases, the fault of the lamp.

The management of these lamps—of all things—is one of the most difficult to get servants to attend to carefully.

If you are not so fortunate as to possess a domestic capable of keeping the lamps in order, do it yourself; and, if you will bear in mind the following short directions, you will never have any *contretemps* in the matter of lamps. Fill up the lamp every day and *neatly* trim the wick—a jagged wick never gives a good light. When not in use, keep the lamp covered up, and never let more than two or three days go by without lighting it even for a short time.

When the lamp is lighted, the wick should be a good half inch above the metal sheath which incloses it, and the flame should be regulated by raising or lowering the chimney. If you only turn up a small portion of the wick, although you get a good light at first, the metal sheath soon gets very hot, the lamp begins to smoke, and the light to diminish; and moreover the oil is consumed much quicker. Lastly, you should send your lamps to a "*lampiste*" once a year, to be cleaned thoroughly; and I hardly need say that you should buy good lamps, and not trumpery cheap things, which are always dearest in the end.

Many people make their dining-room a sort of morning sitting-room, and, as a natural consequence, it gets filled with books, desks, workboxes, and other odds and ends, which are in the way and out of place in a dining-room. Few houses do not contain, besides the drawing-room and dining-room, a third room, which can be used to sit in during the morning. The dining-room should be a sort of temple dedicated to GASTEREA, the tenth muse (according to Brillat-Savarin), and no furniture nor anything should be placed in it, but what is requisite for the daily celebration of her mysteries.

An oval table appears to me the most sociable one at which to sit down to dine; and although it is against all precedent, I believe, I would have the host and hostess sit at the two sides instead of at the two ends of it. By this arrangement they would be nearer to their guests, and better able to enjoy their society and to entertain them. Of the chairs, I will only say, that no pains should be spared to have the most comfortable to sit upon that can be made, and each chair should have a stool or hassock placed under it for ladies, or for such as may require it.

The table linen should be got up by all the resources at the command of the laundress; but the table-cloth only may be lightly starched; starching napkins, as some do, although it allows of their being folded up more elaborately, renders the use of them disagreeable, if not impossible; and here let me mention, that whenever civilised people eat—be it dinner, breakfast, luncheon, or supper—they should have napkins. This point, although often disregarded, is of some importance.

The table-cloth should not overlap the table too much, for it would otherwise be in the way and would interfere with the guests when sitting down to dinner. Under the table-cloth there should be a piece of thick green baize, the exact size of the table. When carving is to take place on the table, a large napkin should be put before the carver, to be removed in case of accidents; and it is also advisable to have a supply of napkins at hand, to throw a veil upon any misadventure happening to the purity of the cloth during dinner. If the table is a square or long one, pieces of cloth (called slips) are laid along the two sides—an arrangement I dislike; the table looks much better when it presents an unbroken surface of white damask.

One of the greatest elements of success in a dinner party is the uniform harmony which should exist in all the *mise en scène*, so to speak, of the dinner. The plate, the dinner and dessert service, the glass, &c., go a great way towards making the dinner table look pretty and inviting; and those who aspire to a reputation for good taste, have ample scope to attain it in selecting these things. Electro-plate is a sham which we must put up with, but I would have all the plate of the same kind and pattern : if you cannot have all silver, have all electro-plate, but not half and half. In selecting the china and glass have an eye to form first, and to colour and ornament afterwards. The most fashionable dinner services are of plain white, with a small fillet of gold and the arms or the crest and motto of the owner painted on the flat rim of the plates and dishes. The glass may be also quite plain, but engraved with the same heraldic device.

Dessert services made entirely of glass are sometimes used, and they have a very pretty effect. But I will not enlarge farther upon this subject, beyond pointing out the great mistake of having fine services of china and glass, to be used *only* when " company is coming," as servants say. The man of taste should have pretty and handsome things for his own sake, as well as for that of his friends. Besides, if the servants are accustomed to handle trumpery china and glass every day, they get into a careless habit, and when the fine services are put forth—accompanied with great admonitions to be careful—the servants become nervous : smashes follow as a matter of course, so that, in the end the number of breakages is perhaps greater than if the fine things were in every-day use.

On the same principle, people should have good bread every day for their dinner; and not provide, when they have friends, those conventional spheroids of dough which have the double disadvantage of being unpleasant to eat and difficult to digest. A neat piece of good bread is much better in all respects; but, if you will have *des petits pains,* get them at a French baker's, and you will have something more presentable and eatable than the conventionalities referred to.

The use of the mats, with which some people strew their dinner table, is to be deprecated. The thick green baize under the table-cloth should protect the table from the heat of the dishes. Mats, besides being unseemly, are very apt to make the dish unsteady, to the annoyance of the carver. Nor should a dish ever be placed upon the table with the cover on. Some people possess most elaborate besilvered dish covers, but these simply spoil the appearance of the table, besides often sending a puff of fast condensing vapour into the next person's face when they are taken off.

I believe the ancient English custom of placing the fish on the table, to wait till the soup is served and eaten, still obtains pretty extensively. What a mistake this is I need not point out. In the first place, the soup should never be put upon the table at all, but should be served by a servant from the sideboard, and handed round to the guests in plates. This is the practice at all the dinners, Russian or not, of people who do things as they ought to be done. Secondly, can any fish be otherwise than spoiled by standing ten or fifteen minutes on the table before it is eaten?

But before I go farther, I would impress upon all never to omit a delicate attention, which is indispensable to the enjoyment of a good dinner. I mean the bill of fare; the *menu* of the feast. Those who do things regardless of expense have *a menu* printed in most elaborate style—one for each guest; but a written *menu* will do quite as well, if the former method be thought too ostentatious. At any rate, let the guests know at the beginning of dinner what they are going to have to eat.

When by the force of circumstance it happens that a score or more people assemble at the same table to dine, the least disagreeable way of getting through the ceremony is to serve the dinner à la Russe; but even in this case I would spare the dessert, and only put it on the table when it is wanted.

For dinners properly so called, where people meet to enjoy their food and the society of their friends, the style called by the French *demi-Russe* is the best mode of serving. It is a compromise between the entire Russian, and the old English fashion of placing every dish upon the table. I will describe the proceeding, giving at the same time a sort of skeleton bill of fare for a dinner of ten people.

The soup having been handed round and disposed of, two dishes of fish are placed upon the table and helped by the host and hostess. Upon the removal of the fish four *entrées*, judiciously selected, and each a complete dish in itself, are handed round, and when the consumption of these is drawing to an end, two *relevés* or *pièces de résistance* appear on the table, each being likewise a complete dish in itself. These give place to a couple of roasts of poultry or game, and then two or more *entremets de légumes* (not vegetables à l'Anglaise) should be served.

A well-made salad should always be handed round with roasts of all kinds, except game. Neither does a salad go badly with plain boiled or fried fish.

The French counterchange this order of things: they would serve the *pièces de résistance* after the soup, then the fish, then the *entrées*, &c.; this is according to the teaching of Brillat-Savarin, who says, that the order of food should be from the most substantial to the lightest, and that of drinks from the lightest to the strongest.

If game and poultry do not figure in the *menu*, one of the *pièces de résistance* should be a roast, and the *entremets de légumes* should be served with it, or they may form part of the *second service*. In this also, in the *demi-Russe* fashion, the two principal dishes are put upon the table and the rest handed round. Of *entremets sucrés* there should be at least four, two hot and two cold, and one or both of these latter should be iced.

Then comes the cheese question. I cannot but think it a most incongruous proceeding for people, after having eaten sweets of various kinds—may be an ice pudding— to discuss a piece of ripe Stilton or strong double Gloucester. Cheese, I hold, should be eaten *before* the *entremets sucrés* or sweets, and then it should be eaten in the form of *ramequins* or a *fondue* ; or, if you will have cheese *au naturel*, have some Parmesan, Brie, Gruyère, cream-cheese, &c. I mean no disparagement to Stilton, Gloucester, Cheddar, &c., but they are not after-dinner cheeses, and the mode of serving some of them which certain people affect—viz., putting half a cheese of ever so many pounds weight on the table, is as ridiculous as it is offensive. The cheese should not be put upon the table at all, but should be handed round, cut in very thin slices, if it is Parmesan or Gruyère. The *raison d'être* of the English custom of eating cheese after sweets, lies in the now declining fashion of wine-drinking after dinner: in France cheese is always served at dessert.

In hot weather it is indispensable that all the drinkables should be cooled and even moderately iced, but this should be done, except in the case of water, by external application. Putting a lump of ice in a wine-glass may help to disguise bad sherry, but it is always an objectionable practice.

A variety of wines is no doubt desirable in a good

dinner, but before you attempt variety, consider whether your purse can stand the expense of obtaining dry sherry, sound claret, first-rate champagne, clean hock, and good port wine. In the matter of wine no mediocrity is tolerable; small beer or even water is infinitely preferable to bad wine. When people have friends to dinner they *will* have champagne, and so long as it has the appearance of that sparkling beverage, and can be had cheap enough, they are satisfied.

A white wine with soup, fish, and sweets, and a red wine with meats and made dishes, are all that are wanted, if they be good wines, in the best of dinners. Good dry sherry and sound claret can be got at no greater expense than the half a dozen deleterious compounds of gooseberry which some give to their friends under the names of champagne, hock, Sauterne, &c., &c.

A very big book might be written upon this subject, for drinking is one of the exclusive attributes of man, who alone, it is said, can drink when he is not thirsty,—provided, of course, no Act of Parliament makes it penal to do so. The moral of such a book, however, can be stated in very few words. In the choice of your drinks, more than in anything else, avoid shams.

The selection and disposition of the dessert is one of the most difficult things in the arrangement of a dinner. As I have said before, unless people are rich enough to have the services of a good *maître d'hôtel*, it is the lady of the house who should undertake all that part of the dinner. Each dish, fruit especially, should, with the help of flowers and leaves, be made into an elegant ornament. Fern leaves are very well adapted for this purpose, but when practicable it is more artistic to use the leaves of the fruit which compose each dish. Artificial leaves should never be employed.

No fruits, confectionery, &c., should appear on the table but such as are good to eat, and although there is no limit to the number of dishes which go to form a dessert, it is always better to have less rather than to put on the table such fruit as shaddock for instance. Candied fruit and other many-coloured productions of the confectioner are to be avoided, unless you get the very best that the best shops sell. A dish of fruit, made up into a sort of salad with wine or liqueurs and sugar, is a very acceptable addition to all desserts. A dish of dry biscuits, and one of olives should never be omitted, but the latter should be served in water, and not with the liquor they were preserved in.

The position each dish is to occupy on the table ought to be planned carefully beforehand, with a view not only to effect, but also to the accessibility of each dish by the company; and to that end some of the dishes should be doubled when it is practicable.

The dessert never ought to be placed on the sideboard; it should be kept ready prepared, until wanted, in an adjoining room, or in the pantry, and, in the case of delicate fruit, in the cellar or some cool place, when the weather is hot. This is the plan usually adopted in France, and I need hardly point out its advantages.

The important business of the dinner being concluded; people at dessert can devote themselves more entirely to conversation; therefore it is a bad plan to keep the servants in the room at that concluding stage of the feast.

At dessert it is imperative that the wines should be good, and port wine, which is generally considered *de rigueur* at all English tables, is every year becoming more difficult to obtain at all fit to drink, except at very high prices. Burgundy is no bad substitute for it; but if your means do not allow of your having two or three sorts of wine at dessert, be not ashamed to produce only *one* kind of wine, and that one good. All your friends, whose good opinion is worth anything, will thank and respect you for this departure from the usual routine.

The water in the finger glasses is sometimes coloured with some harmless ingredient, such as cochineal. I am doubtful, however, about recommending this; but I would always use water perfumed with a few drops of rose water or lavender water.

Coffee, bright as well decanted wine, is the proper conclusion of every dinner. It should be served in the dining-room, at any rate to the gentlemen, and liqueurs, one of which should be first-rate cognac, ought to be handed round with it.

The attendance or waiting at table is of the greatest importance. A servant thoroughly well up in dinner-drill is indeed a *rara avis*. He should combine the most imperturbable *sang froid* with the greatest activity, and the only way to possess and keep up these qualities, is by carefully studied method. Too many servants, even if well up to their work, create a bustle by their very presence. For a dinner of ten people two are quite enough to be in the room; a third one may be helping outside, but no farther than the dining-room door, and in fact it is better to have only one servant in the room if the second one is not well drilled, for he or she would only be in the way and create confusion. When there are two, each should attend to a certain part of the work arranged previously, or the guests should be apportioned between the two. If the servants know their work well, nobody ought ever to have occasion to ask for anything —the great aim of a good servant should be to watch with tender solicitude each guest allotted to him or to her, and to anticipate his wants or wishes.

A servant who knows the familiar friends of the master and all their peculiarities and fancies connected with the dinner table, is an invaluable treasure which cannot be too highly appreciated. Those who wish to do their duty by the friends they ask to dinner ought to spare no pains to secure and train up such a servant; and, degenerate as some people may think the present breed of domestics, there are yet as good fish in the sea as ever came out of it. Servants will take an interest in their work, if they see the master and mistress do the same instead of expecting them to do exactly as they wish by mere intuition. Let employers consider the number of good qualities which are requisite to make even a tolerable servant, and 'et them be very thankful that there are not more bad ones, nay, that there are any good ones at all.

As much care is necessary in selecting and assorting guests as is requisite for arranging the dinner they are asked to eat; but, although this is entirely a matter of taste and feeling, I cannot help pointing out that people of an argumentative turn of mind, people who will " argufy" *à propos de bottes* if needs be, until they are black in the face, should never be asked to dinner. Arguing is all very well in its proper place and season, but at dinner it makes the best of sauces lose their taste, and turns the wines sour.

STEPS IN COOKERY.

The great fault of English cooks is that they are not clean at their work. The only excuse to be made for them is, that open ranges and coal fires are more calculated to produce dirt than are the *fourneaux* and charcoal fires used abroad, or even coal fires when burnt in a close range or kitchener. These improved appliances, however, are only within reach of the rich. The working man's wife—and even those in a higher grade of life, but who live in houses below £100 a year—must put up with open ranges such as they are; and this matter of cleanliness becomes more difficult for them, though none the less important. Dirt will mar the success of the simplest dish, and will make the production of any but the simplest impossible.

Without wishing to enter upon the various modes of cleaning kitchen utensils, I will merely observe that the best plan is to clean them, as far as possible, as soon as they have been used, and that, when I say "clean," I mean to make them absolutely free from dirt and grease. I will venture to say that, in a majority of the kitchens of our middle classes, the cooks would pronounce vessels "clean" which no amount of sand, soda, and soap could ever make fit for use, and yet, as a rule, English servants are not dirty, for see how bright the door plates and how white the door steps (no easy matter in a climate like this) are kept by them. That they do not keep their saucepans clean is purely a matter of habit, which, like most bad habits, is difficult to eradicate; but yet it is not an impossibility if mistresses will but insist upon the *batterie de cuisine* being kept in good order. "Cleanliness," says Gouffé, "is a word which should be graven in capital letters over the door of all kitchens, large or small."

When a young woman has been taught, not only how to clean a saucepan, but also how to know a clean saucepan from a dirty one—to know, in fact, what absolute cleanliness means—then, and then only, should she be permitted to enter upon the study of cookery; an art, or a science, as you please, than which there is none of more importance to mankind. Let those laugh who will, but what would become of us without cooks, bad even as they are?

The next thing to teach an apprentice is the preparation of the materials for cooking, viz., plucking and drawing poultry and game, skinning and drawing rabbits and hares, trimming joints, cutting up loins into cutlets, cleaning and scaling fish, &c., and lastly the trussing of poultry and game. *Pari passu* with the above should be taught the picking, washing, and cutting up of vegetables, from peeling a potato or shelling peas to "turning" carrots for ragoûts with fancy vegetable cutters. All these things appear simple enough, but, like everything else, to be well done they require great care; and there is a wrong and a dirty way of doing them, as well as a right and a clean way. My experience leads me to believe that the former more generally obtains in English cookery. Until a kitchen maid has learnt to prepare everything ready for cooking in a becoming and approved form, she should not be allowed to approach the kitchen range, except perhaps to learn how to light and manage the fire—an operation, by the way, which is by no means unimportant, and requires a certain amount of training and practice.

The first operation of cooking, to be performed by the

tyro, is to boil vegetables in water and salt; then to boil fish, and meat. Her instructor will be able to tell her whether the things to be boiled should be placed in hot or cold water in the first instance, and also when the salt is to be put in; but how much of it to use, and how long each thing should boil, are matters which the learner must find out by her own practice and observation. To have learnt to boil a potato or a trout to a nicety is already a great stride in the art of cookery.

Making stock will be the next step; and by degrees the preparation of soups and sauces should be taught. At this stage a cookery book, if it be a tolerably good one, becomes useful, and the composition of made dishes of meat, of poultry, of fish, and of vegetables can be learnt from it; but the making of these things creditably must be learnt by practice.

Frying, roasting, and broiling come next, and each of these constitutes a special art, which requires special instructions. What is common to all is the management of the fire, and this must be mastered first.

To learn how to do all these things well is the work of years, and even then the learner must have, in addition to her own aptitude and willingness, the good fortune to be under an instructor who knows how the work is properly to be done. In our days women turn cooks just as the fancy takes them, and that such find places is a sign of two things—the great dearth of properly trained cooks, and the inability of employers to distinguish between a cook and an impostor.

The preparation of sweet dishes is quite a separate branch of cookery to master, which requires special training and practice; cleanliness being here more than ever an indispensable condition to insure anything but unutterable failure. It is given to very few to be good cooks and at the same time pastrycooks and confectioners. In fact, what Brillat Savarin says of the roaster may be said of a maker of pastry; for, unless such an one have by nature a light and a cool hand, no amount of teaching and practice will enable her to make good pastry. Still there are plenty and enough of sweet dishes into the composition of which paste does not enter. These should be taught by degrees —from the simplest to the more complicated. But above all things the preliminary operations, such as whisking eggs, buttering moulds, &c., must be learnt perfectly.

Last of all comes the knowledge which constitutes the ethics of cookery, and this will gradually grow upon the cook who is fond of her calling and interested in it. If this be the case, she will lose no opportunity of watching better cooks than herself at work, and of seeing how they send up dinners, and of what these dinners consist. She will also make a collection of bills of fare, and last, but not least, she will study books on cookery—not mere strings of recipes, of which there are too many already, but such works as Gouffé (it has been translated), and a few others. Thus will she become able not only to cook, but also to compose a dinner.

The above is but an imperfect outline of the course of study required by one who would become a good cook. Nor can the scarcity of good cooks be wondered at, when we consider the endless knowledge which must be acquired before you can honestly call yourself a cook at all. In fact, a cook must be an artist in the broadest sense of the word.

GARNISHING.

The scientific branch of cookery comprises the devising of dishes and sauces. The artistic branch constitutes the art of garnishing, and this plays a most important part in the outcome of the kitchen, as, by means of it, dishes please the eye before they please the palate. First impressions go a great way, and when the one sense is captivated by an agreeable and inviting appearance, the dish must be bad indeed which fails to stand the more searching ordeal of taste. Besides, people who suffer from jaded appetites have a better chance of eating their dinner, when the dishes which are put before them are pleasant to the sight.

Art, however, is not a thing to be taught. You may show a man how to mix colours, but you cannot teach him how to use them. Neither will I pretend to teach the British cook how to garnish dishes. I will only attempt to explain that that which in cookery is meant by garnishing is not the traditional parsley of the British cook: and I will describe what cooks, properly so called, mean by garnishing; of what garnishes are made; and how the different materials are prepared for the purpose.

The combinations of these things are too infinite to allow of more than a very general exposition. They wholly depend upon the talent, skill, and taste of the operator. The one and great thing to avoid, as much as possible, is the using for purposes of garnishing, things which are not eatable.

"*Garniture,*" which is rendered into English by "garnish," may be defined as all that is added to the chief material which constitutes the dish. Thus tomato sauce, in a dish of cutlets, or fried potatoes round a steak are garnishes.

These things fall naturally under two great heads. The hot garnishes, which accompany every savoury dish, and the cold garnishes, which go with cold meats, salads, mayonnaises, &c.

Vegetables are the chief materials of hot garnishes. By judicious combinations they will produce very pretty effects of colour. To instance only a few: turnips, potatoes, Jerusalem artichokes, cauliflowers, celery, and vegetable marrows will give whites; carrots, tomatoes, beetroot, supply the reds; truffles and mushrooms the blacks; and then there are the endless shades of green given by French beans, peas, Brussels sprouts, cucumbers, asparagus, &c. To be so used, all such vegetables as will admit of it must be cut into uniform shapes with what are called vegetable-cutters, the successful use of which requires some practice. They may also be cut, with a knife, into the shape of a "quarter" of an orange, or again, into little oblong slabs a quarter of an inch thick, and one inch by three-quarters, with all the edges slightly chamfered. This way is very good for carrots, when the middle part begins to harden, and is not fit to eat. Some vegetables can be sliced, and pieces can then be stamped out of them. French beans should be cut into lozenges, or they may be cut in the shape of peas with a stamp. Cauliflowers should be picked out into little bunches the size of a penny at the top. Vegetables are usually cut before cooking, and each kind should be cooked separately. Great care is necessary to ensure that, when sent up to table, they are all "*cuits à point*" and hot.

Here is a simple example of purely vegetable garnish.

Suppose that a piece of beef be stewed according to art, and put in a dish on a tasteful and velvety gravy. Having all your vegetables ready cooked at hand, you proceed to place four little heaps of cauliflowers at equal distances from each other; then you flank each with carrot cut in slabs on one side, and French beans cut into lozenges on the other; and lastly you fill in the remaining spaces, *i.e.*, between the beans and the carrots, with potatoes cut to the shape and size of Spanish olives, and fried a very light colour in butter. I should here observe that, once cooked, these things should not be touched with the hand, but put into position by means of a larding needle and a teaspoon, or some other instrument. I may also state, for the benefit of those who look to economy before all things, that all this cutting and stamping out of vegetables need not cause the slightest waste. The trimmings of carrots, turnips, &c., should go into the stock pot, those of potatoes make mashed potatoes, and *purées* can be made with most, if not all, of the remnants. In fact, a *purée* composed of a combination of vegetables is no bad thing, either as a soup or as a garnish for cutlets, &c. For purposes of garnishing, potatoes are also mashed, and then shaped into various forms, and they are likewise made into croquets, and fried a golden colour, in which latter case eggs and spices should enter into their composition.

Bread sippets—which are used to garnish many dishes—should be invariably fried in butter. They ought to be cut out of stale bread, and should be of the same thickness and of uniform shape, which, with the help of paste cutters, can be varied *ad infinitum*.

Forcemeat, quenelles, tongue, eggs (hard boiled), olives, &c., are used in garnishing. Parsley should only be used in a fried form: a hot dish garnished with raw sprigs of parsley is ridiculous. The only cold things which may enter into the garnishes of hot dishes are lemons with some fish, and water cresses or garden cress with some kinds of game and poultry.

In the matter of the garnishing of cold dishes there is a wider scope for artistic feeling. Cold meats should always be ornamented with aspic jelly, and, instead of parsley, with the curled garden cress, which, while it resembles parsley closely, has the advantage of being eatable when raw. But it is in salads, mayonnaises, and the like that the artistic feeling of a cook can come out. I will describe the materials she has at hand for ornamentation. First is the aspic, which when well made should rival the finest topaz in brilliancy, and can be so shaded as to approach the deeper tint of the ruby. Then come the white and yolk of hard-boiled eggs, which are both used finely minced, but the former can yield any number of fanciful devices, which are thus arrived at. Several whites of egg are put into a tin previously slightly buttered, and then are made to set in a bain-marie; when turned out they will give you a slab of hard-boiled white of egg, out of which you may cut and stamp what you like. Beetroot will furnish similar devices in red, and so will tongue; olives (stoned), truffles, capers, anchovies, gherkins, lobster coral, &c., will give other colours and shapes. It will readily be seen that many very pretty combinations of many colours can be made with these things. A fair average taste and some patience are the chief requisites.

Flowers (cut out of raw turnips), crayfish, which are not to be eaten, designs wrought in flour and lard coloured in various ways, and such like matters which appertain to what is called grand cookery, belong to the category of shams, and cannot meet with the approval of any true artist.

STOCK.

Stock is to a cook what the medium or the water is to a painter in oils or in water colours. Without it any cooking is impossible, except roasting and broiling, and that much-to-be-deprecated English method of boiling food in water and salt alone.

The stock-pot is a familiar name to the British cook, and a standard article in cookery books. Pounds of meat and bones, cow-heels and calves' feet, and what not, are supposed to be required for the making of stock, and economical people naturally shrink from so expensive an item in the household expenditure; therefore it is that soup is looked upon in English households as an expensive luxury, whereas it is a necessity provided cheaply enough, when people understand how to make it.

Stock, properly so called, may be defined generally as a solution in water of the nutritive and sapid elements contained in meat and bones. Salt and spices added to it make it more savoury, and if to this you add the flavour of various vegetables, you have soup.

For the type of all stock making I would take the French POT AU FEU. A glazed earthen vessel is used in France to make it, and is best; but it can be made in the iron pots used in this country, or in a tinned copper vessel. The proceeding is this. Put a piece of silver side of fresh beef, 7lb. or 8lb. weight (tightly bound with string), and the bones sold with it, into a saucepan filled with cold water, so as completely to cover the meat. Put the saucepan by the side of the fire, and let the contents become gradually heated. As this takes place a scum will rise upon the surface, and this must be carefully removed as it rises. The clearness of the soup will depend upon all the scum being taken off, and upon the water not boiling until it is all removed. This done; have the following vegetables carefully cleaned and cut up in small pieces, which you put into the saucepan a few at a time— viz., a couple of onions, a clove of garlic (not a whole bulb), three or four carrots, three or four turnips, and three or four leeks (all according to size), one head of celery, one root of parsley and leaves, and a couple of tomatoes, either fresh or dried. Then put in, tied up in a piece of muslin, some thyme, marjoram, a bay leaf, a handful of whole pepper and allspice, some cloves, cinnamon, and mace. The proportions of these things cannot be given; the flavour of no one of them should predominate; and to attain this end taste and practice are the only means. You now put in salt *quant. suff.*, one teaspoonful of Worcester sauce, and two of mushroom catsup, the least bit of burnt onion, or some burnt sugar colouring; or, better still, a very small quantity of a French compound, called *Suc colorant*, which is an extract of vegetables, and a most invaluable ingredient to have in the kitchen for colouring soups, gravies, &c., for it imparts flavour as well as colour. I do not know where it can be bought in this country. I got my supply years ago from Paris, where it is cheap enough, a bottle, costing two francs, lasting quite one year. When the *pot au feu* is, so to speak, completed, it must be left to simmer slowly from three to four hours. Then, or before, if, by tasting, the soup is found sufficiently flavoured, the muslin bag must be taken out. As much soup as is wanted for the day is strained into a basin and left to cool, so that all the fat may be effectually removed. Then the liquor is warmed and served with maccaroni, bread sippets, or vegetables, &c., according to the kind of soup you wish to have.

The meat may be served up with tomato sauce, piquante sauce, gherkin sauce, Soubise sauce, &c., &c., as taste may suggest; the string being of course removed before serving. There are some who will say that such meat has no taste, to whom I would respectfully recommend tasting it before saying so. Others will say that it has no nutritious qualities, and to these I would point out that, if the soup be eaten first and the meat afterwards, quite as much nutriment will be derived from it as if the same piece of meat had been roasted, and assuredly a great deal more than if it had been converted into salt junk, as it is the custom in this country to do with the silver side of beef.

The addition of a piece of ham or bacon to the *pot au feu* is a decided improvement; and an ancient fowl, too tough to be eaten, even when boiled, can do good service therein.

The ham or bacon can also be put in in this wise—long pieces of it must be rolled in a mixture of powdered sweet herbs, spices, pepper and salt, and introduced into incisions made in the piece of meat, and passing through and through it. In this case the meat needs to be more carefully tied up.

What remains of the broth should be strained, and will be available for soup for two or three days.

To make any kind of stock the principle is the same as that for the *pot au feu*. Take, for example, the bones of a sirloin of beef and of a leg of mutton. These, broken into convenient pieces, are put into a saucepan, and then covered with water, with the addition of vegetables, salt, herbs and spices, as above, but not in a bag, and the whole is left to boil for four or five hours. The liquor is then strained, and, all the fat being removed, the stock thus obtained is used for the purposes of cooking. If soup is to be made out of it, it may be necessary to clarify it with white of egg, as indeed must be done with all soups, if you wish them to be perfectly clear. A better way, however, of clarifying soup is to put into it when cold some very small pieces of raw beef free from fat. Put it on the fire till it boils, then strain. Or you may use both beef and white of egg. Some employ pieces of raw liver for the same purpose; but, if too much of it is used, it is apt to impart a bad taste; besides, the beef adds to the goodness of the soup, at the same time that it clarifies it.

Into the stock-pot should go all the carcases of poultry and of game, if not high, that are at hand; but a better plan, if the supply of these things allow it, is to make separate stock of meat, of poultry, and of game.

When the supply of meat and poultry bones is not great, the addition of one or two pounds of shin of beef can be made to the stock-pot; this quantity of shin of beef, with the same quantity of bones, will make soup for two days for at least three or four people. The soup may be made all at once, or enough water for one day's supply being boiled with the meat, vegetables, &c., can be strained off when sufficiently flavoured, and the meat, &c., put away till next day, then boiled again with more water.

Another way of obtaining a supply of most excellent stock, purely of meat, is to put into the dripping pan, just before the joint which is roasting is done, from a glass to a pint of hot water, according to the size of the joint and the quantity of the dripping. When this has been put into a basin, and become quite cold, beneath it will be found a glassful or more of pure meat stock, which comes in very well to put into sauces, or to improve common stock. Some of this, put into stock, will also have the effect of clarifying it, nearly if not quite as well as any other method. Of course the stock obtained from a joint of beef, in the manner just described, will be better than that which a joint of mutton will yield; but still this latter is by no means to be despised. Great care must be taken in making stock or soup not to let the meat, bones, or vegetables be over-boiled. It is a mistake to suppose that the more these things are boiled the better the stock will be. A piece of meat, a bone, or a carrot has only so much flavour to give, and, when this is got out of it, it will rather spoil than improve the stock by being further boiled in it.

What is the precise length of time that these things should be boiled, is a matter which—supposing the operator to have average brains—practice alone and not I can determine.

ON SOME ANCIENT AND MODERN SOUPS.

LOBSTERS are accounted by many people to be highly indigestible, and I dare say not without cause; but there are ways of cooking lobsters, which do away with that drawback, and none so palatable, I think, as the one I am about to describe, which consists in making them into soup. By this I do not mean the preparation of a lobster broth, but of a thick soup, to make which some very good stock or meat broth is to be used. The *modus operandi* is as follows:

Pick all the meat from a lobster, and pound it in a mortar, with an almost equal quantity of butter, until you obtain a fine orange-coloured pulp. This you flavour with white pepper, salt, and grated nutmeg, according to your taste; you then melt a small piece of butter in a saucepan, and mix up with it about one tablespoonful of flour; with this you amalgamate your lobster paste; on the other hand, you take a quantity of bread crumbs equal to that of your lobster paste, and soak them in a good allowance of stock; then you mix them gradually with the lobster paste in the saucepan, adding more stock until you get your soup a little thinner than the consistency you wish it to be when sent up to table. You now put it on the fire, and keep stirring it until it boils and thickens, when you take it off the fire, and let it stand for a while to allow the superfluous fat to come to the surface. Having carefully removed all the fat, you strain the soup through a fine hair sieve, and put it by until it is wanted, when you make it hot and serve with small dice of bread fried to a golden colour in butter.

The above formula cannot fail to be successful if the following points are attended to : thorough pounding, judicious flavouring, and rigorous skimming of all superfluous fat.

This soup is termed BISQUE DE HOMARD in the Gallic tongue, and is a preparation many hundred years old. By using crayfish instead of lobster, you will produce what is called *Bisque aux écrevisses*.

Another very ancient soup is the POTAGE À LA REINE.

According to the traditions of the kitchen, this soup owes its name to no less a personage than the wife of Henry IV., Margaret of Valois, who was said to be immensely fond of it. The ancient formula for preparing this soup is simple enough, and I shall transcribe it here, before setting forth the latest forms which it has been made to assume, at the hands of those who are authorities in such matters.

Soak in a pint of clear stock a piece of bread crumb the size of a large egg. Pound in a mortar the breast (the white) of a roast fowl, with twelve sweet and three bitter almonds and six yolks of hard-boiled eggs. When the whole is thoroughly pounded into a paste, add the stock and bread crumb with a pint of cream or milk; season with pepper, salt, and spices, and pass the whole through a tammy. The *coulis* thus obtained is to be kept very hot in a bain-marie until the time of serving, when it is poured over some toasted slices of bread and served.

The more modern form of this soup in the grand style is as follows :

Stew a couple of fowls with carrots, onions, sweet herbs, spices and salt to taste, and a pinch of sugar. Keep on adding some good stock until you have added a quart or more, according to the quantity of soup you want. When thoroughly done, take out the fowls and let them and the stock get cold. Remove all the white flesh from the fowls, and pound it in a mortar with half its quantity of bread crumbs soaked in the stock (from which all fat has been previously removed); then add the rest of the stock, pass the *purée* through a fine hair sieve or tammy, and put it by till wanted. Just before serving pound in a mortar a couple of dozen sweet almonds with half a pint of cream. Squeeze this in a cloth, and into the juice thus obtained beat up a couple of yolks of egg, previously strained. Let your *purée* come to the boil, but mind you do not let it boil; take it off the fire, and stir into it the mixture of almond juice, cream, and eggs, and serve at once over sippets of bread, fried in butter and cut in the shape of small dice. Or, you may instead put into the soup some peas, or some carrots or cucumbers cut into the shape of peas, and previously cooked in stock. Or again, you may put into your soup some very diminutive quenelles of fowls.

A less expensive way of making this soup is the following; and, with proper care and judicious flavouring, the result will leave nothing to be desired:

Remove the flesh from the remains of a couple of roast or boiled fowls, taking care to exclude all the skin; add half the quantity of bread crumbs, soaked in stock free from grease, and pound thoroughly in a mortar; season with pepper, salt, and a little nutmeg; pass through a hair sieve, add as much stock as you want soup, and you have your *purée* of fowls, which at the time of serving you make warm without letting it boil, and stir into it the yolks of a couple of eggs strained and beaten up with half a glass of cream or milk. Serve with sippets, or peas, &c., as stated above

Supposing no stock to be available, the way to proceed would be to put the remains of the fowls bodily into a saucepan, with carrots, onions, sweet herbs, a little bacon, and any bones, veal trimmings, &c., which may be handy; moisten with a quart or so of water, and let the whole simmer away slowly. After about three hours' simmering take out the pieces of fowl, which you treat as directed above, and strain the broth in which they have been boiled; when it is cold remove all fat from it, and use it instead of stock.

The above formula will apply to the making of soup with remnants of any kind of poultry or game, with such variations as taste and practice may suggest, as, for instance, if wild ducks were thus treated—and a truly toothsome *potage* they make—no cream should be used, but the yolks of egg should be beaten up with a wineglassful of sherry or claret, and little or no bread crumbs should be used. Another variation consists in pounding the fowls, bones and all, and after having passed the result through a sieve, adding the bread crumbs. Some use boiled rice instead of bread crumbs.

The following is a very good form of white thick soup.

Boil a few Jerusalem artichokes with salt, and when quite done pass them through a fine hair sieve. Take as much milk as you want soup, and boil in it a handful of pepper, some mace, cloves, nutmeg, &c., also some parsley, and the smallest bit of shalot. The success of the soup depends upon the proportions of these things, and these, as I have said before, practice can best teach. When the milk is well flavoured, strain it; then melt a good-sized piece of butter in a saucepan, and stir into it first a handful of potato flour, if you have it, or if not, corn flour, then the milk and the pulp of the Jerusalem artichokes, each in such quantities as will give your soup the desired consistency. Lastly, stir into it half a pint of cream, more or less, according to quantity, and after it has given a boil or two, serve with sippets of bread fried in butter, to be handed round with the soup. The cream is by no means necessary to make the soup good, but it is an improvement, nevertheless.

This is the PALESTINE SOUP of English cookery, and affords an amusing instance of the eccentricity of nomenclature. The Italian word *Girasole* being first corrupted into the English "Jerusalem" artichoke, by a masterpiece of blundering the soup made with this vegetable became "Palestine."

The above formula is what is called *au maigre*. If it is desired to produce the soup *au gras*, this is easily done by using white stock instead of milk.

Most kinds of soups *au gras* can be dressed *au maigre* by using, instead of meat, VEGETABLE STOCK, prepared as follows:

Take carrots, turnips, onions, leeks, and celery in equal quantities. Cut them into small pieces, and toss them in plenty of butter for half an hour; then add two heads of lettuce, shred fine, some parsley and chervil, a little thyme, marjoram, and tarragon in judicious proportions, toss them a little longer; then add as much water as you want stock, pepper, salt, cloves, and mace to taste, and a pinch of sugar. Let the whole stew gently for some hours, then strain the liquor through a cloth. If the stock be not wanted for a white soup, a couple of tomatoes, either fresh or dried, are an improvement.

The following are some formulas for soups, which can be made *au maigre* or *au gras*:

POTAGE À LA PURÉE DE LÉGUMES.—Boil in some stock with a bundle of sweet herbs, pepper, salt, and spices to taste, any combination you like of such vegetables as carrots, turnips, potatoes, parsnips, leeks, onions, celery, &c. When thoroughly done, pass the whole through a fine hair sieve. Mix in a saucepan a piece of butter and a little flour, then add a little of the *purée*, and when this is well mixed add the rest. Finish by stirring in (off the fire) the yolks of a couple of eggs, strained and beaten up with a little milk.

This is a very good way of using the trimmings of vegetables, cut with fancy cutters. The vegetables used to make vegetable stock should always be utilised by the thrifty in making this soup.

POTAGE À LA CRÈME D'ORGE.—Boil half a pint of pearl barley in a quart of white meat or vegetable stock till it is reduced to a pulp, pass it through a hair sieve, and add to it as much white stock (meat or vegetable) as will bring the soup to the consistency of cream. Put the soup on the fire, and when it has come to boiling point stir into it (off the fire) the yolks of two eggs, beaten up with a gill of cream; add half a pat of fresh butter, and serve.

A homely but no bad soup withal is what is termed

POTAGE AU PAUVRE HOMME.—Put an ounce of butter into a saucepan, with three large onions, shred fine, and fry them a pale brown colour, add half a tablespoonful of flour, stir for a few minutes, but do not allow the mixture to darken, then add one quart of stock, stir until the soup boils, and season it to taste with powdered pepper and salt. Peel one or two potatoes, cut them into small dice, and put them to boil with the soup. Cut some crust of stale bread in long pieces, the size and half the length of French beans, dry them in the oven, and, at the time of serving, throw them into the soup; then stir into it (off the fire) the yolks of two eggs, beaten up with a little milk and strained.

A *pendant* to the above is POTAGE À LA BONNE FEMME, which is made in this way:

Cut up a good-sized onion into very thin rounds, and place these in a saucepan with a good allowance of butter. Take care not to let the onion get brown, and when it is half done throw in two or three handfuls of sorrel, a lettuce, and a small quantity of chervil, all finely cut, add pepper, salt, a little nutmeg, and keep stirring until the vegetables are nearly done. You then add a tablespoonful of pounded loaf sugar, and half a cupful of stock or broth, free from fat, and not coloured. Let the mixture reduce nearly to a glaze, when you throw in about a quart of stock or broth of the same description as used above; and, after the soup has given a boil, it can be put aside until the time of serving. You now must prepare about a dozen and a half very thin slices of bread, about an inch wide and two inches long, taking care that they have crust along one of their long sides, and you must dry these thoroughly in the oven. When it is time to send up the soup, you first remove the superfluous fat from it, then set it to boil, and when it boils stir into it (off the fire) the yolks of two or three eggs beaten up with a quarter of a pint of cream, or even milk. Pour the soup over the slices of bread, and serve in three minutes.

A simpler kind of soup is made chiefly with onions, and this is the recipe for it as a *maigre* soup.

SOUPE À L'OIGNON.—Slice a couple of Spanish onions, powder them well with flour, and let them take a turn or two in a frying-pan with plenty of butter; before they begin at all to brown, add water, pepper, and salt *quant. suff.;* let the whole boil till the onions are well done, and serve over slices of bread or toast. The addition of grated Parmesan cheese, or thin slices of Gruyère cheese, is an improvement, only if the latter be used the soup should be allowed to stand a few minutes before sending it to table. The grated Parmesan need not be put into the soup at all, but may be handed round with it, for those to take who like it.

This soup has also the advantage of being beneficial to people suffering from colds, and, in fact, if a little garlic be added to it, it becomes a sovereign remedy for such complaints. If it is to be eaten medicinally, however, cheese of any sort should be left out.

Here is another soup, which does not pretend to obtain at the tables of the wealthy, but which is withal toothsome in the extreme. I have often dined off it, having previously cooked it myself, and have found both operations productive of infinite satisfaction. The *modus operandi* is this:

SOUPE AUX CHOUX.—Take a couple of nice summer cabbages—having removed the outside leaves—cut them in quarters, put them into a saucepan with a good-sized piece of bacon (cut into pieces an inch wide down to the skin, which is to remain intact, and is easily cut through with the ladle when helping the soup), a few pork sausages, or, better still, some Bologna sausage, or some *mortadella* (a form of Italian sausage, procurable in this country, and delicious above all sausages), and a bag containing spices, sweet herbs, plenty of pepper, a clove of garlic, and salt if necessary; add a sufficient quantity of cold water to cover the whole, and then let the soup simmer till the cabbages are quite done, serving with a few slices of bread under it.

The skin of bacon or ham—generally thrown away in this country—is very good eating when properly cleaned and boiled, and any amount of such skin or rind may be put into the above soup. In Bologna they make a kind of sausage called "*zampone*," chiefly from such material. It is eaten boiled, and very delicate eating it is.

The liquor in which a leg or a neck of mutton has been boiled, in the English fashion, can be turned by the economical housewife, to very good account to make soup in this wise:

Remove all fat from it, which is easily done when it is cold; then add to it the pulp of dried or fresh peas, or haricot beans, and put into it a muslin bag containing some spices, whole pepper, and sweet herbs. Let it boil a short time, add salt if necessary, and serve with bread sippets. The practice of serving mint with peasoup is barbarous; it should be boiled in the soup in the bag aforesaid.

The liquor in which a knuckle of veal has been boiled can be put to the very same use as the above, as can also that obtained from boiling fowls: it can in fact be made into stock by boiling a judicious selection of vegetables in it, and otherwise flavouring it with herbs and spices.

A very good soup can be made with some of the liquor aforesaid by the following process:

Put a root of parsley and a piece of celery into the liquor, with pepper, mace, a few cloves, a piece of lemon peel, and salt if necessary. Let it boil for an hour; then strain and boil in it some filleted soles, cut up into small pieces. Serve when the soles are done, with a few sprigs of parsley or chervil thrown in at the moment of serving.

This is a more elaborate form:

CONSOMMÉ DE SOLES.—Remove the fillets from a pair of soles, cut them out with a cutter in pieces the size of a penny: put the bones and all the trimmings of the soles in a saucepan with one quart of plain white stock, a large handful of parsley, a piece of celery, one onion, two or three cloves, a blade of mace, pepper and salt to taste. Let this boil slowly from three to four hours.

Carefully skim and strain the liquor; then put it on the fire again, and when it boils put in the cut pieces of sole. When they are cooked take them out, put them into the soup tureen with a few sprigs of chervil or parsley, and, having strained the liquor once more, put it over them and serve.

Passing now to clear soups; these may always be prepared with the *bouillon* of the *pot au feu*, or with ordinary stock. If this latter is more highly flavoured by the addition of ham, veal, or poultry, you will have what is called *consommé*, which is the highest form of clear soup, not to be confounded with the liquefied glue which goes by the name of gravy soup. A well-made *consommé* should have an aromatic and appetising flavour about it, and should be as clear and light as the palest sherry; indeed, a *consommé* of fowls should not be darker than hock. This is an economical mode of preparing

CONSOMMÉ DE VOLAILLE.—Cut up into small pieces the remains (bones and all) of a couple of roast fowls, removing all skin or browned parts, put them into a saucepan with a pound of knuckle of veal and a piece of lean ham, cover with plain white stock, add salt to taste, and put the saucepan on the fire, skimming carefully any scum that may rise. Just before it begins to boil put in three or four carrots, two or three onions, a head of celery, some thyme, parsley, marjoram, and bayleaf, in judicious proportions, a few cloves, a little mace, and whole pepper, to taste; then place the saucepan at such distance from the fire as will let the contents simmer, but not boil. In about four hours time strain the liquid through a napkin, free it from all fat, and clarify it with raw meat and white of egg.

If a couple of uncooked fowls are used, a more expensive but rather better *consommé* will be produced: assuming that in either case the cook has the talent of so proportioning her vegetables and condiments, as to get the right combination of flavours. A *consommé* of fowls may be served simply with a few sprigs of chervil or of tarragon floating in it; or it may be garnished with a variety of things ready cooked, added at the time of serving, and it will be named accordingly:

CONSOMMÉ DE VOLAILLE AUX POIS.—A few green peas boiled in stock, and strained.

AUX POINTES D'ASPERGES.—Asparagus heads treated in the same manner.

AUX HARICOTS VERTS.—French beans boiled as above, and then cut or stamped out in uniform shapes.

AUX CHOUXFLEURS.—Cauliflowers picked out in small sprigs, and boiled as above.

AU RIZ.—A small quantity of well boiled rice.

AUX PÂTES D'ITALIE.—Any kind of small *paste* or maccaroni cut into convenient pieces, then boiled in plain stock and strained.

AUX QUENELLES.—Small quenelles of fish, of meat, or of poultry.

Here is a formula for making QUENELLES DE VEAU as an *entrée*:

Remove the skin from a pound of veal cutlet, and cut it into small pieces. Put into a stewpan a gill of water, a pinch of salt, and a small piece of butter; when boiling stir in as much flour as will form a paste; when it is smooth put it away to get cold, then take half the quantity of butter that you have of veal, and half the quantity of paste that you have of butter; put the veal into a mortar, pound it well, then add the butter, pound it, then add the paste, pound well for ten minutes, add one whole egg, the yolks of three eggs, salt, pepper, a little grated nutmeg; work well together, pass through a wire sieve, stir in half a gill of cream, shape the quenelles with two tablespoons, place them in a well-buttered *sauté-*

pan, leaving a clear space on one side; put a good pinch of salt in that space, pour in sufficient boiling water to cover the quenelles, and leave them to poach for ten minutes; then drain them carefully on a cloth, arrange on a dish, and serve them with rich gravy or any sauce you like. When wanted for soup, the quenelles should be shaped to about the size and form of an olive, and they will obviously require less time to be poached than the above. It is not imperative to use a *consommé de volaille* for these soups, a plain *consommé* or the *bouillon* of the *pot au feu* will do just as well; but in that case the respective soups will simply be *potages à la* whatever the garnish thereof may be.

That very hackneyed soup, JULIENNE, may be prepared also with the *bouillon* of the *pot au feu*, in default of a more elaborate foundation. The chief point to be observed is that the vegetables should be properly cut up and prepared. This is my notion of it:

Take about equal parts of carrots, turnips, and of leeks, onions, and celery, cut them all into thin strips, not much more than one-eighth of an inch square and one and a half inches long; put them into a saucepan with a lump of fresh butter, a good pinch of powdered lump sugar, and pepper and salt to taste. Toss them lightly on the fire until they begin to colour, then add a head of lettuce, shredded fine, and a small quantity of chervil and sorrel, also finely shredded; and, after giving the whole a tossing on the fire for about five minutes, moisten with some stock, and keep the soup hot by the side of the fire for a couple of hours. At the time of serving add as much stock as is necessary.

The POTAGE À LA JARDINIÈRE is but a slight modification of *Julienne*. I make it as follows:

Cut equal quantities of carrots and turnips into the shape of small olives, cut up a similar quantity of small sprigs of cauliflower, cut some French beans into diamonds, some celery into round pieces with a cutter, and have some very small onions—about equal quantities of all. Boil each vegetable, separately, in salted water, with a small piece of butter, till it is cooked, but not overdone; lay the vegetables on a hair sieve, and throw a little cold water over them. At the time of serving put them all into a saucepan with a pint of well-flavoured stock, or of *consommé*, and when it is on the point of boiling add as much of it as you want soup, and a few sprigs of chervil or of tarragon.

Another hackneyed soup is POTAGE PRINTANIER, or, as it is sometimes called, À LA PRINTANIÈRE. This is but a variety of the above, as will be seen by the following, which is one of the very many ways of making it.

Cut some carrots and some new turnips in the shape of peas; put them into separate saucepans with enough stock to cover them, and a pinch of sugar. Keep them on the fire till the stock has nearly boiled away, but mind that they do not catch or burn; cook some peas and some asparagus points in the same way; you should have equal quantities of each. Cut out of lettuce and sorrel leaves pieces the size of a sixpence; let them give one boil in some stock. Put all the vegetables so prepared into the soup tureen, add a few sprigs of chervil and a few tarragon leaves, pour some well-flavoured *consommé* over, and serve.

To produce what is called BRUNOISE, the carrots and turnips should be cut in the shape of small dice, and no other vegetables should be added to them but celery and onions cut in the same manner; then the vegetables should be prepared in this wise.

Put the carrots into a saucepan with a large piece of butter, a teaspoonful of powdered loaf sugar, and pepper and salt. Toss them on the fire until they begin to take colour, then put in the celery; after a little time the onions; and lastly the turnips. Toss them altogether for a few minutes longer, then add as much stock as you want soup, and set the saucepan by the side of the fire to simmer very gently for a couple of hours. Skim it well before serving.

Another soup akin to the above is the NIVERNAISE, which is made thus:

Cut some carrots to the shape of olives, or any fancy shape of that size; boil the trimmings with some stock, so as to give it a very strong flavour of carrots. Toss the cut carrots in some butter, with a pinch of sugar and pepper and salt, moistening after a while with a little of the stock; when they are cooked and almost glazed add the remainder of the stock.

A very effective soup for a dinner party is what is called CONSOMMÉ À LA ROYALE, which is naught else but pieces of custard floating in a clear and judiciously flavoured *consommé*. What gives it effect is the artful ordering of the custard, which is done thus:

Mix the yolks of six eggs with rather less than a gill of cold water and a pinch of salt; strain the mixture, and divide it into three equal parts; colour one with some cochineal, the other with spinach greening, and leave the third plain. Put them into three plain moulds, previously buttered, and place these in a pan of hot water, which you put on the fire to boil just long enough to set the mixture. When the water in the saucepan has become quite cold, turn out the contents of each mould on a wet napkin, and you will have three cakes of custard, green, red, and yellow respectively. Cut them into small dice, and, handling them in the gentlest possible manner, spread them out on a plate, to be kept covered until wanted to be put into the soup tureen with the *consommé*.

POACHED EGGS are sometimes put into clear soup. The length of time it takes to poach eggs is perhaps difficult to determine, but I can at any rate describe the way to set about it. Fill a shallow *sauté*-pan with water, and salt *quantum suff.*, a few peppercorns and some leaves of parsley. When the water is on the point of boiling (it should never be allowed to boil) break two or more eggs into it (according to the size of the pan) and put on the cover. When you judge they are done, take them out carefully, brush them clean on both sides with a paste brush, and cut each egg with a round fluted paste cutter, so as to get them all of a uniform shape, and to leave neither too much nor too little white round each egg. This done put them into the soup.

Were I to continue describing all the soups thick and clear, *au maigre* and *au gras*, which are made or could be made, I should leave myself no room for anything else; but I cannot conclude this part of my subject without telling my readers how to prepare that homely but delectable *potage*, the

CROÛTE AU POT, which is simply a more artistic form of putting pieces of toast into soup. Cut off the bottom crust of a quartern loaf, with the same thickness of crumb as there is of crust; cut it out in rounds the size of a sixpence; soak them in some stock or broth from the *pot au feu*, put them (in a buttered tin) in the oven, and let them remain until they are dried up (*gratinés*). Take some carrots and turnips out of the *pot au feu*, cut them out in rounds the size of a shilling and of the thickness of a penny; put these into the soup tureen, with as much stock or broth as is wanted; pick out the pieces of bread with a knife from the tin, put them in the soup, let it stand for five minutes, and serve. Celery and leeks out of the *pot au feu* may likewise be added, being cut in the same manner, and also a few leaves of tarragon, which latter herb is an improvement to most clear soups.

BROTHS FOR THE SICK.

BEEF-TEA is the favourite form in which food is given to the sick in this country. When properly made it is undoubtedly a very good but also a very tasteless thing to drink, and one is apt soon to tire of it. When the tongue is as dry as a piece of blanket, however, it matters not whether what is put into the mouth has a pleasant taste or not, for then all things taste pretty much alike. Still there are other stages of illness when it would be an advantage to give patients some kind of food, pleasant to the taste, as well as nutritive and wholesome. The formulas for such a preparation are very numerous, and Brillat Savarin's *magistères restoratifs* are about as elaborate, and perhaps as good, as any, although I should not administer them to invalids without the doctor's advice. The two restorative broths which I am about to describe are based upon the best formulas which exist for such things, and have been by repeated experiments and constant practice reduced to their present simple and economical form.

No. 1. Slice three onions, and dispose them in a saucepan so as to completely cover the bottom of it; over them place a layer of fat bacon in slices a quarter of an inch thick; over that put three carrots, also cut in slices, so as to form another layer; on this again put the following condiments judiciously proportioned—viz., salt, whole pepper, cloves, parsley, marjoram, and thyme. Upon this pile up two calves' feet, chopped in small pieces, and one pound of beefsteak, free from all fat and finely minced. Cover the saucepan and put it on the fire, there to remain for one hour. There should be no fire at the side, it should be fairly under the saucepan. The next step consists in filling up the saucepan with boiling water so as just to cover the contents; and then it is put by the side of the fire to simmer for one hour; after that the liquor should be poured off without disturbing the other contents of the saucepan. The steam, which arises during this operation, gives out a most appetising perfume, which will fill the hearts of those present with gladness. The liquor should now be strained through a napkin; the little fat which will float on it should be removed with the help of some clean blotting paper; and the broth can be administered to the patient. A teaspoonful of sherry and a small quantity of sugar may be advantageously added to each cupful. This restorative when cold will be a firm jelly, and it can then be administered in a solid form.

No. 2. Proceed as in the above as far as the layer of carrots, and in putting in the spices substitute mace and a little nutmeg for the cloves; put in the calves' feet; and instead of the beefsteak have a fowl, which must be cut and chopped up into small pieces. Finish this restorative in the same manner as No. 1.

The great secret for successfully preparing these nourishing restoratives consists, almost entirely, in the proportions of sweet herbs and spices which enter into their composition. As I have often said before, it is by practice alone that perfection can be reached in these as in most things in this world; and it would be as ridiculous as it would be useless if I were to specify how many cloves and how many grains of pepper should be put in.

After the liquor is poured off, the contents of the saucepan must not by any means be thrown away; for if you fill it up again with hot water, and add a few more spices and sweet herbs, a couple of hours' boiling will produce a second edition of the restorative, nearly, if not quite, as good as the first. When cold this second edition will also set in a firm jelly.

What is now left in the saucepan presents an excellent foundation for making some very good soup. The way to do it is this. All the odds and ends of meat, bones, poultry, and game that may be at hand, are put into a saucepan with the residuum aforesaid; more spices, herbs, pepper, salt, and vegetables, are added in due proportions. The whole is set to simmer for five or six hours, after the familiar fashion of the stock pot of cookery books. The liquor is then strained and cleared with white of egg, and you have a capital clear soup as the result.

The quantities given for these two restoratives would yield from two to three pints of each edition, besides a foundation for about four pints of excellent good soup. The cost even of the more expensive one, in which a fowl is used, would not be over 6s. or 8s. at most.* No. 1 would not exceed 5s.; and this money would hardly buy the same quantity of calves'-foot jelly as sold by confectioners.

In conclusion, I will describe a way of making BEEF TEA, which was imparted to me by a medical friend, and which will be found the most effectual mode of extracting all the nourishment out of the meat.

Take 2lb. of beef, free from all fat; mince it as fine as you can, and put it into a jar, with one pint of cold water, to stand inside the fender for a couple of hours; now strain off the water, and put it by, replacing it by another pint of tepid water. Put the jar nearer the fire, or on

* This was written in 1866

the kitchener, so as to keep the water hot without boiling. After the lapse of another couple of hours strain this off, and mix it with the first pint you strained off. Transfer the minced meat into a saucepan : add one pint of boiling water to it, and let it boil for one hour ; strain and mix with the first two pints. Let the whole give one boil; add salt, and the beef tea is ready for use.

The *théorique* of the above process is this. Meat contains various substances, all of them nourishing; but some, as albumen, are only soluble in cold water, others tepid water alone will dissolve, and others again can be brought out by the action of boiling water alone. By treating the meat with cold, tepid, and boiling water separately, all that is to be got out of it is obtained ; and the result is, as it must be, the best beef tea that can be made.

ON A PINCH OF FLOUR.

ONE of the common failures of ladies who strive to improve the plain cook of English households is embodied in the production of a Crécy soup, or, in plain English, a carrot soup. When this is prepared by amateur cooks it usually presents the appearance of those draughts of the doctor which bear the direction " to be well shaken before taken." The carrot pulp *will* separate from the stock or broth, and lie at the bottom of each soup plate. That this should be so is not the fault of the well-meaning amateur; the fault lies with the compiler of the cookery book that she has chosen as her guide. Writers of recipes generally, seem to assume that those who will use them have an instinctive knowledge of cooking, and therefore they are satisfied with giving, as it were, a slight sketch of each dish, leaving out those "little nothings" upon which depend the success and excellence of all dishes.

In making Crécy soup a pinch of flour stands between failure and success; but is that enough? The tyro requires to be told when and how to introduce that flour. Of course there is a great deal in cooking which no amount of writing can teach; nay, even more, there are some things which nothing can teach, such as, for example, the making of paste. You must be born with the gift. A person may be a first-rate cook in all respects, and yet not be able to make paste satisfactorily. Details of manipulation cannot be too abundant in a recipe; details of quantities of ingredients, such as a quarter of a teaspoonful of salt, three peppercorns, one clove, and so forth, are simply ridiculous. Tastes differ; and the proportions of salt, spices, and such things, can safely, and indeed should, be left to the taste of the operator. But it is much more to the purpose to state when and how to put in these things. Take, for instance, the case of salt, which should be put into most things when they are first set to cook; whilst with dried haricot beans it should only be put in when they are nearly boiled, or else they will all split and break—every one.

Plain melted butter is another instance. In its simplest form it is a mixture of flour, butter, water, and salt. The proportions of it should be, butter and water, with just enough flour to thicken the mixture, and salt *quantum suff.* The way in which your plain cook usually sets to work, is to dredge some flour, generally a good deal of it, into the water, adding a small piece of butter and salt, and stirring the whole on the fire. Another way is to roll a piece of butter in flour, and then to put it into the water with the salt. The result of these manipulations most people know too well, and rightly deplore. Sometimes, by chance or extra care and the use of a colander, the butter may be free from little round lumps of flour, and be less like paste than it usually is.

Now, with these very same ingredients, and less trouble, good eatable melted butter can be made. The whole secret lies in the *modus operandi*, and it is this—the butter should be melted first, then the flour added, which will amalgamate with it almost of itself, and thereby render impossible the lumps above referred to; the water (boiling) is now put in with a proper quantity of salt, and the mixture being stirred on the fire until it thickens, your melted butter is made.

This is the simplest form of MELTED BUTTER, which may be varied in several ways, viz.:

1. Beat up the yolk of an egg and the juice of half a lemon, strain, and stir them in just before serving, *off the fire*. The result is what is called SAUCE BLANCHE.

2. Use milk, or milk and water, instead of water.

3. Beat up the yolk of an egg with a little cream, and stir (off the fire) into the melted butter just before serving.

4. Throw in, just before serving, some fennel, minced fine, or some chervil, picked out in little leaflets, or parsley minced fine, or capers chopped up. Caper sauce made with whole capers is, I think, a mistake.

These additions are also compatible with the three first arrangements.

5. Let the butter and flour get a good brown colour, then add water, and—when the sauce is made—Worcester Sauce, catsup, pepper, and other spices and condiments to taste.

6. Stir into plain melted butter, after it is made, a sufficient quantity of anchovy sauce.

7. Cut up some onions and shallots, and a very small piece of garlic, boil them in milk, with whole pepper, mace, a few cloves, and some parsley. When the mixture is well flavoured, strain and use the milk instead of water to make your sauce; egg and lemon may be added if wished. Without these two last it is not a bad substitute for onion sauce. Fillets of soles, boiled in the flavoured milk, and served with the sauce over them, are not bad eating. The great rock to be avoided is excess of any one thing in flavouring the milk, chiefly in the spice line.

8. For puddings and sweet dishes melted butter is made in the same way—except that the salt is replaced by sugar, in larger quantities of course—and should be

made with milk, or milk and water, and an egg or two used, with or without lemon, according to taste; or the eggs may be beaten up with brandy or wine. I prefer myself a custard by way of sauce over cabinet puddings; but for Christmas puddings brandy sauce or the pure spirit are the correct thing.

To thicken soups, such as Crécy, which are made with vegetables, not containing enough starch to float their pulp in the broth or stock, this starch is supplied by the addition of flour, and the way to put in the flour is the same as that just described for melted butter. But I may as well give the whole process of making the soup in question.

POTAGE À LA CRÉCY.—Boil a few carrots in water and salt, or in broth; when they are thoroughly done, drain them, and pass them through a hair sieve. Mix the pulp thus obtained with broth or stock in sufficient quantities to produce a *purée* rather thinner than the soup should be when sent up to table. You now melt a piece of butter, and mix a small quantity of flour with it, then gradually put in your *purée*, and stir it on the fire till it comes to a boil, when you put it by the side, and presently remove any superfluous fat. Serve with sippets of bread, the shape of dice, fried in butter.

ON NAMES.

In cookery, as in natural history, nomenclature is a vexed question. Cooks will keep on giving new names to old dishes, *à propos* of nothing or to suit particular occasions : and much confusion and disappointment are the result of this practice. If one sees on a bill of fare, say *filets de soles à la "Atlantic cable,"* and orders the dish, fondly thinking that a new method of dressing soles has been invented, what must be the disappointment experienced when the dish turns out to be the well-known *filets de soles à la "Electric telegraph."* When the French revolution changed so many things in France, the names of dishes did not escape ; but then the cooks of the period took care to put the old name with the new, thus : *Sauce à l'homme de confiance, ci-devant maître d'hôtel ; Bifteck à l'insulaire, ci-devant à l'Anglaise ;* something or other *à la bonne femme, ci-devant servante*, and so forth. Now, as the "Divine Williams" said of the smell of the rose, it may be said of the taste of a good dish, that by any other name it will taste as sweet ; but as you cannot generally taste of a dish at the time of ordering it, it would be very desirable that cooks and makers of books on cookery should be brought to agree in this matter. As a contribution towards such an agreement, I propose to describe some sauces with fine names, the foundation of all of which is the very simple form known as melted butter in this country, and as *sauce blanche* in France.

If you add to plain melted butter a small quantity of

parsley, minced very fine, and a little grated nutmeg, you have what is called SAUCE À LA MAÎTRE D'HÔTEL, *anglicè*, parsley and butter. A more artistic form consists in adding, instead of parsley alone, the following herbs, judiciously proportioned, and finely minced: chervil, garden cress, and parsley in equal parts, and a few leaves of tarragon; a little burnet may also be used.

In either case it is always better to finish the sauce by the addition of the yolk of an egg, and lemon juice.

But melted butter *à la maître d'hôtel* must not be confounded with MAÎTRE D'HÔTEL BUTTER, which is prepared in the manner following:

Put a couple of ounces of fresh butter into a basin with the juice of a lemon, white pepper and salt to taste, and a small quantity of parsley freed from moisture, and minced fine. Incorporate the whole together effectually and quickly, then put it by in a cool place till wanted, *ex. gr.*, to put on a broiled steak or on a kidney.

The addition to plain melted butter of a quantity of capers or gherkins, chopped small, will give you a SAUCE AUX CÂPRES, or AUX CORNICHONS.

If, in making the melted butter, gravy or stock is used instead of water, a SAUCE BLONDE is produced, and to this may be added Worcester sauce, and any other condiments that taste may suggest.

The pulp of a few onions, obtained by passing them through a hair sieve after they are well boiled, when added to the original melted butter, constitutes what is called SOUBISE SAUCE in France, and onion sauce in England.

The more elaborate form of this sauce is the following:

Boil some onions in milk, with pepper, salt, and nutmeg. When quite done pass them through a sieve. Put some butter and flour into a saucepan. When the butter is melted and well mixed with the flour put in the pulp of the onions, and add either milk or cream, stirring the sauce on the fire until it is of the desired consistency.

And here are two more:

1. Parboil some onions a few minutes, mince them roughly, and put them into a saucepan, with plenty of butter, a pinch of sugar, pepper, and salt to taste. Let them cook slowly, so that they do not take colour, and stir in a tablespoonful of flour. When they are quite tender, pass them through a sieve. Dilute the onion pulp with sufficient milk to make it into a sauce. Make it hot, and serve.

2. Put into a saucepan parboiled onions, butter, sugar, pepper, and salt as above. Add a tablespoonful or two of rice (previously boiled in water for ten minutes). Let the whole cook slowly, and, when the onions are quite tender, add a tablespoonful of grated Parmesan cheese. Stir the mixture well, and pass it through a sieve. Add as much milk or cream as may be necessary.

SAUCE HOLLANDAISE, in its homely form, is but a plain *sauce blanche*, into which a larger quantity of yolks of eggs has been put; but, in its more glorified form, it may be described as a custard made with yolks of eggs, water, vinegar or lemon, and butter. I prefer using lemon, and would proceed as follows:

Boil a small quantity of mace and roughly-pounded allspice in some water. Beat up, and strain the yolks of three eggs with about a tumblerful of this water when cold. Add salt to taste, and about three ounces of fresh butter. Put this mixture into a bain-marie, and never cease stirring until the sauce thickens. Should it get too thick, add a few drops of cold water. Lastly, stir in (off the fire) the juice of a lemon.

When vinegar is used, a small quantity of it is put to

reduce in a saucepan on the fire with the spices. Then it is strained, and butter and yolks of eggs being added, with salt to taste, the mixture is stirred for some time at a gentle heat.

In any form, however, this sauce is one of the most difficult to make with success; and a great deal of practice will be required to ensure perfection.

So much for what is called *Sauce Hollandaise;* the Hollanders themselves, however, affect a simpler preparation to eat with their fish, and that is simply butter melted. A large piece of butter is put into a saucepan with the juice of a lemon, and a due quantity of pepper and salt. As soon as the butter is well liquefied it is allowed to settle, and poured out clear (from the sediment at the bottom of it) into a piping hot sauceboat.

What is called SAUCE À LA POULETTE is only plain melted butter, with rather more egg and lemon stirred into it, and the addition of a few button mushrooms.

When a larger quantity of mushrooms is used you have a SAUCE AUX CHAMPIGNONS, or mushroom sauce. This may be made white or brown by using as the foundation of it *sauce blanche* or *sauce blonde.* If you fry some slices of onions or shallots until they assume a very light brown colour, taking care by frequent stirring that none get burnt or done too much, and having added to them either broth or water *q. suff.*, and a small quantity of vinegar, let the whole give one boil, and then stir this mixture into a saucepan containing butter and flour, as if to make plain melted butter, and add pepper, salt and some minced parsley, you will produce what is called SAUCE AU PAUVRE HOMME, "poor man's sauce," the simplest form of several other sauces, which, in spite of their names, are only slight varieties of it—viz.:

SAUCE PIQUANTE.—Having fried your shallots, or onions, add a small piece of garlic and some sweet herbs; use a mixture of equal parts of vinegar and water, or of vinegar and broth, strain and proceed as above. Any condiments and flavours, such as mushroom catsup, Worcester Sauce, tomato sauce, truffles, nutmeg, &c., may be advantageously added to this sauce by a capable cook. Chopped gherkins are sometimes added to this sauce, and they improve it.

SAUCE ROBERT is almost identical with the above; save in the addition of a small quantity of mustard, and if it be French mustard all the better.

SAUCE À LA TARTARE is produced by adding a larger quantity of mustard to a *sauce piquante*. The cold *tartare* is a different preparation, of which I shall treat in another place, as also of *poivrade* sauce, *remoulade* sauce, and *ravigotte* sauce, which are cold sauces. But there are likewise hot forms of these.

SAUCE POIVRADE may be described as a plain *sauce piquante* without gherkins, but in which pepper predominates.

SAUCE REMOULADE and SAUCE RAVIGOTTE are almost one and the same thing, except that a small quantity of oil is put into the former. This is the way to proceed:

Take some parsley, chervil, burnet, garden cress, tarragon, and any other green herbs you can get; chop them up very fine; slightly rub a saucepan with garlic or shallot; melt a piece of butter in it; add a little flour; mix thoroughly; add broth or stock *q. suff.*, pepper, salt, and a glass of white wine. A few minutes before serving throw in the herbs, a squeeze of lemon, and a pat of fresh butter. This constitutes *ravigotte*. By omitting the wine and the lemon, and putting in a tablespoonful of salad oil, and the least bit of mustard, you produce a *remoulade*.

The following is a somewhat different and more artistic form of

SAUCE PIQUANTE.—Put half a pint of vinegar into a saucepan with one clove of garlic, a couple of shallots minced fine, a sprig of thyme, a bay leaf, pepper and spices to taste, and, if liked, a little cayenne; let the whole boil till reduced to one-half, then add half a pint of stock or broth. Melt a piece of butter the size of an egg in a saucepan, mix a little flour with it, then add the above liquor, strained. Stir the sauce till it boils, add salt if required, and a little parsley minced fine, and some chopped gherkins and capers.

Yet another form of sauce, akin to the above, is Italian sauce, of which the following are two formulæ:—

SAUCE À L'ITALIENNE.—Mince a couple of shallots quite fine, and fry them in a little salad oil. When they are a pale straw colour add two or three mushrooms and a little parsley minced in the same manner, then moisten with enough stock and white wine, in equal parts, to make the sauce; put in, tied up in a small bundle, a clove of garlic, some sweet herbs, and a bay leaf; add pepper and salt to taste, and let the sauce boil for half an hour. Remove the bundle; melt a piece of butter, add a very little flour, then gradually mix the sauce with it. Stir it well on the fire, and as soon as it is hot it is ready.

2. Fry in butter some onions chopped fine till they are a golden colour, add some ham and mushrooms finely minced, moisten with some good stock; put in a clove of garlic, a few cloves, pepper and salt to taste, a bay leaf, a little thyme, and some parsley. When the sauce has boiled an hour or so, add one glass of white wine and a squeeze of lemon; let it boil five minutes more, then strain it carefully, and finish it as the other.

The following is one of the simplest formulæ for SAUCE À LA PROVENÇALE:—

Put into a saucepan a small quantity of fine salad oil, some onions or shallots, a little garlic, some tomatoes, and mushrooms, all chopped up; add parsley and sweet herbs tied up in a bundle, pepper, salt, nutmeg, and a few cloves; when the whole is well warmed, add a table-spoonful of flour; mix well, and throw in gradually a mixture of white wine and stock, in equal parts; let the sauce boil ten or fifteen minutes; strain and serve.

SAUCE À LA PÉRIGUEUX (in other words, truffle sauce) should be as simple as possible. Having chopped up the truffles very fine, throw them into a saucepan previously rubbed with garlic, but very slightly, and containing either oil or butter; toss them in this for a few minutes; add pepper and salt, and moisten with a mixture of half stock and half white wine in sufficient quantity to make your sauce. Let it boil till the truffles are done; then serve.

The fundamental preparations of the higher walks of the art, called by the ancient professors *coulis*, or *mères sauces*, now called *grandes sauces*, are the *Espagnole, Mirepoix, Allemande, Velouté, Béchamel,* and *Suprême*. They are used chiefly for *ragoûts*, and to improve other sauces, and there are in reality but two of them, the *Espagnole*, a brown one, and the *Velouté*, a white one. All the others are but slight modifications of these two. To be well made they should not be greasy, and they should have just enough fat in them to present the velvety appearance of the petals of a full-blown damask rose.

BROWN SAUCE OR ESPAGNOLE. — Proceed as directed elsewhere to make aspic jelly, and, having strained the liquor and removed all the grease from it, warm it, and pour it gradually into a saucepan, in which you have previously made a *roux*, which is done by melting a piece of butter and adding to it a handful of flour, stirring on the fire until the flour begins to brown. Let your sauce give a boil or two, add any condiment according to taste, and the sauce is made. Truffles or mushrooms, or both, may be added with advantage in the first part of the process.

The addition of the juice of a lemon, and a glass of white wine, at the second stage of the proceedings, will produce what is called MIREPOIX, a very good sauce for all hashes or fricassees of pigeons, fowls, ducks, and birds in general.

WHITE SAUCE OR VELOUTÉ, is made much in the same way as *Espagnole*, only, as it is a white sauce, all ingredients tending to give it a colour, such as *suc colorant*, should be excluded, and in the first part of the process the meat and vegetables should not be browned at all; also in making the *roux* the flour should not be allowed to brown, and mushrooms, at least, are *de rigueur* for this sauce.

By stirring into your *velouté* two or three yolks of eggs beaten up with a little hot water, and adding a pat of butter, with a little finely-powdered nutmeg, you will have a SAUCE ALLEMANDE.

SAUCE SUPRÊME is nothing else (according to no less an authority than CARÊME) but some *sauce Allemande*, to which, at the moment of serving, a pat of fresh butter and a couple of tablespoonfuls of *consommé*, or clear gravy or stock have been added.

The BÉCHAMEL, or rather one kind of *Béchamel*, is made by adding half a pint of cream to a well made *velouté*.

I will now give the recipe for a sauce which I recommend to those who love the flesh of that useful animal the pig. Having procured the livers of any kind of poultry, or of rabbits, or of hares, scald and proceed to mince them as fine as you can. Incorporate some butter and a little flour in a saucepan, throw in a small quantity of finely minced shallots, and the least bit of garlic (or you may rub the saucepan with a clove of that fragrant bulb); let the shallots fry a short time without taking colour, add as much gravy or stock as you want sauce, with parsley, pepper, salt, thyme, marjoram, nutmeg, and a very little cloves, all finely powdered; when the sauce boils, put in the minced liver, a glass of port wine, and, at the moment of serving, the juice of half a lemon, and a pat of fresh butter. Many other things besides pork are improved by the aid of this LIVER SAUCE.

Here is another sauce, which in my opinion is preferable to the traditional port wine sauce with wild ducks. It is called BIGARADE SAUCE, and is made thus :

Pare off as thin as you can the yellow rind of two Seville oranges, cut it into very thin shreds, and boil them in water for five minutes. Melt a piece of butter in a saucepan, mix with it a tablespoonful of flour, and stir until it begins to colour; add a gill of stock, pepper and salt to taste, and the juice of the oranges, with a good pinch of powdered loaf sugar, then put in the boiled rinds, stir the sauce until it boils.

Lastly, here is a sauce imparted to me by a friend, whose eulogiums upon it I fully endorse; it is "rich" but good.

"LADY PEG'S SAUCE," for pike and other fish. Half a pint of cream, two tablespoonfuls of walnut catsup, and one of essence of anchovy. Boil these together, and just before you take them off the fire, add a little butter, rolled in flour, and a little cayenne; stir all the time after the butter is added.

ON SOME ANCIENT FOOD.

BRILLAT SAVARIN had a great respect for fish. He says that "they are truly antediluvian creatures, for the great cataclysm which drowned our great uncles in the eighteenth century of the world, or thereabouts, was for the fish a time of joy, conquest, and festivity." I must refer my readers to Savarin's book for his inimitable and philosophical remarks upon that venerable article of food, my object now being only to point out some cunning ways of dressing fish other than the boiled and fried forms, which—with the exception perhaps of stewed eels—generally obtain in the households of people who cannot afford to pay more than £20 a year to their cooks.

Some fish, especially salmon, need only to be plainly boiled in salt and water, with a little vinegar; but in my opinion most fish, excepting salmon, are greatly improved by being boiled in a COURT BOUILLON, and this is how it is done:

Having placed the fish in the fish-kettle, with enough cold water to cover it, add a glass of vinegar, slices of carrots and onions, and a clove of garlic; then sweet herbs, spices, and a laurel leaf tied up in a muslin bag, with pepper, salt, and a root of parsley. The proportions of all these must depend on the quantity of fish to be boiled, the skill of the cook, and the taste of the company. When the fish is cooked, pour a jugful of cold water into the fish-kettle, and do not take out the fish till the moment of serving. A mixture of wine and water, or milk and water, in equal parts, may be used instead of the water and glass of vinegar.

It is better, when fish is intended to be boiled, to clean it from the gills, without splitting it open. This is an operation not understood, I believe, by English fishmongers; but it is not more difficult than skinning eels, and is easily learnt by a little practice.

Fresh-water fish are very much improved by being boiled in a *court bouillon*, and the muddy taste which some have can be got rid of by pouring a small quantity of vinegar down the throat of the fish while it is still alive.

Plain melted butter, made with egg and lemon, is the best accompaniment to every kind of boiled fish in a general way. Some fish, however, require a more elaborate sauce, but the choice of it must be left to the discrimination and taste of the cook. Lobster sauce is decidedly too rich.

The remains, or, as the French say, "*reliefs*," of most boiled fish can be turned into very nice dishes when you know how to do it. The first principle is to pick out carefully all the bones, skin, &c., leaving nothing but the flesh. This done, you can simply put it into a saucepan, with a goodly piece of butter and minced parsley; keep shaking till the fish is warmed, and then add a little lemon juice, pepper, and salt, and cayenne, if liked. This makes a capital dish for breakfast. To make a dinner dish of it I should proceed in this way: flavour some milk, by boiling a few spices and herbs in it, with pepper and salt; then strain and thicken it, as if to make melted butter; put your sauce and the fish in a saucepan, and keep shaking round on the fire (not stirring) until the fish is thoroughly warm; then serve. There should not be too much sauce; and a few sliced gherkins (pickled *à la Française*, not the mixed pickles of this country) put round the dish, are an improvement to the taste and appearance of it. Another way is to place the fish, when warmed, on a dish, and to cover it with a layer of bread crumbs; then brown the top and serve: or a layer of well-seasoned mashed potatoes may be put on instead.

All the above refer more particularly to the remains of salmon, cod, turbot, brill, and even haddock.

FISH CROQUETTES can be made with the remains of any boiled fish, and if well-flavoured and cooked can hold their own at any table. This is one way of proceeding:

Having carefully picked out the flesh of your fish, pound it in a mortar, moistening with a little cream or milk, and a little butter; add one or more eggs, according to quantity, pepper, salt, and a few pounded spices to taste. When you have got the mixture to the consistency of a very smooth thick paste, roll it up into balls or any other shape you may fancy; they should be floured in rolling them up; and they may be either boiled and served with a sharp sauce, or they may be fried and served without sauce, with a garniture of fried parsley. To boil them they should be dropped gently into a saucepan containing just enough boiling milk, or milk and water, or plain water, to cover them; they take a minute or two to cook. Their fine name in this form is QUENELLES of whatever the fish is, *à la* whatever the sauce which is served with them. When fried they are *croquettes*; before frying them they should be dipped in a beaten egg and bread-crumbed, and this operation should be repeated after a little while. They should not be fried too much, but just enough to warm them and give them a light golden colour.

And this reminds me of that popular English preparation, the LOBSTER CUTLET, for which I append several recipes.

1. Pound the flesh of the lobster in a mortar with a fourth part of its bulk of fresh butter till you reduce it to a smooth paste; season with pepper, salt, and nutmeg, add two yolks and one white of egg; melt a small piece of butter in a saucepan, mix it with a tablespoonful of flour, and then with the lobster paste. Perfectly amalgamate the whole, and when warm spread it out on a marble slab to the thickness you wish your cutlets to be. When cold cut out the cutlets, dip them carefully in beaten egg, and then bread crumb them with fine baked bread crumbs. After the lapse of an hour or so, repeat this operation; then fry to a nice gold colour; insert in each cutlet bonewise a short piece of the small claws or of the antennæ of the lobster.

2. Mince the flesh of a lobster to the size of small dice, season with pepper, salt and spices; melt a piece of butter in a saucepan, mix with it a tablespoonful of flour, add the lobster and some parsley finely minced; moisten with some good stock till the mixture assumes the appearance of minced veal; then stir into it, off the fire, the yolks of a couple of eggs. Spread out the mixture to cool, and proceed as above. Those who like it may introduce into either of these dishes the slightest flavour of shallot or even of garlic, which is done by simply rubbing the saucepan with it before beginning operations.

3. Cut up, as in the foregoing, of the flesh of lobster three parts, and of mushrooms and truffles mixed one part, add pepper, salt, and spices to taste and minced parsley. Put the whole into a saucepan on the fire, moisten with some well-flavoured white sauce (*velouté*), add a small piece of glaze, and when the mixture is quite hot, take it off the fire, and stir in a sufficient number of yolks of eggs to set it when cold. Then make it into cutlets as above.

The lard in which these cutlets are fried must be very hot, else they will prove failures, especially if made according to the last two recipes.

By shaping any of the above into balls you will produce CROQUETTES DE HOMARD, and by treating remnants of salmon in the same manner you will have, according as you shape the mixture, CROQUETTES DE SAUMON, or one form of SALMON CUTLETS. The artistic form, however, of salmon cutlet is a different affair, and of this the following recipe is an example:

SALMON CUTLETS AUX CONCOMBRES.—Take a slice of salmon two inches thick, carefully remove the bones and skin, cut it into slices half an inch thick, and flatten each on the chopping board with a cutlet bat dipped in water. From these slices cut as many cutlets of a uniform shape as you can. Place them quite flat on a well-buttered baking tin, sprinkle pepper and salt over them, and, ten minutes before they are wanted, put them into the oven with a sheet of buttered white paper over them. Put all the trimmings of the salmon into a saucepan with carrots, onions, thyme, parsley, a bay leaf, a few cloves, some whole pepper, salt to taste, and a little more than a pint of good stock. Leave this to boil gently till reduced to one-half, then strain the liquor into a basin, and remove any fat there may be. Melt a piece of butter the size of an egg, add to it a little flour, and stir it on the fire till it is well coloured; add the liquor to this, and continue stirring until the sauce boils. Cut a large cucumber in rounds an inch long, cut each round into four quarters, remove the seeds and rind, and trim each piece to a uniform shape, then throw them into boiling water with a little salt; let them boil until nearly cooked. Strain them, and throw them into cold water, then strain them again, and put them into a saucepan with a little butter, pepper, salt, and chopped parsley, to be kept covered up and warm until wanted. To dish up; pour the sauce on a dish, arrange the cutlets on it, overlapping each other in a circle, and fill the hollow space in the middle with the cucumber.

There are a great many ways of stewing fish known to professors of the art, but I will confine myself to a few, which, as modified by me, are very easy to accomplish:

1. Butter liberally a silver or metal dish; strew it with a mixture of bread crumbs, minced sweet herbs, pepper and salt, and a little powdered nutmeg; lay the fish on it, put more of the bread crumbs, &c., over it, and a few pieces of butter; add the juice of a lemon, and bake till the fish is done, serving in the dish itself.

2. Butter plentifully a dish, as above; make a mixture of mushrooms, shallots, and parsley, minced very fine, place a thin layer of it on the dish, then a thin layer of what is called CHAPELURE (baked bread crumbs—produced best in this way: pound some well-baked "pulled bread," and pass it through a fine strainer or colander), then the fish, then the rest of the mushrooms, &c.; cover the whole with *chapelure*, adding pepper and salt, and enough gravy or stock and white wine, in equal parts, to come up to the fish but not over it, taking care that the *chapelure*, &c., on the fish be moistened but not washed off in the process. To be baked as above.

This form of dressing fish is what is called AUX FINES HERBES; but if the fish is baked until hardly any gravy remains, then you will have a fish AU GRATIN. Soles, or fillets of soles, are best cooked in either of the above ways. Remnants of turbot or codfish are very good dressed *au gratin*, but the process is somewhat different.

CODFISH AU GRATIN.—Rub a dish slightly with garlic and butter it, lay on it some boiled codfish, picked out in flakes, and perfectly free from bones, pour over it a judicious quantity of melted butter, made with milk and cream; sprinkle pepper and salt, to taste, over (those who like may add a little cayenne); cover the fish all over with very fine *chapelure*, then put the dish in the oven to get hot, and when the top is well browned it is ready.

Some Parmesan cheese introduced into the melted butter, and also sprinkled over the fish, produces a pleasant variety of the above.

The following are various forms of the French MATELOTTE:

1. Put into a saucepan any kind of fresh or salt water fish, or both (cut in pieces a couple of inches long), a muslin bag containing sweet herbs and spices, a laurel leaf, and plenty of whole pepper; a root of parsley, and a clove or two of garlic; add salt *quant. suff.*, with broth or gravy and claret, in equal parts, sufficient to cover the fish. Let the whole boil till the fish is done, not overdone. Fry a dozen or more small onions in plenty of butter, add a handful of flour to it, and a sufficient quantity of the liquor the fish has been boiled in to make a thick sauce. Take out the fish and serve with the sauce over it, and sippets of bread fried in butter round it.

2. MATELOTTE D'ANGUILLES.—Take a couple or more eels, cut them up into pieces two inches long. Put half a pint of stock and the same quantity of claret into a saucepan with a sliced onion, a clove of garlic, some whole pepper salt, cloves, thyme, bay leaf, and parsley, all according to taste; lay the eels in this, and let them boil gently till done. Strain the sauce and add to it a liqueur glass of brandy. Melt a good-sized piece of butter in a saucepan, stir into it a tablespoonful of flour, then add the sauce; let it boil, pour it over the fish, and serve with sippets as the above.

3. Cut up the eels as above, flour them, and fry them a light brown in butter. Melt a quarter of a pound of butter in a saucepan, mix with it a tablespoonful of flour, add half a pint of stock and the same quantity of claret or burgundy, a bundle of sweet herbs, two or three shallots, whole pepper, cloves, and salt to taste, and the least bit of cayenne. Let this sauce boil a quarter of an hour, strain it over the eels in a saucepan, add a few button mushrooms, and let the whole stew gently for twenty minutes, squeeze in the juice of half a lemon, and serve.

Another Gallic preparation of fish, peculiar to the south of France, is the BOUILLABAISSE, than which there are few dishes more delicious or more difficult to get at. In its own country, especially in Marseilles, most people who can cook at all know how to make it; but in this country, I am afraid, it is not to be had for love or money, although the excellence of it has been praised by Thackeray, who thus describes it in his ballad of " Bouillabaisse:"

> This bouillabaisse a noble dish is,
> A sort of soup, or broth, or brew,
> Or hotchpotch, of all sorts of fishes
> That Greenwich never could outdo—
> Green herbs, red peppers, mussels, saffern,
> Soles, onions, garlic, roach and dace,
> All these you eat at Terré's tavern
> In this one dish of bouillabaisse.

I have eaten it in the greatest perfection at the *Trois Frères Provençaux*, in the Palais Royal, where it had to be ordered the day before.

The following is one way of making it, which will produce a dish not devoid of merit, although inferior to the production of the *Trois Frères*—now, to the unspeakable grief of all lovers of good food, unhappily extinct.

Take any sort of both fresh and salt water fish, not too large, such as whiting, soles, small haddocks, plaice, mullets, small doreys, and carp, roach, dace, perch, &c., the greater the variety the better, say in all about 4lb. or 5lb. weight, a couple of dozen mussels, three or four onions sliced, the same number of tomatoes peeled, emptied of their seeds, and cut up in quarters (or dried tomatoes), a slice or two of lemon, from which remove the skin, a small bag containing plenty of whole pepper, a few cloves, a laurel leaf, a clove of garlic, a piece of lemon or orange rind, a pinch of saffron, and half a chili or capsicum pod. Put the whole into a saucepan, and add to it some fine salad oil, some light white wine, and some water, in the following proportions: one part oil, one of wine, and three of water, salt to taste, and on the point of serving throw in a handful of minced parsley. It takes about an hour to cook, and, when cooked, may be served either altogether in a deep dish, over slices of stale bread, or the best part of the liquor may be served thus, and the fish with the rest separately. The muslin bag must be of course suppressed at the time of serving.

Broiled fish is by no means a bad institution, especially for breakfast; but there is broiled fish and broiled fish. I should place the fish in a "*marinade*" (pickle) for some hours, and then broil it wrapped up in a piece of oiled paper, not printed paper. The pickle I should compose as follows: fine salad oil, a very little vinegar, pepper, salt, parsley, and any fresh sweet herbs that are obtainable, minced very fine, as well as a few shallots, all, of course, in due proportions; and I may here again mention that onions, shallots, and garlic are as dangerous as they are useful to the cook's art, for a little of them goes a great way, and if a certain limit be overstepped they spoil instead of improving the dish.

A slice of salmon, or a red mullet, which has lain in the above pickle three or four hours, and is then inclosed in oiled paper, broiled over a clear fire, and served either with a lump of *maître d'hôtel* butter over it, or with a brown caper sauce, is a dish fit for a king.

Here is another form somewhat akin to the above for dressing that excellent fish the red mullet:

ROUGETS EN PAPILLOTE.—Cut one carrot and two onions into thin slices; add thyme, parsley, and marjoram, with pepper and salt to taste, and three tablespoonfuls of salad oil; mix these well together, cover each mullet with the mixture, and roll it up in a piece of white paper, previously oiled; bake them in a moderate oven half an hour, then carefully open the paper, place the fish neatly on a dish, ready to be served, and keep it warm. Melt a small piece of butter, add a large pinch of flour, half a tumblerful of good stock, and the vegetables, &c., the fish were cooked in. Let the sauce boil five minutes, add salt if wanted; strain, skim, pour it over the fish, and serve.

FRYING.

Some twenty years ago, in a street where I lived in an Italian town, was a wine-shop, at the door of which stood a man who got his living by vending various kinds of vegetables and sundry preparations of flour fried in oil or lard. The operation of frying was conducted on the spot in the open air. The trade was brisk at all times, and this frying man was a great ally of the wine-shop, for his wares, being plentifully sprinkled with salt, helped to draw custom. But it was not to all of his customers that he was so bountiful of that condiment; for if any of the neighbouring gentry sent to him for a dish of *frittura*, as many often did, he would produce a *piatto*, of which any cook might have been proud.

In Italy *un piatto di frittura*—a dish of fried things—seldom fails to appear at most tables. The things are almost too numerous to mention; leaves and sprigs of borage, flowers of vegetable marrow, flowers of acacia, sliced vegetable marrow, potatoes, celery, artichokes, &c., &c.; then some small fish, like whitebait, called *fravaglie*, and molluscs of various kinds, *purpe* (a species of octopus) and several varieties of *calamari* (a sort of sepia); but the latter are among the best. All these are either floured or dipped in batter before frying, and with the batter itself (*pastetta*) many oddly-shaped morsels are prepared, with or without the addition of Indian corn flour, semolina, &c.

The frier above referred to knew his business right well, and I will endeavour in this paper to set forth some of the first principles thereof, premising that I write for those who know nothing whatever about it, and that what may be fulsome truisms to professors of the art, are valuable hints to the uninitiated.

Frying is of two kinds, which may be termed the dry and the wet process. The former is typified by the cooking of an omelette or a pancake, and butter only should be used for this purpose. Fish, vegetables, rissoles, croquets, fritters, &c., should be wet fried—*i.e.*, in plenty of fat, so that they swim in, and are completely surrounded by it. Lard, oil, or dripping may be used, lard being unquestionably the best frying medium. Only such things as do not require long frying may be fried in oil, for at a certain temperature it acquires a disagreeable taste, and cannot be used again; whilst lard, if properly attended to, will remain sweet and fit to use, for frying purposes, for many weeks. This is what is to be done. As soon as you have removed the things fried, throw into the frying-pan a handful of salt, and pour off the lard into an earthen pot, leaving out the sediment which will have formed at the bottom. The way to manage is to have three pots with a supply of lard. No. 1, you will use to fry sweets (fritters, &c.); No. 2, to fry savouries (croquets, &c.); No. 3, to fry fish. Begin with fresh lard in pot No. 1; having used it once or twice, transfer it to No. 2; and when it has done duty there pass it on to No. 3. Dripping may be all very well, but, clarify it as you like, you can never produce the same golden tints as when lard—good, sweet lard—is used; but, of course, good dripping is better than bad lard.

Carême prefers beef fat to all other frying mediums, but what he means, however, is not the dripping collected from joints during the process of roasting, but *lard* made by melting and clarifying the fat and suet of beef instead of that of pork. Mutton dripping is an abomination never to be used under any circumstances, except by tallow-chandlers.

This wet frying business may be described as boiling things in fat, and what makes it a very attractive mode of dressing food is, that the juices of each morsel are kept in it instead of a large part of them being dissolved, as in the case of boiling in water. The cardinal point of successful frying is to let the fat become sufficiently hot before commencing operations. All the merit of a good *friture*, says Brillat Savarin, depends upon the *surprise*—*i.e.*, upon the fat being hot enough; and I would refer all those who have any wish to improve in the art to the Professor's Seventh Meditation, The Theory of the *Friture*. This Gallic word *friture*—*frittura* in Italian—means in those languages, not only frying or the action of doing so, but the medium used in frying, and also the thing fried, be it what it may. I am not aware of any English words to render these two significations.

But, to return to the frying-pan. If the fat is not sufficiently heated, the things to be fried, instead of being "surprised" by it, will get soaked with it; and you will produce a flabby, greasy mess, instead of a crisp, appetising dish. Until practice has been acquired the heat of the fat should be tried with a sippet of bread, and if in a few seconds it assume a light yellow colour, then proceed.

The things to be fried should themselves be as free from moisture as possible, as otherwise they will lower the temperature of the fat suddenly, and prevent their *surprise* and the success of the cook. In the case of potatoes, they should be dried thoroughly in a cloth after being cut up for frying. Fish and other things are egged and bread crumbed, floured, or dipped in batter. For fish, eggs and bread crumbs are a mistake; flouring is the proper thing, and this should be done at the moment of frying, and not before. To flour successfully whitebait and other small fry, oysters, &c., you should possess the instrument I am about to describe, which, if it is not to be bought in this country, can easily be made to order. It is in shape like a long drum, and consists of four parts, which fit into each other. The bottom compartment is like a deep sieve, with a piece of parchment stretched across it, instead of tammy or wire. On this fits another sieve, also with a parchment bottom, but pierced with holes the size of a pea, and on this again fits another sieve, the parchment of which is pierced with very small holes, or a piece of tammy is stretched across it instead; then comes a fourth piece, with whole parchment, which is simply a cover. When fitted together, the four pieces present three chambers, the bottoms of which are respectively a piece of parchment, the common bottom of the whole apparatus, another piece with large holes, and another with small holes, or made of tammy. If you place some flour in the top compartment, your whitebait in the second, fit the pieces together, put on the cover, and shake the apparatus from side to side on the table, a cloud of flour will descend on to the fish from the third floor, and the superfluity will fall through the large holes into the first floor, leaving the fish in the second floor, floured to a nicety.

If you *will* bread crumb your fish, the process should be carried out some time before frying, and it is better always to do it a second time after the lapse of an hour or so; and any other things which have to be bread crumbed, such as cutlets, &c., should be treated in like manner.

Some vegetables, such as slices of vegetable marrow, or bottoms of artichokes, need only to be floured in the machine aforesaid before frying; but, as a general rule, they are better dipped in batter.

When the thing fried is done it should be placed on a cloth or on several sheets of blotting paper in front of the fire to let all the grease evaporate and drop from it. If savoury it should be sprinkled freely with salt, as fine as can be procured, and this should be done at once; the sweets should be covered with finely-powdered sugar at the time of serving.

The best fire to fry upon is a clear wood fire when this can be managed. Frying with a coal fire on an English fireplace, such as exists in most houses, is an operation trying alike to the patience and to the back of the operator.

That the frying-pan should, as everything else in a kitchen, be scrupulously clean I need hardly say; but, to fry successfully, this point is of some importance, and there are as many people, if not more, who require to be told of it as there are who do not.

In conclusion, I will tell you of a homely conceit of a floury nature which is used in the land of the Gaul.

Put about a pint of water in a saucepan with a few grains of salt, a piece of butter the size of an egg, and as much sugar, with plenty of grated lemon peel. When the whole boils, throw in gradually sufficient flour to form a thick paste; then let it remain ten minutes, and work into it (off the fire) three or four eggs, reserving the white of one or two, which you whisk into a froth, and mix into the paste. Let it rest a couple of hours, then proceed to fry by dropping pieces of it the size of a walnut into very hot lard. The paste will swell in the process of frying, and hollow balls of a fine golden colour will be produced if the lard is at the right temperature, and they are fried long enough. Serve piled up on a dish with a good sprinkling of powdered sugar, and you will have BEIGNETS SOUFFLÉS, a cheap and effective sweet, sometimes adorned with the poetic appellation of "*soupirs de nonne.*"

BATTER.

INNUMERABLE dishes, both savoury and sweet, owe their *raison d'être* entirely to batter. By means of it most kinds of vegetable and fruit can be made into savoury or sweet fritters. Remains of flesh, fowl, and fish can be turned into dainty morsels, and in some cases inviting *entrées* can also be served at first hand in a coating of batter. Lastly, several *entremets sucrés*, as, for instance, pancakes, are composed of nothing but batter.

The forms of the batter itself, as may be imagined, are many, and they vary according to the use for which it is required. Frying, of course, is the mode of cooking these preparations, and to be a master hand at this is indispensable to insure success in the production of any dish of which batter is an element.

What it is intended to now expound is how to make batter, and how to compound various cunning dishes which will be found as effective and tasteful as they are inexpensive and simple.

First as to mixing the batter; my favourite form is this:

1. Beat up the yolks of two eggs with two tablespoonfuls of brandy or rum, one tablespoonful of olive oil, and four or five tablespoonfuls of cold water. Incorporate with this mixture three tablespoonfuls of flour and a pinch of salt. Take great care to make it into a smooth paste, and to keep on beating it for at least ten minutes. If the batter be too thick, more water is to be added, to make

it of the desired consistency. At the time of using stir into it quickly and thoroughly the whites of two eggs, beaten into a stiff froth.

There are other forms, which in their way are not devoid of merit—viz.:

2. Beat up equal parts of salad oil and brandy, say a tablespoonful of each, add the yolk of an egg, and incorporate with this sufficient flour to make a thickish paste, which you afterwards thin to the requisite consistency by the addition of water; at the time of using add the white of an egg beaten up into a froth.

3. Equal parts of milk and of vinegar and water, with sufficient flour to make a batter, and a pinch of salt, are thoroughly mixed and well beaten.

4. Beat up two tablespoonfuls of dissolved butter with the yolks of two eggs and a pinch of salt and some warm water; add to this as much flour as will make the batter of the required consistency. Keep on beating the mixture till it is perfectly smooth, and then at the time of using add one or two whites of egg whisked into a froth.

5. Mix thoroughly two tablespoonfuls of salad oil, the same quantity of water, a pinch of salt, and enough flour to make a thick paste, then gradually thin it by adding water, and at the time of using it add the whites of two eggs beaten up into a froth.

6. The yolks of two eggs are beaten up with two tablespoonfuls of milk; to this is added a small pinch of salt and two tablespoonfuls of dissolved butter, then enough flour to make a thickish paste, which must be well beaten, and then thinned, by the addition of milk, to the desired consistency; the whites of the eggs beaten up into a froth being added at the end.

7. Melt two ounces of butter in a pint of water, add a pinch of salt, and, removing the saucepan from the fire,

incorporate sufficient flour to make the batter; when quite cold, mix thoroughly with it one tablespoonful of orange-flower water, and the whites of two eggs beaten into froth.

8. Add to a tumblerful of French or Rhenish wine a liqueur glass of brandy and the same quantity of oil; then make a thick paste with the yolks of four eggs, a little water, and some flour; it should be so thick that by adding thereto the wine, brandy, and oil, it will become a batter of the proper consistency. One white of egg beaten into a froth should be added before using the batter.

9. Reverting to the first recipe, instead of rum or brandy, use the same quantity of any liqueur you may fancy, putting only half the quantity of oil and no salt.

10. Make a smooth paste with flour and a glass of ale, then add a tablespoonful of dissolved butter and a pinch of salt; the yolks of two eggs are then worked into the mixture, and then the white of one or two eggs beaten into a froth.

Taste and circumstances must determine which of the above forms of batter is to be used. I now proceed to describe the composition of the FRITTERS themselves, the number and varieties of which are many.

Apples should be cored, cut in slices a quarter of an inch thick, and laid for at least a couple of hours in a marinade of brandy and sugar, to which the thin rind of a lemon, or some cinnamon cut in pieces, is added; sherry may be substituted for brandy, but the effect will not be so good. At the time of frying drain each piece of apple, dip it in batter, taking care that it is covered all over, and fry. Another form consists in rolling each piece of apple in finely powdered sugar before dipping into the batter.

Pears are treated in the same way as apples.

Oranges.—Peel carefully, so as to remove every vestige of the white part of the rind; divide into quarters, remove the pips, roll each quarter in powdered sugar, then dip in batter and fry; or peel and core as you would apples, cut in slices, and fry as above. Another form is to make a syrup as follows: Beat up a white of egg in a pint and a half of water; in this put two pounds of loaf sugar, and set on the fire in an untinned copper vessel called a sugar-boiler. Keep on removing the scum—adding a few drops of cold water until no more rises—then let the syrup boil for a few minutes, and strain it through a piece of tammy. When cold, dip the pieces of orange in the syrup, drain them, dip in batter, and fry.

Lemons are treated in this way by those who like them, but they should be dipped into very thick batter, and not a sprinkling, but "no end" of powdered sugar should accompany these fritters.

Another form of treating both oranges and lemons is to put the pieces in a marinade of brandy or rum with some sugar. When they have been in it for some hours proceed as before.

Peaches, Apricots, Nectarines, Plums, Greengages.—The fruit should not be quite ripe, the three first less so than the two last. Split each fruit, remove the stone and the skin, roll each half in powdered sugar, dip in batter, and fry. They may be dipped in syrup instead of being rolled in powdered sugar; or, again, they may be put into a marinade of brandy. In the case of peaches and nectarines, if noyau or maraschino take the place of the syrup, the process, though expensive, will produce agreeable results.

Strawberries, Raspberries, and Currants.—Remove the

stalks, roll in sugar, dip in batter, and fry. Strawberries may be steeped in brandy, or the above syrup may be used for all three. Except in the case of large strawberries, the plan is to put the fruit all at once into the vessel containing the batter, then to take out two or three at a time with a spoon, and to skilfully drop them into the hot fat, so as to form one fritter.

Pine Apple.—Peel, cut in slices of convenient shape, steep for some hours in brandy, or, better still, good old rum; roll in powdered sugar, dip in batter, and fry.

Rhubarb and Celery.—Cut into pieces an inch long, which you boil in sugar and water, or plain water, for a few minutes; then drain and put them into cold water: when they are quite cold lay them in a marinade of brandy and sugar, there to remain some hours; then proceed as for other fritters.

Fruit, such as peaches, apricots, &c., preserved in tins or in spirit, are made into fritters in this way: Take some sheet wafer, such as confectioners use, moisten it, and wrap each piece of fruit very carefully in it, then dip in batter and fry. By a similar process you can make fritters with any sort of suitable jam or marmalade, and also with various kinds of creams prepared as under; but in this case the use of wafer is optional. Make a smooth paste with three tablespoonfuls of potato flour, and part of a pint of milk, then gradually add the rest of the milk, or the same quantity of milk and cream, then two whole eggs, the yolks of three or four more, a pat of the freshest butter, and sugar to taste. If necessary, strain the mixture, and set it on the fire, where you must keep stirring it until it is quite thick. When nearly cold spread it out on a buttered slab to the thickness of about half an inch. When quite cold cut it into fritters, which you may either egg and bread crumb, or dip in batter before frying. This cream may be flavoured with vanilla, orange flower, &c., or it may be made with chocolate, by dissolving in the first instance, enough of it in the milk to both flavour and colour the cream.

All fritters should be well dried in front of the fire before serving, and sweet fritters should always be well powdered with fine sugar; and, after being so powdered, they may be glazed by holding a red-hot salamander over them.

The composition of PANCAKES differs little from that of frying-batter; and the following are various formulæ for producing this traditional Shrove Tuesday dish.

1. Mix two tablespoonfuls of flour with half a pint of cream, add two eggs, and beat the whole well till quite smooth; put in a tablespoonful of powdered sugar, a little powdered cinnamon, and a little grated nutmeg.

2. Mix half a pint of cream with three tablespoonfuls of flour and half a pint of white wine; add the yolks of ten eggs, a teaspoonful of salt, and some powdered cinnamon. If too thick, dilute the batter with milk.

3. Make a thin batter with a pint of cream and some flour, put in half a pound of fresh butter melted, eight eggs well beaten, half a nutmeg grated, and a little salt.

4. Beat six new-laid eggs with half a pint of cream, half a nutmeg grated, and as much flour as will make the batter of the proper thickness.

5. Mix a pint of milk with as much flour as will make a thin batter; add a glass of pale brandy, a little grated nutmeg, a little powdered ginger, and a pinch of salt; then add four eggs, beat all well together till smooth.

6. Make a thin batter with a quart of milk and some flour, put in six eggs, a pinch of salt, and a tablespoonful of powdered ginger.

7. Boil a quart of milk for half an hour with a stick of

cinnamon and the peel of a lemon; break six eggs into a basin, and beat them up for a minute, add four tablespoonfuls of flour, then the milk strained, and a liqueur glass of brandy.

8. Put into a basin four eggs, four tablespoonfuls of flour, one of pale brandy, one of olive oil, and two of orange-flower water; mix the whole into a smooth paste, then dilute it to the proper thickness with either milk or water.

9. Make a smooth paste in a basin with the yolks of six eggs, the whites of three, and three tablespoonfuls of flour; add a pinch of salt, a wineglassful of orange-flower water, and dilute the paste into a batter by the addition of milk.

10. Take half a pint of ale, half a pint of water, and add sufficient flour to make a batter; then put in a pinch of salt, a wineglass of brandy, and work into the mixture the yolks of six eggs.

There is no great difficulty in mixing the batter for pancakes, but in the cooking of them much practice is necessary. Turning a pancake is an operation requiring the same suppleness of wrist as the " nice conduct " of a fencing foil. One great point to be attained is to fry your pancake in the smallest possible quantity of butter; the neglect of this important rule sometimes entails disastrous consequences at those family meetings where the old custom is kept up of compelling each guest to fry his own pancake—a custom which goes far to ensure a great desideratum in the successful treatment of this dish; *i. e.*, that it should be eaten the instant it is done. Powdered sugar and a squeeze of lemon are the legitimate adjuncts of a pancake; but some powdered cinnamon, and peradventure a dash of apricot or any other jam are not devoid of merit. The one great thing to bear in mind is the utmost swiftness in any operation which takes place between the pancake leaving the frying pan and being served.

Coming now to savoury fritters, the most elaborate form of these is—as its fine name "Kromesky" implies—a dish of Russian or Polish origin; and, when well executed, a most excellent dish it is.

A KROMESKY may be defined generally as a teaspoonful of cunningly-devised mincemeat, called *salpicon* (not the mincemeat of Britain), wrapped either in a slice of bacon or of calf's udder, or in a piece of wafer, then dipped in batter and fried. It is the SALPICON which gives the character to the kromesky, and this element of it can be prepared in many ways from a variety of things.

1. Given some of the dreaded cold mutton of British households—and here I must remark that, in all preparations of cold meat to be warmed up again, all fat and parts which have "seen the fire," *i.e.*, been browned, must be carefully excluded, else the dish you are making will betray its origin by its taste. Mince a small quantity of the said mutton until each piece is the size of a small pea. Having fried in butter to a pale straw colour some shallot or an onion finely minced, you throw in your minced mutton, give it a turn or two, then moisten with some good gravy or stock; add spices, pepper, and salt to taste, and a pinch of minced parsley; let it reduce a little till it presents the appearance of what is called minced veal; then put it to cool, to be used as directed further on.

2. Veal, beef, or pork may be treated in the same way, and the addition of minced truffles or mushrooms, and also (in the case of veal or pork) of a *liaison* of yolks of eggs and lemon juice, cannot but add to the success of the dish.

3. Remains of poultry and game, or of the two combined, make a very good *salpicon*, and the addition of some tongue or ham to the former is desirable; but the preparation must be somewhat different, and a *liaison* of yolks of eggs and lemon juice is imperative; in fact, to make a good *salpicon* of fowls, you should have some good *velouté* sauce wherewith to bind your minced fowl and tongue, to which the addition of minced truffles, or at least mushrooms, is almost indispensable if you wish to produce a truly artistic dish.

4. With fish, particularly salmon, excellent *salpicon* for kromeskys is made; and it is for these that the wafer instead of bacon or calf's udder is used. To make *salpicon* of fish, all that is needed is to mince the fish to the desired size; then give it a turn on the fire with a well-made white sauce, add a little spice, and set it to cool.

5. Sweetbreads, cockscombs, and all other things which are used to make a ragoût for a *vol-au-vent* can also be employed to make *salpicon*.

6. Lobsters and prawns, minced to the required size, and bound with a good white sauce and a *liaison* of yolks of eggs, constitute another variety of *salpicon*; but for these, wafer should be used in preference to bacon.

Having your *salpicon* ready, the mode of proceeding is this: Cut some slices of previously parboiled bacon as thin as you possibly can, and to the size of about an inch and a half by two or two and a half inches; place on each slice a teaspoonful of *salpicon*, and roll it up in the bacon very neatly: keep the kromeskys in a cool place till the time of frying them, when much dexterity is required to dip them in batter and lay them in the frying pan without unrolling them. Some clumsy people tie up their kromeskys with a bit of thin thread before dipping them in batter: this should be avoided. If a cook cannot make kromeskys without thread, she had better not make them at all.

When calf's udder is used it should be previously boiled in the stock pot; then very thin slices of it should be cut as described above.

To use wafer is the easiest of all; it need only be dipped in cold water. In all cases, however, great care must be taken to pack, so to speak, each kromesky neatly and evenly.

Oysters make also very good kromeskys, but I doubt whether they are not better as a simple fritter, viz., dipped in batter and fried. If, however, you wish to proceed artistically, you should, having parboiled and bearded your oysters, put them for two or three hours in a marinade composed of the juice of two or more lemons, slices of onions, a bay leaf, and some whole pepper and cloves.

Another very toothsome form of FRIED OYSTERS is this. Beard and parboil your oysters; when quite cold split each oyster nearly in half, insert in each a piece, the size of two peas, of the following composition, then close them again, dip in batter, and fry. Mince very finely some mushrooms and shallots, and truffles; give them a turn on the fire, with some butter, pepper, salt, and a small quantity of glaze or savoury jelly; set the composition by stirring into it the yolks of two eggs, and the juice of at least one lemon, then let it get cold and use it.

The remains of any firm-fleshed fish, such as soles, turbot, &c., cut into neat collops, steeped in a marinade such as that described above for oysters, then dipped in batter and fried, constitute a homely but useful form of fritter.

Now, as to vegetables. There are many which may

make the foundation of good savoury fritters. They should mostly be previously parboiled, and of course cut into convenient shapes; and as all that need be done then is to dip each piece in batter and fry it, I shall content myself with enumerating some of those vegetables which make the best fritters—they are cauliflowers, vegetable marrow, artichokes, Jerusalem artichokes, celery, seakale, and asparagus, &c. Artichokes proper alone require special treatment. The upper part of the leaves and the small leaves in the centre should all be cut off, and the stalk trimmed away until nothing is left but what is good to eat. Then each artichoke should be cut into four "quarters," or more according to its size. During this operation of trimming the pieces should be kept in water in which the juice of a lemon has been squeezed, else wherever the knife has touched them they will turn black. They also should be parboiled longer than any other vegetables, some of which, such as vegetable marrow, require no parboiling at all, if cut in sufficiently small pieces.

In Italy, as I have before remarked, they also make fritters with the leaves of spinach, of sorrel, of borage, the flowers of vegetable marrow before it blooms, and the flowers of white acacia. The way to proceed is first to wash and thoroughly dry the leaves or flowers. Then, taking by the stalk a couple of leaves, or only one, according to the size, you dip it in batter, see that it is well covered, and then drop it into the frying-pan. Vegetable marrow flowers, or rather buds, are fried one by one, and acacia flowers in small bunches.

Another description of savoury fritters is made with a kind of paste, which, being allowed to cool, is cut into shapes, which are dipped in batter and fried. Here are several forms of it.

1. Pass some potatoes through a sieve, and stir into

them a little butter melted and enough yolks of eggs or whole eggs to form a stiffish paste; season with salt, pepper and a little nutmeg; form into the shape of little balls, dip in batter and fry. This may be varied by adding a little cream, or some ham or Bologna sausage finely minced, and some chopped parsley.

2. Put into a saucepan about a pint of boiling water and 1oz. of butter; drop into this gradually with the hand some Indian corn flour, stirring all the time until you get a liquid paste. Take care not to put too much flour, and to put it in gradually, else it will form into knots and spoil the dish. Removing the saucepan from the fire, you stir into the paste a good allowance of grated Parmesan cheese, and a little salt and pepper, and then pour out your paste on a marble slab to cool. When cold, cut it out in any shape you like and fry. The addition of ham or sausage can also be made to this.

3. Make the paste as above, only with common corn flour; when half cold stir into it some yolks of eggs, and flavour it with pepper, salt, and nutmeg; add chopped parsley and minced ham; then treat as the others.

4. Put about a pint of water into a saucepan with a piece of butter the size of an egg, the least bit of cayenne and plenty of black pepper. When the water boils throw gradually into it sufficient flour to form a thick paste, then take it off the fire and work into it about ¼lb. of grated Parmesan cheese, and then the yolks of three or four eggs and the whites of two beaten up to a froth. Let the paste rest for a couple of hours, and proceed to fry by dropping pieces of it the size of a walnut into plenty of hot lard. Serve sprinkled with very fine salt.

The first three of these pastes may also be fried without being previously dipped in batter, but it is more difficult to so fry them creditably.

BOILING MEAT.

This is one of the simplest and most economical modes of preparing food. Meat loses less weight in boiling than in any other process of cooking, and the water it has boiled in can always be turned to good account; besides which, although it may be an open question whether boiled meat is more nutritious than roast or broiled meat, it is beyond dispute more wholesome and easily digested.

Without entering upon the *théorique* of the chemical process which takes place in the operation of boiling meat, I propose to dilate upon the practical part of the operation, which naturally divides itself into three heads :— (1) When the object is to extract the juices of the meat, which is not itself to be used; (2) when both the broth and the meat are to be eaten; and (3) when the meat alone is to be served. The two first constitute the process of making stock, broth, or soup. Of this I have treated in another place, so I shall here confine myself to the last head, in which the mode of operation differs from that used in the making of soup in the very material point that, whereas in the former the meat should be put to cook in cold water, and then heated gradually, in this the meat should not be put in until the water is hot; but yet, in neither case, should the meat ever be allowed to boil fast: what is called simmering is the thing. And here let me observe, once for all, that water cannot be heated beyond a certain temperature; and that therefore, when once the water boils, to increase the fire can only accelerate evaporation, but will not make the water hotter —on the contrary, it will not only retard the cooking, but will help to make the meat tough, and is therefore pure waste. The talent in boiling a piece of meat consists in so regulating the fire as to keep the water always at the same temperature, and this should be a gentle simmer. When meat is put to cook in hot water the scum will not rise in such quantities as in the process of making stock; but it should be as carefully removed, and no salt put in until the water is perfectly free from scum. Then also should be added a due proportion of certain vegetables, such as carrots, onions, celery, and also sweet herbs, according to the kind of meat which is being boiled; but by no means in such quantities as would be used in making soup. The next point which demands attention is, that the piece of meat be completely covered with water; and if during the process of boiling it should evaporate so far as not to cover some part of the meat, more boiling water should be added. The time that a joint of meat should boil is set down usually at the rate of fifteen to twenty minutes for every pound which the joint weighs; but this is a very rough rule to go by. The only reliable rule is that which the experience of the cook supplies. A very good way to boil meat is to boil it in the pot in which stock is being made. It should be put in after the stock has gone through the process of skimming, and all the vegetables have been added to it. The joint should always be neatly trimmed and tied up with twine before being put to boil; and the English practice of salting beef which is intended to be boiled should be avoided. Such a practice cannot be too strongly condemned; for while it impairs the wholesomeness of the meat, and makes it less digestible, it considerably diminishes the nutritive properties of it; and, boil it as you will, a piece of salted beef is never so tender as a piece of fresh beef. The same principles apply to boiling all kinds of meats and poultry. In the case of the latter, and of such joints as it is desirable to get quite white when boiled, washing and even soaking in cold or lukewarm water before they are put to boil is resorted to, and the water in which they are put to boil should be boiling hot. The washing and soaking take away some of the nourishment of the things so treated, but usefulness must sometimes be sacrificed to appearance. In order to preserve the whiteness of fowls in the process of boiling, various methods are suggested. Some cookery books recommend a slice of stale bread being put in the water; others that the fowls should be tied up in a floured cloth, or in a cloth without flour, or inclosed in a tin made for the purpose, and this plunged into boiling water, which latter process I should call steaming, not boiling. To preserve the whiteness of a fowl or turkey that is to be boiled, the one essential point is to wash it well in tepid water with a lemon squeezed in it, to rub it all over with a lemon cut in half, and then to put it to boil. When all the scum that may rise is removed, a round of buttered paper should be placed over the pot, and the lid put on close. Poultry cannot boil too slowly. Onions, sweet herbs, and whole pepper, as well as salt, should always be put in the saucepan with any kind of poultry.

An old French way of boiling a fowl is to parboil it first, then to pack it up in slices of fat bacon tied on with a string, and then to put it in boiling water with vegetables, &c., to finish cooking. To use instead of water either stock or the liquor in which a joint of meat has been boiled, provided it is strained and freed from fat, can but be an improvement to boiled poultry. This is one of the uses to which the liquor meat has been boiled in can be put; but the chief use of it—and if it have been used to boil a fowl all the better—should be to make stock proper, by being boiled with all the odds and ends of meat and poultry which are at hand, and a proper addition of vegetables and spices. Again, there are more elaborate forms of boiling poultry, calves' head, &c., such as what is called a *blanc;* but these would come more properly under the head of braising.

Although the same principles apply to the boiling of hams as to that of joints, it is very essential that hams should be soaked in water for from twenty-four to forty-eight hours, and that the water should be changed two or three times; then they should be washed, and scraped, and scrubbed perfectly clean, and, being properly trimmed, they should be laid in a boiler filled with cold water, with the addition of carrots, celery, onions, garlic, parsley, thyme, marjoram, bay leaves, cloves, and mace—the proportions of which things must be regulated by the size of the ham, and the skill or taste of the cook. Many other things are put in by those who like them—coriander seeds, juniper berries, a small wisp of hay, and even leather shavings, which latter, in the words of an ancient authority, are supposed to give the ham a high flavour. Some put in a small handful of saltpetre, to give the flesh a good colour. If the ham is a good one, the colour will be good without the addition of saltpetre, neither is it necessary to tie up a ham in a cloth; but what is undoubtedly an improvement to a boiled ham is the addition of a bottle of sherry to the water it is boiled in. Great attention must be paid to the removal of the scum, and the temperature of the water should never be allowed to rise above simmering. An ordinary sized ham will take from four to five hours to cook. When it is done, it should be allowed to remain in the liquor until it is nearly cold, it should then be taken out, the skin removed, and the top covered with baked bread crumbs, or glazed, or ornamented as fancy may suggest with aspic, &c. If it is intended to cut a ham hot, then it should only be partly boiled, and finished by braising.

I cannot conclude this part of the subject without giving a recipe for boiling ham that I came across the other day, and which is, to say the least of it, quaint. Well wash the ham in rough claret or strong beer, pack it up in several cloths soaked in either of the above liquors, and bury it four feet deep in the earth. At the end of two days exhume the ham, unpack it, trim off all parts that may be the least tainted, and put it to boil, tied up in a cloth, in a mixture of half rough claret and half water, with the usual vegetables, and as much hay as the boiler will hold. When done tighten the cloth, and turn the ham and the whole contents of the boiler into a large basin, there to remain till the next day.

ON A TIN OF BEEF.

A PORTION of the press has been loud in its praise of Australian meat, and an eminent muscular Christian, who has written favourably of it, is said to have, in truly clerical fashion, added example to precept by becoming a regular consumer of this new meat. That it is cheaper than fresh meat is obvious enough; that it is as good as fresh meat is very much a matter of taste and opinion. All agree that the meat is over-done, and this fact alone renders it a difficult problem to dress it in palatable form. When it is a question of no meat or Australian meat, it matters little whether the meat be over-done or not. There are many people, however, who would gladly use tinned meat occasionally, but only if it could be so dressed as to be appetising. I am one of these, and I determined to make a trial of this meat, and see what I could do with it. I purchased a 4lb. tin of beef, and this is what I did with it.

The meat tasted well enough when cold, but it was decidedly over-done. There was plenty of melted fat and jelly about it. Having removed the cover, I placed the tin in a saucepan full of boiling water, and in a few minutes the fat and jelly were melted. I then removed each piece of meat, pouring a little hot water over it as I did so, and letting this water fall into the tin. When the meat was all removed I filled up the tin to the brim with hot water, and strained the contents into a basin. When cold I removed the cake of fat from the top, and put the liquor, which presented the appearance of very excellent beef tea, into a saucepan with a couple of carrots, one onion, some celery, parsley, and sweet herbs, adding salt, pepper, and a few cloves. A couple of hours' boiling produced, when the liquor was strained, as good a gravy soup in taste, colour, and clearness as any housewife need wish to put upon her table. It was not the liquefied glue which is sometimes called a gravy soup, but it was what gravy soup ought to be; and if it satisfied the present writer, those who will not like it must be indeed hard to please. I had it served with crusts of bread *gratinés* in the form of *croûte au pot*.

Turning now to the meat, I first cut neat collops out of all the best pieces, as I would out of a cold leg of mutton to make hashed mutton. Then I devised a rich brown sauce, thick, velvety, and aromatic; when the sauce was finished I made it boiling hot, and laid the pieces of meat in it, leaving the saucepan on the hob just sufficient time to make the meat hot. This is how I made the sauce: having sliced an onion, I fried it in butter till it assumed a light brown colour, then I put in a tablespoonful of flour, stirred the mixture well, and added about half a pint of stock, a sprig of thyme, a bay leaf, a few cloves, some whole pepper and some salt. When the sauce had simmered half an hour I strained it, and put into it judicious proportions of walnut catsup and Worcester sauce.

The dish was served with bread sippets fried in butter, mashed potatoes being handed round with it. The meat was certainly over-done, but the tastiness of the sauce made up in some measure for that drawback. What meat was not used for the above, formed the foundation of a mince, wherewith some tiny patties made of puff paste, flaky as talc, were furnished. I need not describe how the mince was prepared, beyond stating that the juice of a lemon and the yolk of an egg put into it at the right moment gave it a piquancy of flavour, which made it quite a distinct dish from the other.

From this experiment I opine that the best use of Australian beef is to make soup such as I have described. It will without doubt be a great saving, for to make soup means, with English cooks, the expenditure of pounds and pounds of meat. As for the Australian meat itself, the ugly fact will always remain that it is overdone; overdone meat is not nice to eat, and no amount of sauce, ever so tasty, will make it a desirable dish. Scores of people, however, pronounce it excellent, but there are degrees of excellence, and tastes differ. I have no doubt that in time some better method of "tinning" the meat will be found, and what I think above all a great desideratum is that the joints should be cut by some competent person, as then we should get out of a tin a presentable piece of meat, instead of a "hunk" cut anyhow, with a few bits put in to make up the weight.

When prepared in the form of a mince, the overcooking of the meat is not so perceptible, and in this way a variety of dishes can be produced. Besides patties of puff paste, cases or borders of potatoes or of rice may be used. With poached eggs it makes a nice dish, and it will also make very fair croquettes and rissoles.

To make hashes, haricots, and stews which shall be good in an artistic sense, we must wait till some improvement has been effected in the manner of tinning Australian meat, and this, I am confident, we may look for at no very distant time.

As to eating the meat cold, it would be better to make it into a salad than to eat it with a salad; and I would suggest the following as a simple form:

Take equal parts of meat, cut in neat pieces, and of cold boiled potatoes, sliced; beat up together some olive oil and tarragon vinegar, in the proportion of two to one, add powdered pepper and salt to taste, one shallot, with a pinch of chervil and one of tarragon minced very fine; lay the meat and potatoes in the mixture, and ornament with some hard-boiled eggs and some gherkins. I need not add that this kind of salad may be varied *ad infinitum.*

MUTTON CUTLETS.

Mutton Chops are without doubt as great—if not a greater—institution of British cookery than the roast beef of old England. Ask any English cook to suggest something for dinner, and you have chops; ask any other English person, and the answer will be chops again. So great an institution are chops in this country that having a chop, in familiar parlance, has got to mean having dinner. Thus one man will ask another to come and have a chop with him, when he wishes to invite him to dinner in a friendly way. *Toujours perdrix*, however, becomes monotonous at last; besides, if the chops are cooked with tomato sauce they may lead to unforeseen complications of a disagreeable nature, as befel Mr. Pickwick. The Gauls affect chops as much as Britons; with the former, however, they not only assume a more refined and artistic shape, but they are dressed in such a variety of charming ways that one could almost live upon nothing else for months together.

Such chops as I operate upon are those called neck chops or cutlets. The chops of chop-houses and British cookery in general are very well in their way, but I prefer eating them *en bloc* in the shape of a well-roasted saddle or haunch of mutton.

The most economical way of proceeding, is to purchase a piece of the best end of a neck of mutton and divide and trim your chops at home. With the trimmings—with the addition, if necessary, of a piece more of what is called the scrag end of a neck of mutton—a very good dish of Irish stew or haricot mutton can be made for the kitchen dinner; or the said trimmings can be used to make gravy or stock, or even simply mutton broth or soup.

Every particle of gristle and almost all the fat should be removed from each cutlet, the bone or rib should not be more than two inches long from the cutlet itself, or "nut," and should be scraped quite clean. The said bone ought to be neatly sawed off, not chopped off, at the end.

Having prepared your cutlets (which should not be thicker than about one-third of an inch), in the neatest manner, and given them a gentle beating with a cutlet bat, you have your choice of cooking them by various methods, which may be classed under two heads—the plain process and the bread-crumb process. There are also more elaborate ways of cooking cutlets, of which hereafter. The plain process consists in broiling them on the gridiron over a clear fire, or they may be done in front of the fire, and this has the advantage, that the bones are less likely to become burnt or charred. The fire should be a brisk one, and the cutlets should be turned frequently during the operation. They should be underdone inside and juicy, instead of having the appearance and about the taste of a piece of soaked leather. There is no golden rule for learning to cook cutlets well by this method; practice and love of the art alone can enable the cook to approach perfection.

Frying in butter, oil, or even dripping, are other modes of cooking coming under this head, but none are better in the plain form than broiling. It is easier, however, to fry a cutlet creditably than to broil it.

The bread-crumb process is more elaborate. It has

one great advantage for those whose principal object is economy. The streak of meat, with the fat and gristle which adhere to the bone of the cutlet, need not be cut off, but simply detached from the bone, leaving one end attached to the nut of the cutlet. It is then turned back round the said nut, the cutlet is plentifully smeared with egg, and thickly plastered over with bread-crumbs. Frying consolidates the whole mass, and you have as handsome a cutlet, at all events in size, as ever graced the window of a cheap restaurant. This meretricious process, however, is never resorted to by true artists and professors; they trim their cutlets just as for broiling, then, holding them by the bone, they dip them into an egg well beaten up, or butter melted for the purpose, or hot gravy, or olive oil, either warm or cold; or, lastly, in the *pot au feu*, or stock pot; then they turn them over and over in a plateful of bread crumbs with a due amount of pepper and salt, and put them by, to repeat both operations after a lapse of about half an hour. The bread crumbs are sometimes mixed with finely-minced parsley and sweet herbs. Minced shallots in small quantity may also be added, and sometimes baked bread crumbs (*chapelure*) are used instead of plain bread crumbs. Cutlets thus prepared are generally fried, but they may also be broiled. They should be fried, not too brown, in plenty of butter or fat.

Cutlets cooked in any of the above forms can be served with a plain clear gravy, a thick brown sauce such as *Espagnole*, tomato sauce, *sauce piquante*, *Soubise* (onion sauce), *sauce ravigotte*, *tartare*, *sauce aux cornichons*, *sauce Robert*, *sauce provençale*, *sauce Périgueux*, *maître d'hôtel*, &c., &c.

They are served also with mashed potatoes, or spinach, and likewise with *purées* of potatoes, celery, carrots, turnips, sorrel, lentils, peas, beans, &c.; also with combinations of vegetables (not in the *purée* form) and some of the above-named sauces; or with the *garnitures* called a *jardinière*, a *macédoine*, &c. In short, there is no end to the variations of which a dish of mutton cutlets is susceptible, and I will now describe some ways of dressing them still more artistically.

1. The cutlets being trimmed *sec. art.*, they are dipped in egg and then turned over in a mixture of ham and truffles very finely minced. After a lapse of a quarter of an hour they are dipped in egg again, and then bread-crumbed with *chapelure*. After that cut some pieces of white paper into the shape of a heart, and large enough when folded in two to enclose each cutlet. Oil each piece of paper with butter or fine salad oil (the latter is best), place a cutlet in each and bend up the edges securely. Broil them on the gridiron till done, and serve in the paper.

The above formula is varied by dipping the cutlets in batter instead of *chapelure*, and frying them instead of broiling them in paper.

2. Make a *marinade*, with equal parts of oil and vinegar, slices of onion, whole pepper, salt, some spices, and sweet herbs, all in due proportions. Lay your cutlets, ready trimmed, in this pickle, which should cover them. When they have lain in it four or five hours, dip them in butter, melted for the purpose, and proceed to broil them in front of the fire, basting plentifully with butter. To be served with a *sauce piquante*. A few mushroom or truffle trimmings, or both, are an improvement to the pickle. Some cooks pretend to give mutton the taste of venison by putting into a pickle, somewhat similar to the above, a handful of juniper berries.

3. Mutton cutlets may also be stewed in a variety of ways, of which the following may be taken as the common form: Put some butter in a stewpan, and place your cutlets in this, turning them over and over until they are well *saisies* ("set") by the butter; then add a small quantity of well-flavoured stock or gravy, and let them simmer in this till done, when they should be served with the gravy, which you thicken if necessary with a little flour. Vegetables may be cooked with the cutlets, and served with them, or a *garniture* of vegetables, cooked separately, can be put in the midst.

4. Place your cutlets untrimmed into a saucepan over some slices of bacon, with some onions, carrots, sweet herbs, pepper, salt, and spices to taste, moisten with a very small quantity of stock or even of water, and let the cutlets braise gently till done. Then lay them out flat between two plates, with a weight over them, to remain till cold, when you proceed to trim them neatly without scraping down the bone, but cutting it off short. On the other hand strain the gravy they were braised in, and after removing all the fat, put it on one side. Mince equal quantities of shallots and mushrooms. Fry the shallots a light gold in butter, then add the mushrooms, pepper, salt, spices to taste, and minced parsley; moisten with a little of the gravy, add a squeeze of lemon, and put this mince by to get cold. Cut some paper, and oil it as mentioned above. Cover your cutlets on both sides with a thin coating of the mince, enclose them in their papers, and broil them just long enough to make them quite hot, or if more convenient, they may be made hot in the oven.

The above is my version of the well-known dish said to be due to the inspiration of MME. DE MAINTENON.

EPIGRAMS.

THE essence of epigram consists in neatness and the faculty of producing an agreeable surprise. The culinary epigram, and occasionally its literary brother also, present to us "old friends with a new face," and charm the languid palate with a new and startling combination of well-known elements. And this, perhaps, is the reason why such familiar viands as lamb and mutton, dressed in small compass and in a fanciful manner, constitute what in cookery are called Epigrams. The mode of making these is by no means difficult, and is what I now propose to describe.

Braise a piece of breast of lamb or mutton in a stew-pan, with some water, onions, carrots, celery, whole pepper, salt, a few cloves, and a *bouquet garni*, i.e., parsley, thyme, marjoram, in proper proportions, and a bay leaf, all tied up in a little bundle. When sufficiently done to allow it, pull out all the bones, and put the breast, between two dishes, under the heaviest weight you can get, there to remain until perfectly cold. In the meantime, the liquor in which it has been braised should be strained, and freed from fat, either to be used as I shall presently state, or to be kept for other purposes. The breast, being cold and stiff, is now neatly cut up into the shape of cutlets or collops, and these are egged and bread-crumbed; after an interval of at least one hour they are again egged and bread-crumbed; but this last time there should be a little salt and white pepper mixed with the egg.

When this second bread-crumbing has had time to dry, you must fry your EPIGRAMS a light brown colour, and serve them on a *purée* of turnips, spinach, turnip tops, &c., as you may fancy, or with tomato sauce, piquante sauce, &c., or lastly, simply with fried parsley.

I can safely assert that epigrams, if properly cooked, are not bad eating; and to my mind they are a better use for the breast of lamb and mutton than are roasting the one with the fore quarter and making Irish stew or mutton broth with the other. The two last-named dishes I by no means wish to disparage; but I like them made with mutton chops or cutlets; and as for roast lamb, heterodox as I may seem, I think the brisket the worst part of the fore quarter.

The only difficulty I can see in producing successful epigrams is in the frying of them. It should be borne in mind that the meat, being cooked, only requires warming, and yet the bread crumbs round it must be browned to the desired colour. The talent consists, therefore, in having the fat or lard in which they are fried—and there should be plenty of it—at the right temperature, and in knowing the exact moment at which to take the frying basket out of the frying pan.

It would be too long to set forth at length the way to make the *purées* of turnips, spinach, turnip tops, &c., and I will only generally say that the vegetables should, when well boiled, be passed through a sieve, and the *purée* thickened by being warmed, at the time of serving, in a saucepan in which you have melted a goodly piece of butter and stirred a small quantity of flour; the proper seasoning of the *purée* with salt, pepper, and spices, not being omitted. To *purée* of turnips an onion may be added when they are first boiled.

Epigrams, like games of chess, are capable of many

variations. One of them consists in this, that mushroom trimmings are added to the liquor in which the breast has been braised, and being well reduced on the fire, then strained, and skimmed of all fat, a *liaison* of two yolks of eggs and the juice of a lemon is added to this sauce, off the fire. The breast being cut up into cutlets, each is dipped into the sauce, instead of into eggs, in the bread-crumbing process; but the sauce must be applied hot, and the bread crumbs when it is cold.

Another form is to fit to each epigram, before breadcrumbing, a small neck-chop bone, and—having cooked some cutlets in the same fashion—to serve, them round some potatoes *sautées*, in a circle composed alternately of an epigram and a cutlet.

Another way is this: When the breast is cold, instead of being cut up, it is neatly trimmed, then anointed with butter melted for the purpose, bread-crumbed, and grilled. It is then served very hot, with a pat of butter under it, the juice of a lemon over it, and a good sprinkling of white pepper—those who like it may introduce cayenne.

A simpler way of cooking the breast in the first instance is to put it into the soup or stock pot; but, the instant that the bones can be pulled out, it must be taken out.

Breast of veal also may be treated in the manner detailed above; only, when it has been pressed and is cold, if it is found to be too thick, it must be neatly split in two with a sharp knife, and then cut into cutlets. Epigrams made of veal should be served with a *purée* of sorrel or of spinach; a *purée* of turnips or of turnip tops would not go well with them.

COLD MUTTON.

THERE are not many people who object to eating cold beef, but there seems to be a popular prejudice against cold mutton. As far as looks go, when two or three persons have dined off a leg of mutton the day before, no amount of parsley, be it ever so curly and fresh, can make it look nice; but, as a matter of taste, cold meat, be it beef or mutton, is by no means devoid of merit at certain seasons, and with a proper accompaniment of salads, pickles, and sauces. Only, to be perfect, a cold joint should not be touched until it is cold; the joint of yesterday's dinner is quite a different affair. It is not everybody who can indulge, however, in such niceties of taste. Given a leg of mutton, it must in certain cases be made to go as far as possible to furnish the second, and even the third day's dinner. Some mistresses, bolder than the rest, may dispose of cold legs of mutton for the servants' dinner; but all servants are not so meek as to submit to such an indignity. The kitchen dinner must have joints of its own; these the servants do not mind "finishing up," as they say, and they do it pretty rapidly too.

If you wish to be very economical with a leg of mutton, you should carve it very much as you do a ham; then the next day put it for twenty minutes into a vessel containing boiling water; take it out, sprinkle some salt and a little flour over it, and put it to roast for twenty minutes before a good fire, basting frequently with some dripping melted for the purpose. The result will be a very fair second edition of roast leg of mutton. Some, however, may object to carving mutton after the fashion of ham; and in that case a hash, or a mince, are the only ways of turning cold mutton to account; but there are many ways of hashing mutton and other meats, and of mincing them too.

The great desideratum of a second-hand dish, is, that it should not betray its origin. Nothing is more abominable than the *réchauffé* taste so prominent in the attempts at warming up cold meat, which your plain cook is pleased to call "minced veal," "hashed mutton," &c. The only means to avoid that taste is to remove carefully from the cold meat you are going to use, every part that has seen the fire, as well as the gristle and fat. Let each slice be carefully trimmed, and let them all be as nearly as possible similar in size and shape. Then make your hash, and, even if you are not expert at combining sauces, it will not at any rate have a warmed-up taste. The following are various formulæ for HASHED MUTTON, equally applicable to other meats.

1. Cut an onion in slices, and fry it in butter till it assumes a deep brown colour; then put in a tablespoonful of flour, and, when it is well amalgamated with the butter, add a little less than half a pint of hot stock, broth, or even water; stir a few minutes on the fire, and then proceed to flavour your sauce with walnut or mushroom catsup, tomato sauce, Worcester sauce, spices, pepper and salt, in such proportions as taste may suggest and practice teach. A little *suc colorant*, or some burnt onion browning, may be put in, if the sauce be not of a sufficiently deep colour. When the flavouring is completed, strain the sauce through a fine colander into a saucepan, and place in it your slices of meat. Keep

the saucepan at a moderate heat till it is time to serve, and send up your hash with a garland of bread sippets, fried in butter, round it. The longer the meat lies in the sauce the better will the dish be.

2. Rub a saucepan with a piece of garlic, or of shallot; put in it a piece of butter and some flour, which you amalgamate as if to make melted butter; "lengthen" the sauce with a sufficient quantity of stock or broth, and a certain allowance of vinegar, not too much, adding Worcester sauce, spices, pepper, and salt, to taste; strain, and lay your slices of meat in it. Half an hour before serving put in some pickled gherkins cut in slices, or in any other shape, and, when they are thoroughly warmed, serve, with or without bread sippets. Capers may be used instead of gherkins.

3. Proceed as in either of the above recipes, as far as the butter, flour, and onions are concerned; then add to the sauce a moderate allowance of mustard, either French or English—or both may be used; then add the stock and a wineglass full of white or red wine; season with Worcester sauce, spices, pepper, and salt; strain, and put in the meat, serving with pickles or not, according to taste. Beef and pork are best warmed up in this way.

4. A homely Gallic mode of warming cold meat is in this wise. Fry some slices of onion in butter, and when they begin to take colour put in your slices of meat, pepper, salt, and a sprinkling of flour; keep on frying, till the onions are thoroughly done and the meat warmed; then add a small quantity of stock, broth, or water, with a *filet de vinaigre*, and serve.

Minced parsley may be added to any of the above dishes with advantage.

5. Butter plentifully a tin or a dish that will stand the fire, having previously rubbed it well with garlic or

shallot; dispose upon it your slices of meat; pour on them a mixture of half white wine and half stock or broth, pepper and salt *quantum suff.*, and strew over them a couple of mushrooms chopped fine—or button mushrooms may be used whole; then cover up the whole with bread crumbs, and having placed a few lumps of butter over all, put the dish or tin into the oven. About twenty minute's baking will produce a very desirable result, which should be sent to table as it is.

6. If the state of the joint you have to work upon will allow it, cut your slices the thickness of a finger; trim them all nicely, and as near as possible to the same shape; then dip them in egg, and cover them with a mixture of bread crumbs, powdered sweet herbs, pepper and salt in due proportion. Let them rest a couple of hours, and then egg and bread-crumb them again; then fry them in plenty of lard till they are a nice colour. Serve either alone with fried parsley as an ornament, or with any sauce, such as tomato sauce, piquante sauce, &c., which taste may suggest. Cold veal or pork treated in this way make a very toothsome dish.

Of course it is necessary, to carry out these warmings up, that the cold joint should not have been too heavily punished when it first appeared on the dinner table. When a joint has not enough left upon it to cut neat slices, then mincing is the best way to utilise it.

The common form for MINCE is as follows. Having picked out the meat free from fat, &c., mince it as fine as you can with a double-handled mincing knife; sprinkle it with flour, pepper, salt, and a little powdered spice, according to taste; then put your mince into a saucepan with a lump of butter, and moisten it with stock or broth till it is of the desired consistency. Some tomato sauce, walnut, or mushroom catsup, *suc colorant*,

Worcester, or any other sauce, may be added with advantage, if in due proportions. A squeeze of lemon or a little tarragon vinegar may be used instead of tomato sauce, but no acid imparts so pleasant a flavour to a dish of this kind, and in fact to all kinds of hashes, as that of tomatoes. The main thing is to know how much of it to put in, and this can only be learned by practice. The mince should be kept in the saucepan at a gentle heat for an hour or two before serving; it should not be allowed to boil. There are numerous ways of dishing up or serving mince besides simply putting a circle of bread sippets fried in butter round it. Poached or fried eggs may be disposed on the top of a mince. An omelet can be made, and, instead of doubling it up in the frying pan, as soon as one side has taken the least colour, you can slip it into a very hot dish, place the mince upon half of it, double over the other half, pass a salamander over it, to give it a better colour should it require it, and serve. A clove of garlic, or a shallot should be placed in the mince when first put into the saucepan, and removed at the time of serving; or onions, or shallots, minced very fine, may be added to it, as well as finely chopped parsley. If you are an adept at making puff paste, you can manufacture a *vol-au-vent* case, or small patties, and fill them up with meat minced as above. Of course your *vol-au-vent* will not be so *recherché* a dish as if it contained an elaborate ragoût of sweetbreads, cockscombs, truffles, and what not; but nevertheless, if the paste be light and crisp, and the mince nicely flavoured, the dish will have its merits.

Another way is as follows: Cut out of the crumb of stale bread half a dozen cylindrical pieces an inch deep and two inches in diameter. Make an incision round the top of each, about the eighth of an inch from the outside, as deep as you can go without coming through at the bottom. Fry these a gold colour in pure lard, and plenty of it. Then, when they are well drained and dried before the fire, remove the inside part with the point of a knife, and you will have a small case of fried bread. Fill each with mince, and serve. These are called CROUSTADES.

These cases can also be made with potatoes, and this is the way to proceed :—

CASSOLETTES DE POMMES DE TERRE.—Peel 2lb. of potatoes, boil them ten minutes in water, strain it off, and add a couple of ounces of butter and a little salt; cover them up and leave them to steam till thoroughly done, when you stir into them the yolks of three eggs, add a little grated nutmeg, and keep stirring them on the fire for five minutes. You then pass them through a sieve, pat them into a paste, and flatten them on a marble slab to the thickness of 1½in. When the paste is thoroughly cold, cut it into cylinders with a plain round cutter 2in. in diameter, and egg and bread-crumb each cylinder; mark it on the top with a smaller cutter so as to form the cover, and fry them in hot lard till they are of a gold colour: remove the top, take out the best part of the inside with the handle of a teaspoon, taking great care not to damage the outside. Fill up each case with mince, replace the covers, and serve.

A wall of plain mashed potatoes or of rice can also be used to enclose a mince upon its dish. The mashed potatoes should be made rather hard, so as to stand up well. They may be browned or not, according to fancy. Coating the outside of your wall with a beaten-up egg will help the browning. Rice should, for the purpose, be cooked in this way. Put into a saucepan as much rice, picked clean and washed, as you require, with enough cold water to cover it. Let it remain on the fire until all the water is absorbed. Then add pepper and salt $q.\ s.$, a piece of butter, and a handful of grated Parmesan cheese. Moisten with more hot water if the rice seems to require it. Stir it thoroughly to well mix all the ingredients; then build your wall. Stock or broth may be used instead of hot water. In addition to the above, a certain quantity of tomato sauce may be put in, or, instead of it, a pinch of saffron may be steeped some hours in hot water, and, this being strained, put into the rice. The Parmesan cheese, besides adding to the taste, has the effect of binding the grains together, and thus you are enabled to build up your earthwork firmly. In lieu of cheese one or two eggs may be worked into the rice a few minutes before serving.

With rice so prepared, then treated as the potatoes mentioned above, another variety of small cases may be also made.

With veal a white mince is sometimes made, but this must depend upon the resources of the kitchen. If there happen to be some Béchamel or other rich white sauce in the larder, use it instead of stock or broth to moisten the veal. In other respects proceed as above, omitting of course brown sauces. At the time of serving, the yolks of one or two eggs beaten up with the juice of a lemon should be added. Thin slices of bacon fried and rolled up should be put round the dish, as well as sippets of bread.

Mince is used to make what are called croquets in some English cookery books, RISSOLES in French. The process is simple enough:

Make some plain paste with egg, flour, water, a little salt, and a little sugar. Roll it out flat to the thickness of half-a-crown. Cut it out in small squares. Place a little heap of meat on each so as to be able to fold up the paste over it. Make the edges stick well together with a little white of egg. Trim them a regular shape. Fry in lard, and serve on a napkin with fried parsley. Sticking these things all over with vermicelli, as is done by some, is to me an abomination. The chief element of success of this form of serving mince is the thinness of the paste.

To make true CROQUETTES, the meat should be submitted to a greater degree of trituration—in fact, it should be pounded to a paste in a mortar; and I am not quite certain that the dish just described is not better when pounded meat is used for it instead of minced meat.

When your meat is well pounded, a certain quantity of fine bread crumbs and a little flour should be added to it, then various condiments according to taste, and then two or more eggs should be incorporated with the mixture. The next operation consists in fashioning the pounded meat into any shape you like; that of sausages, cut square at the end, is the best. These you egg and bread crumb (baked bread crumbs are preferable), and repeat the process after an interval of half an hour. Then fry a light colour, and serve.

This last process of pounding the meat can be applied to the remains of poultry and game, of which there might not be enough to make a hash or a mince, as well as to joints, when not much is left upon them. Of course the flavouring must be regulated according to the kind of meat to be operated upon.

Another way is to stew these things a very short time in a rich gravy or sauce, or simply in tomato sauce, serving them with the sauce under. The bread crumbing need only be done once in this case, if at all; flour may be used instead of bread crumbs to shape the *croquettes* with.

But to return to that leg of mutton, of which there should now remain little else but the bone. There is a use for it, and a very important one too; for without stock or gravy of some sort no cooking can go very far. The British cook has an idea that no gravy or stock can be made without shin of beef, and a good deal of it. Of course there is gravy and gravy, and I will not deny that a leg of mutton bone will not make so good a stock, *i.e.*, yield as much gelatine, as a piece of shin of beef; but what I maintain is, that it will make or help to make a very fair stock, quite good enough for the cook to make her hashes and ragoûts with, supposing she knows how to make it and them.

Every bone that is not tainted should be boiled down with a proper addition of vegetables, spices, &c., so as to give a well flavoured broth, or whatever you choose to call it. This is to be the foundation, as it were, of all the soups, sauces, &c., which may be required. Not but that a very good soup can be made out of bones and such like odds and ends. I have eaten a soup, in the making of which no other animal element had been used but a leg of mutton bone, the carcase of a pheasant, and a few scraps of bacon, chiefly skin. That soup was as good as, if not better, than some I have tasted in the making of which the tail as well as the shin of an ox had been used.

ON PAPER CASES.

The British cooks who can truss poultry are not many; therefore, it becomes the duty of the poulterers to perform that operation on the fowls we eat. And this means with them so to smash the sternal bone that, by pressing the sides of the animal, the breast may be so puffed up as to present a plump and inviting appearance. To render this appearance permanent, they insert sideways what is called a skewer, but is in fact, in relation to a fowl, a huge stake; and to this the animal is tied up in the approved form.

People who are fortunate enough to have a cook who knows her business, easily avoid this by ordering the poulterers to send the poultry untrussed, and then, when they come to carve the breast of a fowl, they will find it all beautifully white and fit to eat. Poulterers do not like to send out untrussed poultry—I presume because they derive some extra profit by the sale of the heads, necks, gizzards, and livers; or peradventure they give these things away, and then their objection arises from philanthropic motives. Be it, however, as it may, these things are good to eat; and, in fact, in the case of geese, are consumed in the form of giblet soup and giblet pie. And with the giblets of fowls both soup and pie can be made, almost as well as with those of geese. But there are more artistic uses to which they may be put, one of which I will now describe.

The first thing to procure is some little paper cases,

ON PAPER CASES.

either square or round, of about an inch and a half square, or the same in diameter, and an inch high. The square cases anyone knows how to make. The round, which look decidedly the best, may be bought for 1s. a dozen if you go to the proper shop, that is, a stationer's; for grocers and confectioners will demand 1s. 6d., or even 2s. for them. The cheapest way, however, is to make them at home. It will not be easy at first, but with a little practice the art of making these things creditably will soon be acquired. The tools required are a small round tin mould, without bottom, of the size of the case you wish to make, and a round piece of wood, with a handle to it, fitting into the tin. Take some white foolscap paper of moderate thickness, place a piece, sufficiently large to allow for the sides, on the tin, and press it so as to get a round impression on it; then with the back of a table knife, and in alternate ways, mark out folds, at equal distances and radiating from the round impression, on that part of the paper which will form the sides; then put the paper on the tin, press down the wooden form, and the paper will readily adapt itself to the shape by taking the folds you have marked out. You now trim the top, leaving enough to bend back to form a ridge, whereby the case is prevented from coming open. Having done this, withdraw the piece of wood, and push out the case from the other side.

An intelligent servant will soon learn how to make these cases, and, indeed, the manufacture of them is not beneath the attention of young ladies. It does not require more talent than many kinds of fancy work, costs less, and is perhaps more useful.

Before they are used the cases should be oiled throughout with fine salad oil, and put into the oven for a quarter of an hour. This is an important point, as those who neglect it will find out.

But now for the dish. Given three or four fowls' livers, cut from the best pieces as many neat collops as you have cases to fill; mince finely the rest of the liver, add some shallots, parsley, and mushrooms or truffles, or both if you have them, all finely minced, then some sweet herbs, pepper, and salt. Give this mixture a turn on the fire in a saucepan with a small quantity of butter, and half fill your cases with it; place one of the collops in each, and a small slice of fat bacon over it; fill up with a little brown sauce or rich stock; then put the cases into the oven for twenty minutes, and serve. Another way to make the liver mince is to half cook it first in butter, and then to mince it. It can also be fried with equal quantities of bacon, and, with the addition of the seasonings mentioned above, the whole must then be pounded and passed through a wire sieve.

Foies gras treated in this way make rather a nice dish; but if you go to the expense of *foies gras*, you must not omit the truffles. There is no end of the varieties of which these *entrées* are capable. You may use any forcemeat or *farce* you like; with that of liver, boned larks go very well, and the breasts of pigeons or blackbirds will do just as well for most people, if you only take care to call your dish ALOUETTES EN CAISSES.

But if you wish to produce this dish seriously the following should be the mode of proceeding:

Bone the larks skilfully, put the livers on one side, and set the bones and trimmings to boil with some good stock broth or even water, adding carrots, onions, parsley, pepper, salt, a few cloves, a bay leaf, and a few pieces of ham or bacon. When well reduced, strain the gravy and put it by; cut up the larks' livers, as also some fowls' livers, in small dice; do the same with half their quantity of bacon. Fry a few shallots in plenty of butter, then put in the liver and bacon with minced parsley, pepper, salt, and a little powdered spice, toss the whole on the fire for a few minutes, then turn out on a sieve, and pass them through while hot. Have your paper cases ready oiled, put a layer of this *farce* in each, then a moderate-sized piece inside each lark, which you roll up neatly and place in its case with a thin slice of fat bacon over it; you then bake them in the oven not longer than ten or fifteen minutes. At the time of serving, thicken the gravy mentioned above by mixing a little flour with some butter, and then adding the gravy to it. Fill your cases with gravy and strew a little finely minced parsley over each. The pieces of bacon may be removed or not before serving.

Sweetbreads and many other things can be treated in this way, but of course with a different kind of mince, forcemeat, and sauce.

Fish also, and particularly soles, are not to be despised in these cases, to say nothing of lobsters, oysters, crayfish, crabs, mussels, snails (the large ones they have in France), &c.; but of course each must have its appropriate forcemeat and sauce.

The way to prepare soles is as follows:

SOLES EN CAISSES.—Fillet them, roll up each fillet, and put it to "set" in the oven on a well-buttered tin. Take the trimmings of the soles and put them on the fire with some white stock, or, if you have none, water, and a few carrots, sweet herbs, parsley, mushroom trimmings, mace, nutmeg, pepper and salt, not forgetting an onion or a few shallots; let this boil down, strain it, reduce it well, and thicken it with a little flour and butter. Then make some fish stuffing—having kept back one or two fillets for that purpose—by pounding these with bread crumbs and some butter, and adding the yolks of one or two eggs, grated nutmeg, a very little sweet herbs, minced parsley, pepper and salt. Put a layer of stuffing in each case, with one fillet of sole, and a few minced mushrooms; fill up with the sauce mentioned above, and bake for fifteen or twenty minutes with a sheet of paper over the cases. Instead of, or in addition to, the minced mushrooms, one or two whole button mushrooms can be put on each case; and for the sake of variety the sauce may be made brown by the addition of a little *suc colorant*.

I may mention that calf's liver may be used to make the liver stuffing. These paper cases are used also for what are called savoury dishes, being filled with *ramequin* paste or hard-boiled eggs, chopped up fine with anchovies, a little Parmesan cheese, bread crumbs, and butter, or with many other varieties of similar preparations. When so used the cases should be rather smaller than when they are to contain meat, fish, &c.

These *entrées* in cases, if properly composed and dressed, have a very neat appearance; they are very good to eat, and last, but not least, they are anything but expensive.

STEAKS, AND A PIE.

In private houses, a well-cooked beefsteak is a never-attained luxury; it is only at some chop-houses in the City that such a thing is procurable, but there, not only is it beyond the reach of ladies, but you are compelled to eat it in a crowd and bustle, sufficient of themselves to take away the enjoyment of the choicest efforts of the culinary art.

The great secret of cooking a steak consists in making a roaring fire, and then adding some coke to it: when this is red-hot you have a clear smokeless fire on which to cook your steak. You should cook it on the fire, and not in front of it, otherwise it is only a toasted bit of meat, instead of a broiled steak. How long you are to leave a steak on the fire is so entirely a question of judgment as well as a matter of taste, that it is impossible to give any rule about it. You should turn your steak as soon as it has been on the fire a few minutes, and keep turning it till it is done. This process prevents the formation of a hard rind of overdone meat. For a steak to be well cooked it ought to be equally done throughout its thickness, but not by any means overdone, and consequently dry. There are people, however, who abominate a juicy steak, and will have their meat in any form thoroughly done, or rather overdone, not to say utterly spoilt; but

Non ragioniam di lor, ma guarda, e passa.

Sprinkle the steak freely with salt when serving, not before; and, being done, shall it be sent up *au naturel*—

Anglicé, "as it is?" Such a sacrilege should not be allowed; and I will tell you what I do to steaks at this stage of the proceedings.

1. Mix together a handful of finely minced parsley and a goodly lump of butter, place it on the steak, the heat of which will melt it by the time it is served. This is what is called "steak à la Parisienne." Fried potatoes are usually served with it.

2. Mince very finely equal parts of tarragon, chervil, and garden cress (*cresson alénois*), and use instead of minced parsley as above.

3. Wash thoroughly a few anchovies, and knead them with a lump of butter, and put it on the steak.

4. Mince a number of stoned olives, and knead with a lump of butter, putting it on the steak as it is sent up to table.

5. Mince one or two shalots, put them into a saucepan with a lump of butter and a little pepper, and when they begin to brown pour over the steak.

6. Squeeze the juice of a lemon in a saucepan, add to it a good piece of butter and a very little grated nutmeg; when the butter is quite melted pour over the steak.

7. Mince a few button mushrooms, give them a turn or two in a saucepan with a piece of butter and a little pepper, and pour over the steak.

8. Make a cold *tartare* sauce, and put it over the steak at the moment of serving.

When I speak of beefsteaks I use the word in a generic sense, and mean no disparagement to rumpsteaks, which are considered the best in this country; but the best in reality are slices cut from a fillet of beef—a joint which, I fear, is not within reach of the many. Slices cut off a leg of mutton, and cooked as beefsteaks, are very fine eating; and I may remark that all steaks are improved by being well beaten before cooking.

Another way of dressing steaks is this:

Make a *marinade*, with oil, vinegar, slices of onion, a piece of garlic, spices, pepper, salt, parsley, and sweet herbs, and let the steak (beef or mutton) be steeped in it for ten or twelve hours before cooking—turning it at intervals—then cook it in the usual way, and serve either *au naturel*, or with parsley and butter as above.

Steak and onions is a well-known English dish. I think the custom is to fry the steak with the onions. This is wrong—a fried steak is a mistake. Fry the onions and broil the steak; then serve the two together.

Rumpsteak with oyster sauce is another English dish, and this is how you should proceed to do it creditably. Parboil the oysters, beard them, and give them a turn or two with plenty of butter in a frying pan, then add pepper and salt, a little flour, and the juice of half a lemon, with enough oyster liquor to make up the quantity of sauce you want; stir till the oysters are done, and serve with the steak broiled in the usual way.

The following sauce is also a good accompaniment to a broiled steak:

HORSERADISH SAUCE.—Boil in gravy or broth some grated horseradish, when done stir into it the yolks of one or two eggs beaten up with some tarragon vinegar; add pepper and grated nutmeg, and serve in a sauce-boat. Another form of the above sauce is this:

Having boiled your grated horseradish in gravy or plain water, beat up the yolks of one or two eggs with half a pint of cream, and some tarragon vinegar, stir into the horseradish; let the whole remain on the fire a few minutes, stirring all the time, and before it comes to boil serve in a sauce-boat. This sauce is invariably served in

Germany with all forms of beef, either broiled, roasted, or boiled. I have met with something like it occasionally in this country, as an adjunct to roast beef, instead of the usual raw shavings of the root in question.

I am now going to describe a pie invented, on purely theoretical principles, by a philosophic friend who imparted his views to me upon the subject, and for my part I can strongly recommend it in a practical sense, having made it and eaten it on many occasions.

Take a piece of rumpsteak or of fillet of beef, and cut it up in thin slices; lay all the slices on the table, and place on each a small piece of fine suet or a piece of fat bacon, a pinch of sweet herbs, judiciously proportioned and pounded quite fine, a little minced parsley, pepper, and salt; then roll up your slices of meat, and place a layer of them in a pie-dish, the bottom of which has been rubbed with a shallot. The slices should be so cut that, when rolled up with the bit of fat, &c., each shall form a mouthful for an adult. Over this first layer put a thick covering of calves'-foot jelly, then a second layer of steak as before, and more jelly on the top, covering the whole with a crust made with an egg, butter, flour, and salt; decorate as you like, paint over with yolk of egg diluted in water, and bake in the usual way.

Those who like them can put in oysters and kidneys. With regard to the latter, I will describe how to get rid of the peculiar taste that kidneys always have, and which is certainly not agreeable. Before using them for any purpose whatever, slit them in halves, and throw them into boiling water and salt; let them remain not longer than a minute; then take them out, dry them in a napkin, and either broil or stew—as the case may be. To put in the pie they should be sliced in pieces a quarter of an inch thick. Oysters should be bearded, and they should not be put in until the pie is nearly done, when the cover should be gently raised and the oysters inserted.

A few boned larks are not a bad thing in the above pie, only if anything beyond the rolled-up morsels is put in, it should be peppered and salted separately. Slices of hard-boiled eggs can also be introduced.

HOW TO TRUSS FOWLS.

The ways of putting fowls to death are various. It might be done by shooting; but, presuming that you have first caught your fowl, it is the common practice to stretch, break, or twist the creature's neck—in fact, to slay it by strangulation. This is bad. The best way is to cut the fowl's throat, and to let the animal bleed. It is obvious that by this means it will be better to eat, and if this mode of death be thought cruel, let the fowl be decapitated; and if any one object to this on the ground of cruelty, I will refer him to the account in the *Lancet* of certain experiments made in Paris on the subject of decapitation. The operation of plucking hardly requires explanation. This done; the fowl must be singed by exposing it to the flame of a piece of lighted paper, the object of this being to destroy the minute feathers (hairs as they are called) which cannot be pulled out in the plucking. But this must be done with dexterity and care, lest the skin be singed or blackened. Then comes the trussing; which is of two forms, the one when the fowl is to be roasted, and the other when it is to be boiled or to be braised. I will not discuss the merits of the various ways of conducting these operations, but I will proceed to expound what in my opinion is the proper manner of trussing a fowl.

Having loosened the skin round the vent with the point of a knife, lay the fowl on the table back uppermost, and make an incision in the skin of the neck lengthwise, pull out the neck free from the skin and

HOW TO TRUSS FOWLS.   127

chop it off at the root, then cut off the skin at right angles with the first cut, so as to leave sufficient of it to form a flap large enough to cover the opening made by cutting off the neck. Inserting the fingers through this opening, you must now remove all the entrails, and wipe out thoroughly with a cloth the inside, as well as the inside of the neck flap. If by want of skill or by accident you should happen in the process to break any of the entrails, you must wash out the inside very carefully.

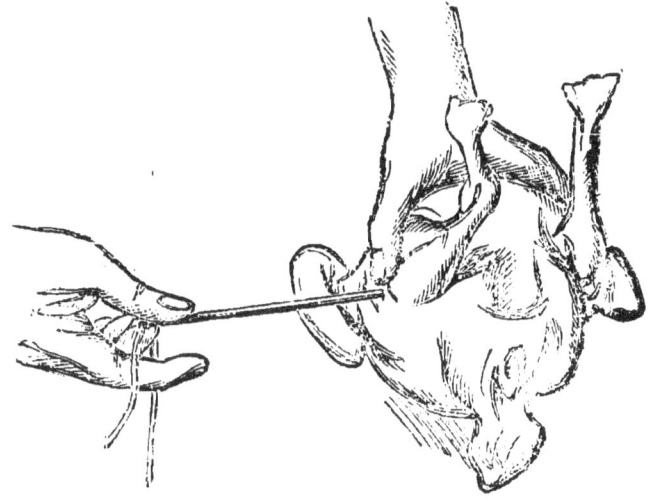

Fig. 1.

You now neatly chop off the end of the claws, the tips of the pinions, and the spur at the end of their second joint; then fold each pinion in a triangle, in which position it will be held by the tip of the third joint catching the first contrariwise.

Some people put the fowl's gizzard between one pinion, and the liver between the other, but this is an absurd practice not to be imitated. The fowl is now laid upon its back: then taking both legs in one hand, you draw them towards the neck (Fig. 1), and with a long needle, in the nature of a packing needle, you pass a piece of white packthread through and through both thighs under the knee; then you carry it along the second joint of one pinion and through the middle of the third joint, then

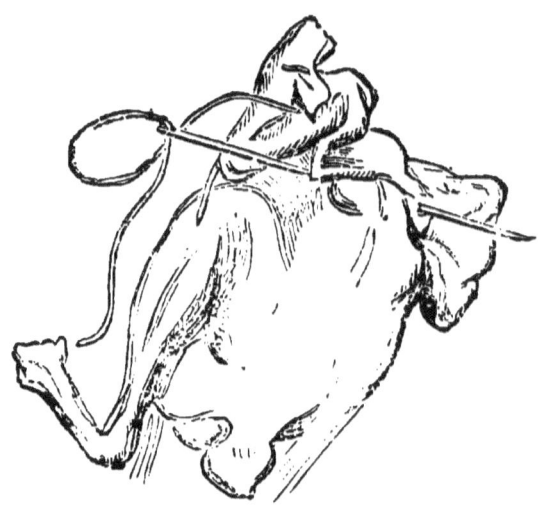

Fig. 2.

through the back under the bone, taking a stitch on the way in the flap, which you have laid flat on the fowl's back (Fig. 2); then you go through the middle of the third joint of the other pinion, and along the second joint. You now tie the two ends of the string tightly, leaving a piece whereby (when the fowl is done) you can, having cut the knot, pull out the whole string.

You must now slightly nick with a knife the tendons of the legs, just above the ankle in front and behind; the object of this being to prevent the feet from sticking up when the fowl is roasted. Some cut off the feet altogether at the ankle joint, and I am not sure that I do not prefer this mode of treatment, but this is a matter of taste.

Taking the fowl in one hand (Fig. 3), you now proceed to

HOW TO TRUSS FOWLS.   129

pass a second string on the same principle as the first, but taking the following road: through the small of the back (Fig. 3), and then through one leg just above the heel, then

Fig. 3.

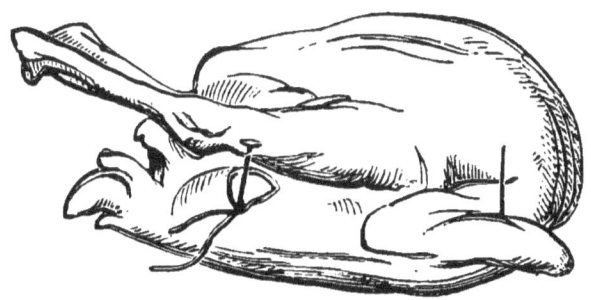

Fig. 4.

under the skin, and under the end of the breast bone and out at the other side through the other leg just above the heel; tying the string tightly as the first was tied (Fig. 4).

K

The only thing which now remains to do, is to make a small incision in the abdomen, just above the vent, and through this cut you must pass what is irreverently called the parson's nose; and if it obstinately refuses to remain in the desired position, it must be tied with a piece of string, to be removed at the same time as the others. If, before stitching down the neck flap, the inside of the fowl has been duly furnished with what those who know the fitness of things are wont, before roasting, to put inside fowls, your fowl is ready for roasting; upon the details and devices of which operation I will not enter on this occasion.

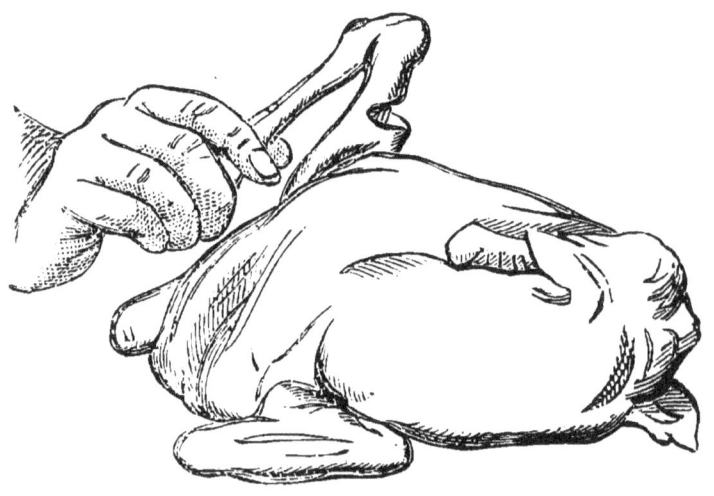

Fig. 5.

When you intend to boil or to braise a fowl, the mode of trussing differs in this: The fowl having been treated in exactly the same way as for roasting; before you proceed to the passing of strings you must make an incision in the leg just above the heel down to the bone (see left leg of the fowl in Fig. 5, being held up), then, inserting the fingers through the vent, you must loosen from the flesh the skin all round the thigh; then, bending the knee, you must push back under the skin calf and thigh together, putting the heel through the opening made by the cut above the heel. The leg will now present the appearance of the right leg of the fowl in Fig. 5. This is one of the most difficult operations in the trussing of fowls, for it is very easy to break the skin, which of course should not be broken. Both legs having been treated thus, the first string is passed and tied as explained above. The second string is also passed and tied in the same way as for roasting, except that it must go over the foot (Fig. 6), catching the ankle under the skin, then the end of the breast-bone, and out on the other side in the same way.

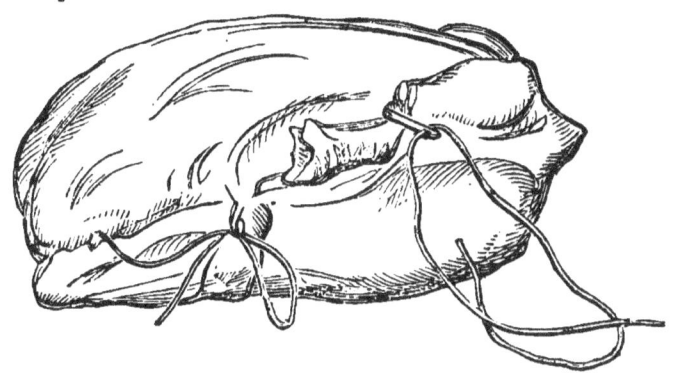

Fig. 6.

By carefully following the above directions, the trussing of a fowl will be found easy enough; but of course, as in all other things, some practice will be necessary before perfection is attained. All cooks, or even kitchenmaids worthy of the name should know how to truss a fowl; but as the desire for higher wages, is in many instances, the only qualification of young women who aspire in our days to a place in the kitchen, such knowledge is not to be always expected. Indeed, it will be a matter of congratulation if any aspirants can be induced by their mistresses to condescend to learn from the above direction what is part of the A B C of the education of a cook.

HOW TO BONE FOWLS.

To make a galantine of fowl or turkey, the first thing to be done is to bone the biped in question. A properly trained cook will, no doubt, be able to perform in the dark this operation, which, like most things, when it is known, is easy enough to do.

To bone a fowl is one of the elements; and is best taught by practice and by seeing a good cook at work; nevertheless, it is not impossible, I think, to explain how the operation is carried out, and this I will attempt to do, with the help of the annexed figures, drawn from nature.

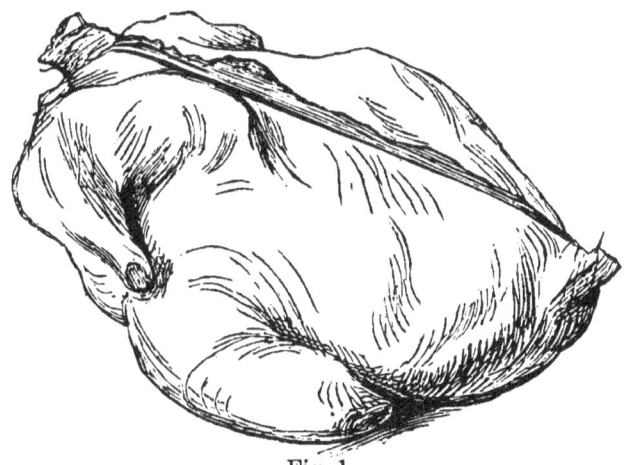

Fig. 1.

Given a large fowl, ready plucked and singed, the process is this. Give a blow to the legs, just above the heel, with a heavy kitchen knife, so as to break the bone; cut the skin round: then, holding the foot, give it a twist, and pull it off, thereby removing the strong sinews of the leg. Chop off the wings just above the second joint, then slit the skin of the neck lengthways, pull this out, cut it off close, and cut the skin square. Lay the fowl breast undermost, and make an incision all along the back, from end to end (Fig. 1); then, with a pointed knife—what is called a vegetable knife will do very well —proceed to detach the flesh from the carcase, beginning

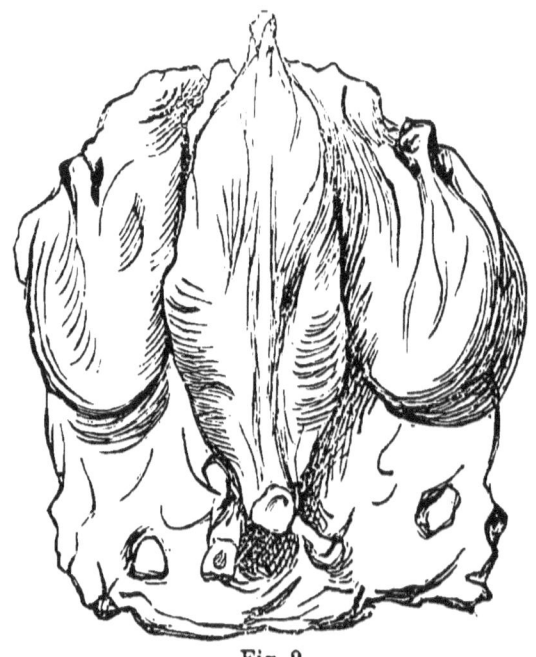

Fig. 2.

at the neck end; when you come to the wing bone disjoint it from the carcase, and then make a slit inwardly along the wing joint, and remove the bone; work along down to the leg, and when you come to the thigh bone disjoint it from the carcase. Operate on the other side in the same way.

Fig. 2 presents a birdseye view of the fowl at this stage. You must now work along each side, detaching the breast; and this requires great care to avoid injuring the skin, especially over the breast bone. When you have worked round both sides you remove the carcase—which can be drawn at leisure, and should be boiled along with the galantine when this is put to cook—and you have the fowl all boned except the thigh and leg bones on each side. The mode of getting rid of these is this: Make an incision along the thigh, as in Fig. 3; dissect the

Fig. 3.

bone from the flesh, as on the opposite thigh in the same figure; scrape the flesh along the leg bone, and finally pull this out, and it will carry the remaining sinews with it. All that now remains to be done is to cut out the "wishing-bone," which will probably have remained in the flesh of the breast, as well as the two large white sinews of the breast; and you may proceed to finish your galantine in the way you think best.

Remember only that a galantine without truffles in it, and a good aspic jelly, clear as amber, round it, is very much a Hamlet-without-the-prince sort of dish.

HOW TO CUT UP FOWLS.

HAVING already attempted to explain the operations of trussing and of boning fowls, I am induced to try a description of the method of cutting them up to make a fricassee. To carve a cooked fowl with any degree of neatness is no easy matter, and one which requires some practice before it can be creditably accomplished. To perform the same operation at a picnic—in a plate on one's knees—is still more difficult. Yet I have heard of expert knights of the carving knife, whose boast it is that they can carve a chicken holding it up impaled on a fork with one hand, whilst they gracefully sever the joints with a knife held in the other. But I have also heard, that on the occasion of a very limited picnic party, held on the top of some high cliffs, a gentleman, in attempting to dismember a roast chicken—the sole *pièce de résistance* of the repast—sent it whirling down inaccessible crags, below all hope of recovery. What the consequences were form no part of the matter in hand, but they were pathetic, serious, awful.

If it is difficult to carve a roast fowl properly, to cut up a raw one is still more so; and, in the latter case, it is of greater importance that the biped in question should be divided into neat and comely joints; for a *fricassée de poulet*, composed of ragged joints, with stumps of bone sticking out from most of them, is an unsightly object, and no amount of excellence in the taste of the sauce can make up for the unpleasant appearance of a dish.

HOW TO CUT UP FOWLS.

The animal is usually divided into twelve or fourteen pieces. What are called the legs make two and sometimes four, but this is seldom done; the wings make four, and the breast and back are cut up, according to the size of the fowl, into two or three pieces respectively. The mode of proceeding is this: Having plucked and singed

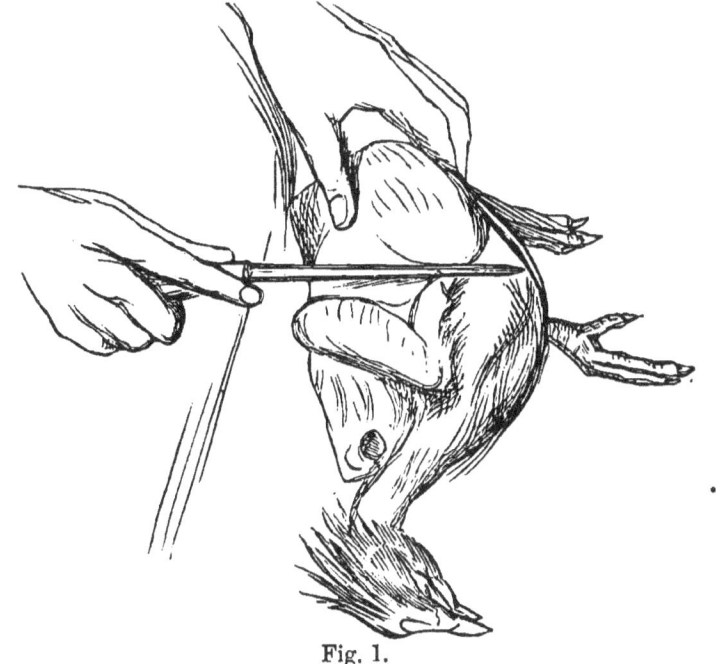

Fig. 1.

the fowl to be operated upon, lay it on its side on a table, grasp the thigh and leg together with the left hand, as in Fig. 1, and with a sharp knife cut down to the socket of the thigh bone; pull the limb back with the left hand, disengage the thigh bone from the socket, cut the skin neatly round the thigh, and put the limb on one side. Do the same with the other leg and thigh. Cut off the head and neck close to the body. To remove the wings; lay the fowl on its back, and make an incision along the breast bone, one inch from the ridge of it, cutting down to the joint of the wing bone, as in Fig. 2, which you disjoint from the carcase; then cut right down, and remove the wing. Take off the other wing in the same way.

Fig. 2.

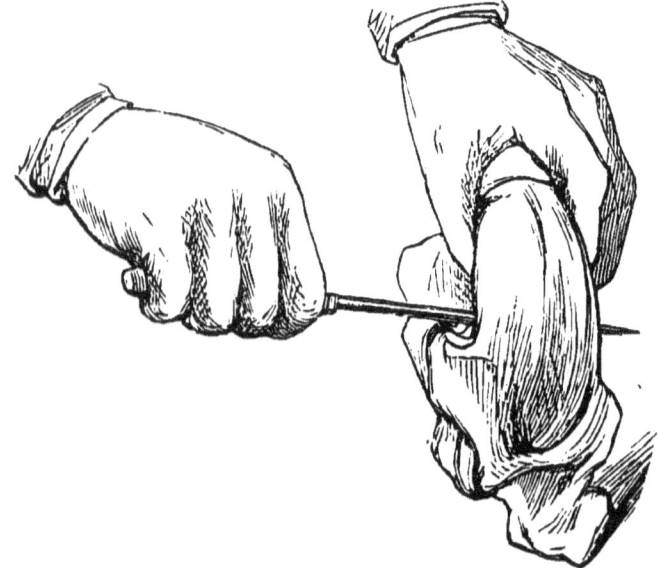

Fig. 3.

You now grasp the fowl with the left hand, and inserting the knife, as in Fig. 3, cut right through towards the vent, then pull the breast back, and cut it off altogether. Having removed the inside of the fowl, you chop off the ribs on either side of the back, and trim this piece

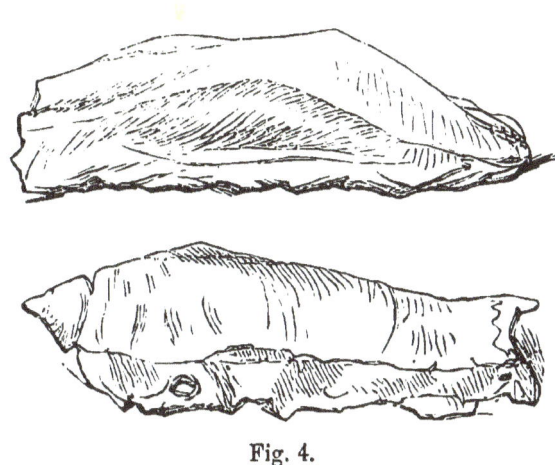

Fig. 4.

neatly, as well as the breast piece. Fig. 4 represents the breast and the back when trimmed. They are each cut

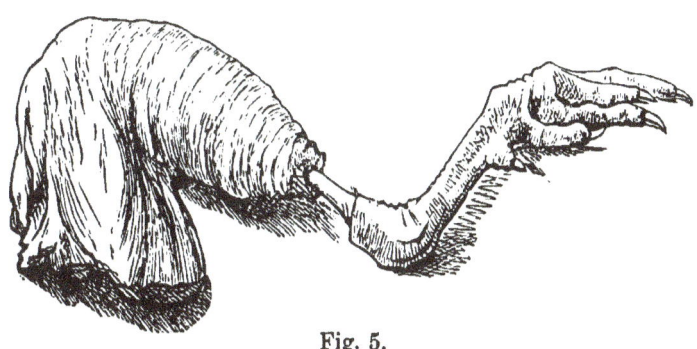

Fig. 5.

across into three or two pieces, according to circumstances.

Taking now each leg in turn, you make an incision round the heel, and pull the flesh back, as in Fig. 5;

chop off the bone above the heel, and pull back the flesh then chop off the head of the thigh bone.

Fig. 6 shows the leg trimmed. The two wings are divided at the second joint, the head of the bones being cut off, as well as the spur at the end of the second joint.

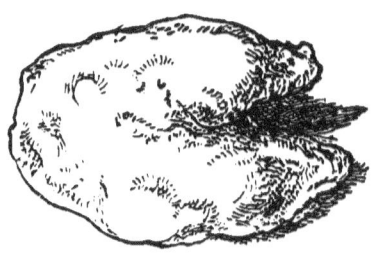

Fig. 6.

Fig. 7 shows the two pieces into which each wing is cut.

Care must be taken in chopping off the bones to do so at one blow, and to have a sufficiently heavy knife to make

Fig. 7.

a clean cut. The blow should be given with the part of of the knife next to the handle; a meat chopper would be too heavy.

Another point, which requires attention, is to let each piece—especially the wings and legs—have its proper allowance of skin. The cuts should be given freely, and at one stroke, so as to avoid little bits of flesh or skin hanging from any of the pieces; for one of the essentials of a *Fricassée de Poulet* is absolute neatness, in the shape of the "joints" or pieces into which the fowl is cut.

TURKEY.

BRILLAT-SAVARIN says that this portly bird is one of the finest gifts made by the New World to the Old. If it is not the first in flavour, among our domestic fowls, it is second to none in the delicacy and agreeable texture of its flesh.

From the time of their introduction into England, turkeys have been intimately connected with Christmas, and, according to Tusser, in his "Five Hundred Points of Husbandrie," Christmas cheer in his time consisted of

> Beefe, mutton, and pork, shred pies of the best.
> Pig, veal, goose, and capon, and turkey well drest;
> Cheese, apples, and nuts, jolly carols to hear,
> As then in the country is counted good cheer.

And so at the present time is a turkey an indispensable adjunct to, if not the chief dish of, a Christmas dinner; and the first question that presents itself is, how shall it be "well drest?" If the bird be of the right sort, and of the right age, there can be but one opinion among those who know how to eat. A turkey stuffed with truffles, or even with the humble chestnut, and roasted *secundum artem*, is a noble roast—indeed, the finest roast of poultry which can be placed upon the table. Still opinions differ; and a Scotchman, to whom I propounded my views upon the preparation of a turkey, met me by quoting a proverb of his country, to the following effect:

> Turkey boil'd is turkey spoil'd,
> And turkey roast is turkey lost,
> But for turkey braised the Lord be praised.

I will describe these three modes of dressing a turkey. The first condition of all is, that the animal should be properly trussed, and not impaled on a couple of wooden skewers. Then comes the consideration of the stuffing, the best form of which is without doubt that expensive luxury the truffle, and this is how TRUFFLE STUFFING should be made.

Take a pound of fat bacon, mince it fine, and put it into a saucepan with a couple of shallots, also minced fine; when the bacon begins to melt add at least 2lb. of truffles, cut up in convenient pieces, pepper, salt, spices, and powdered sweet herbs (thyme and marjoram), to taste. Toss the mixture on the fire for about half an hour, then— before it has time to cool—fill the body of the turkey, sew it well up, and put the bird in the larder to remain a couple of days before it is cooked.

CHESTNUT STUFFING I should prepare in this way: Having removed the outer skin of a number of chestnuts, put them to boil in salted water, with a handful of coriander seeds and some laurel leaves. When cooked (they must be rather underdone) drain them and remove the inner skin, which will come off easily. Sprinkle over them a due allowance of pepper, salt, and spices, and stuff the turkey, inserting while doing so about half a pound of butter cut up into small pieces—the finest beef suet or marrow may be used instead of butter. An onion chopped fine and mixed with the chestnuts, is to my mind, an improvement, but it is not to everybody's taste.

Another way of preparing the chestnuts is to bake them just enough to allow the skin to be removed; then they are stewed with a little stock, some onions, carrots, sweet herbs, pepper, a bay leaf, and salt to taste, until they are quite soft. They may then either be put into the turkey alone, or with butter, &c., as above.

Here are other forms of stuffing:

1. Take two parts of sausage meat, one of chestnuts and one of bread crumbs soaked in milk; pound the whole in a mortar, adding pepper, salt, spices, and powdered sweet herbs to taste, and plenty of minced parsley. Work into the mixture the yolks of two or three eggs, so as to make it of the desired consistency.

2. Take equal parts of ham, beef suet, grilled chestnuts, and mushrooms, and one or two onions; chop them all very finely and pound them in a mortar. Season with grated nutmeg, pepper, salt, and powdered thyme; then add some minced parsley, and as much bread-crumb soaked in milk as you have of ham and suet together. Work into the mixture as many yolks of eggs as may be necessary and stuff the turkey.

3. Take the liver of the turkey with double its bulk of fat bacon, and a couple of onions, all chopped up; give them a turn on the fire, then add equal quantities of truffles, chestnuts, and button mushrooms (either whole or cut up), pepper, salt, and sweet herbs to taste. Give the mixture another turn on the fire, and then use it.

The turkey being duly stuffed and ready for roasting, should be packed up in thin slices of fat bacon (*barder* it is called, from *barde*, a slice of fat bacon) tied on with thread, and buttered paper should be put over all. When once at the fire, the turkey should be basted frequently with butter. About a quarter of an hour before it is done remove the paper and the slices of bacon, whereby the animal will take that golden colour which is indicative of a bird roasted *dans les règles*. Sprinkle it well with salt just before serving.

To braise a turkey; having trussed it as for boiling, and duly furnished the inside of it, I should lay it in a braising pan over a bed of thick slices of bacon, surround it with a calf's foot cut up in small pieces, some onions and carrots in slices, thyme, marjoram, parsley, bay leaves, a clove of garlic, and a few cloves, whole pepper, allspice, and salt to taste, moisten it with about a quart of stock and a tumblerful of sherry, lay a round of buttered paper on the top, cover up the pan, and braise with a moderate fire (over and under) from four to five hours.

Both a roast and a braised turkey may be larded; and when sent to table may be garnished in the same manner. British usage will have sausages as a garnish, but *croquettes* of sausage meat, or Oxford sausages, are a better form. The most artistic sauce, however, is *Périgueux* sauce, *i.e.* truffles minced fine and put into some rich brown gravy. The gravy of a braised turkey, if properly reduced and strained, is the next best sauce; and as for garnishes of vegetables and other things, there is no end of them. The simplest of all is a crown of watercresses, duly seasoned with oil, vinegar, pepper, and salt, and this I consider the best garnish for all roast poultry—even for pheasants, which are neither poultry nor game.

Lastly, I come to boiling, and in this I do agree with the Scotch proverb; for if a turkey is neither fit to roast nor to braise, then it is fit for nothing else but to make soup. But people *will* "spoil" their turkeys, and I may as well tell them how to do it properly. I truly believe that the only *raison d'être* of boiled turkey is that the British housewife, when making out her bill of fare, is guided by no other rule than what I may call the brown-and-white rule; and as roast beef and roast turkey would each be brown, and so would boiled beef in a certain measure, therefore the turkey is sacrificed. The victim should be well washed in tepid water, then rubbed all

L

over with lemon juice, and placed in a saucepan with just enough water—boiling hot—to cover him well. A large piece of butter, a couple of onions, a head of celery, some sliced carrots, whole pepper, mace, cloves, a bundle of sweet herbs and parsley, with salt to taste, should be added. The boiling should be carried on slowly, the pot should be carefully skimmed, and in a couple of hours or less, according to the size of the victim, the sacrifice will be accomplished.

Some people stuff a boiled turkey with oysters, and serve oyster-sauce with it—that is a matter of taste; not to stuff it with truffles is also a matter of taste, but there cannot be much doubt about it. A *purée* of celery, or of chestnuts, or of onions (and why not?—call it *Soubise*, and no one will object), will go very well with boiled turkey. But to my mind the best of all sauces is tomato sauce; nor would I object to a *purée* of endive, or of any other green meat if a proper degree of piquancy were given to it by the admixture of lemon juice.

Many other things are done with turkeys; they make the best galantines; their wings (*ailerons*) make very good *entrées*, and French cookery books—especially the old ones—contain scores of dishes made with these; lastly, the leg of a turkey makes the best "Devil" I know.

ROASTING.

THE national mode of cooking meat in this country is roasting, and such noble joints as a roast sirloin of beef or a roast haunch of mutton can nowhere be found in the same perfection as in England. The quality of the meat has, however, as much to do with it as the skill of the cooks. I fear that, not unfrequently, cooks bake their joints instead of roasting them, and a baked joint is simply a miserable libel upon one which has been properly roasted by a glowing coal fire. But even admitting that the ordinary run of British cooks can roast a joint to perfection, still in the matter of poultry and game, and of small joints which require minute care and attention, they have yet much to learn. I have heard of a cook whose notion of roasting a widgeon, a plover, or a woodcock, was to lay it on a tin in front of the fire.

This matter of roasting appears at first sight simple enough, but the very simplicity of it makes it a most difficult process to carry out; and, in fact, in order to do so successfully, one must be to the manner born, as Brillat-Savarin justly remarks, *"on devient cuisinier mais on naît rôtisseur."* All that seems necessary to produce a roast is to hang a piece of meat before a fire and make the joint continually turn until it is "done to a turn." But to attain this end a proper fire must be provided, the cook must be able to judge, to a turn indeed, how long a time the joint will take to roast, and last but not least, to know to what particular degree those for whom she is cooking like their meat to be dressed. In this matter tastes differ much; what some people would call a joint roasted to a nicety, others would pronounce spoilt. With those who will have their beef and mutton so overdone as no longer to contain a drop of gravy I have no patience. The veriest tyro is aware that beef overdone is as indigestible as veal underdone; and that neither is so nice to the palate as when the former is full of ruddy gravy, and the latter well done through without being dried up. The taste for dried-up meat must have arisen from a continuous era of unskilful cooks, whose legs of mutton were overdone outside and raw inside. This I own to be disgusting, and I can quite understand that a joint overdone right through would be preferable to such an one; and likewise I can understand that a practice adopted in self-defence from bad cooking, may have gradually, by the force of habit, become a confirmed taste. Neither do I hold, on the other hand, with those who carry out almost to the letter the Breton proverb: "*Canard saignant, Mouton bêlant.*" This is, like most proverbs, figurative language, but none the less true for all that. Fancy an over-done wild duck—a wild duck from whose breast the carving knife does not draw one drop of the rosy gravy!

There is an old rule well-known all over the world of cookery, and that is, "white meats well done, black meats underdone;" this applies to all meats of the four as well as of the two-legged sort, but then it means properly well done, and properly underdone. To attain this end the first thing which demands attention is the making up of the fire. It should be regulated according to the size and the nature of the article which is to be roasted, and should be so managed as to last all-aglow the whole length of time that the roasting will take.

In the case of joints of meat the following are the main points to be attended to. The joint should be trimmed neatly, I would cut off the end or flap of a sirloin of beef (this makes a very good stew for a kitchen dinner, or may be used to make stock with greater advantage than roasting it with the joint—in the point of view both of economy and of taste); put a piece of buttered paper, tied on with string over the fat, and do not remove it until just before the joint is done.

If it can possibly be avoided, do not used skewers to fix up the joints, but use string instead; and when practicable perpendicular roasting is preferable to horizontal, as not requiring the use of the spit. Place the meat at first a foot and a half from the fire, or even further off if it be a large joint and the fire greater in proportion. When the meat is well warmed, gradually bring it nearer, and from that time never cease basting the joint at regular intervals, but this you must not overdo.

The time that meat takes to roast is usually set down at from fifteen to twenty minutes for every pound that the joint weighs; but this is a very broad rule, so many circumstances tending to modify it. The quality of the meat, the age of it, whether it be fresh killed or not, the season of the year, the nature of the fire, and the position of it as regards currents of air in the kitchen, must all be taken into consideration. One thing only is certain, and that is that when the joint begins to smoke it is nearly, if not quite, done, and at this stage two or three minutes more or less at the fire will make or mar the success of the joint as a piece of artistic roasting. At the last stage of roasting salt should be sprinkled freely over the joint, and the usual practice is to froth it up, as it is called, by dredging flour over it, then the gravy is made by pouring a cupful of boiling water over the joint. I cannot say that I approve of these two last operations. A properly roasted joint should produce its own gravy when it comes to be carved; and as for white meats, they should have a proper gravy prepared for them with something better than plain water.

It may seem superfluous to mention that the meat screen should always be used to roast anything, from a haunch of mutton to half a dozen quails, but it very often happens that cooks, when about to roast such small fry as the latter, will not take the trouble to place the screen in front of the fire; but the help of it is more necessary in such a case than when a large joint is being roasted. Another point which cannot, however, always be carried out in private houses is that, while the fire is being used for roasting, it should not be employed for anything else.

The Gallic mode of roasting joints of meat differs materially from the English. In the first place, when it is intended to roast a piece of meat, it is always placed for some hours, and even for a day or two, in a *marinade*, in the composition of which oil and sometimes wine play an important part. Whether joints are improved by this treatment is a matter of taste useless to enlarge upon; and I shall content myself by giving a few examples of joints roasted à la Française.

FILLET OF BEEF.—Take a piece of fillet of beef (the undercut of the sirloin), trim off the fat neatly and the thin skin next to it, lard—not too finely—the outside of the fillet with fat bacon, and lay it for a whole day in a pie dish with plenty of olive oil, and some pepper, salt, parsley, slices of onion, and bay leaves. Turn it occasionally. Cover the larded side with a piece of oiled paper, roast it at a brisk fire, and do not let it be overdone. Baste it frequently with butter, or with some of the *marinade*, and a short time before serving remove the paper, sprinkle the fillet with salt, and cease basting, to let the larding take colour. Collect what gravy is in the dripping pan, free it entirely from fat, and serve it under the fillet; which may be garnished either with fried potatoes or with watercresses. If the gravy collected in the dripping pan is not sufficient, some well-flavoured and reduced clear beef stock can be added to it.

LOIN OF MUTTON EN PAPILLOTE.—Take a piece of the neck end of the loin, saw off the chine bone, remove all superfluous fat and gristle, and trim the joint to a nice shape. Lay it for half a day or more in a *marinade* composed of olive oil, and plenty of onions and carrots sliced fine as for *Julienne*, with some whole pepper, cloves, salt, chopped parsley, a couple of bay leaves, and sweet herbs to taste. Then pack up the joint in oiled paper, with the vegetables, &c., composing the *marinade*, and roast it at a slow fire, basting it occasionally with the oil of the *marinade*. Some time before serving remove the paper, brush off the vegetables, let the joint take colour, glaze the top if you like, and serve either with potatoes *sautées au beurre*, or with a *ragoût* of any suitable vegetable cooked in a rich gravy. Red wine is sometimes used for the above *marinade*, either in equal parts with—or instead of—oil; in the latter case, butter is used for the basting.

The neck end of a loin of veal trimmed in the same manner, then larded, put into a *marinade*, and roasted in paper, makes a very nice dish. It need not necessarily be garnished with a *ragoût* of vegetables, but in that case it should be served with some well-flavoured and well-reduced gravy.

Legs of mutton are put into a *marinade* for two or three days, and basted with it when roasted. A clove of garlic inserted in the knuckle gives the joint a flavour very agreeable to those who do not object to that bulb.

To roast fowls and chickens, an onion and a large piece of salted butter should always be put inside them, unless they are otherwise stuffed; and it is best always to tie over their breasts a large slice of fat bacon, which should be removed a short time before they are done. Capons, turkeys, and guinea fowls are best larded, and the two first ought to be furnished with an appropriate stuffing; but all larded poultry should have a piece of buttered paper tied over the larding, to be removed in time to let the larding take colour. Basting with butter is an essential part of the process of roasting poultry, and the fire ought by no means to be so fierce as that for roasting a joint. All white fowls, be they tame or wild, should be roasted slowly. Black poultry, *i.e.*, ducks and geese, require to be quickly roasted, and at a brisk fire. These latter do not require any larding, nor a slice of bacon to be tied over them; but, at the first stage of roasting, it is well to tie a piece of buttered paper over the breast. The basting should be done with butter, and should be almost continuous towards the end of the process; and this applies also to all kinds of wild ducks. The young domestic duck, which it is the traditional custom in this country to eat with peas, is to my mind an insipid viand. Domestic ducks are only fit to eat when they are full grown, and then they should be stewed or braised; and in that form the accompaniment of peas is all very well. But as a roast your skinny domestic duckling is not to be compared to a wild duck. This, however, is a matter of custom as much as of taste; moreover when young ducks are in season, the choice of winged animals for roasts is very limited. Still, quails are in season then, and who would prefer a roast duckling, of the domestic sort, to a roasted quail?

Pheasants and partridges, the former of which ought

to be classed in our days with domestic poultry, should be treated in the same manner as fowls. Partridges, however, being a dark-fleshed bird, require to be less done; but they should always be roasted with a slice of fat bacon tied round them, and the introduction of a couple of bay leaves inside them is said to improve their taste. Pheasants are of course always finely larded and stuffed with truffles by the true gourmand.

Woodcocks, snipes, and plovers, and every other kind of winged game not of the duck tribe, should be enclosed in a slice of bacon while roasting, and should be judiciously basted, neither too much nor too little. Trail birds should have one or more slices of buttered toast placed under them, to catch the trail, and great care must be taken not to overdo them under pain of rendering them uneatable.

It is a bad plan to "spit" any small birds; they should be tied to the spit, and, if roasted in the contrivance which the French call a *rôtissoire*, they stand a better chance of being artistically roasted. This machine is simply a diminutive meat screen holding a horizontal spit, which is set in motion by clockwork. I do not know whether such an apparatus is to be procured in this country; but I well remember how, in days gone by, this machine had a bell, which began to toll slowly some time before the works had run down, and gradually increased to a mad peal as the stoppage of the machinery drew nigh. Then there was a kind of arm with a ladle at the end attached to a spit in the *rôtissoire*, which at every revolution of the spit gathered up the gravy, and then discharged it over the bird. Of course this machine would not do to roast large joints nor a bird with toast under it; but in this latter case the self-acting baster could be removed.

In roasting venison, the great point to attend to is to

preserve the fat, and to this end, that part of the joint should be covered with some buttered paper, a sheet of paste made with flower and water over that, and then another piece of paper.

Opinions are divided as to the propriety of roasting a hare; and I must say that a *civet de lièvre à la Française*, or even the English jugged hare, are better forms of eating a hare, if it be not true that hares were solely invented to be made into soup, as I have heard Scotchmen say. If, however, you *will* roast your hare, you should lard him very thickly all over the back and thighs. He should be basted plentifully and continuously with butter, and he should not be overdone; but the most important thing in the roasting of a hare is—in the words apocryphally attributed to Mrs. Glasse—"first to catch him."

ASPIC JELLY.

Aspic is the French name for the asp—sacred to the mane of Cleopatra. This appellation, although it may appear at first sight fanciful as applied to a savoury jelly, is probably referable to the singular concoctions of vipers and other snakes, recommended to persons of delicate health by the medical authorities of the middle ages. On the other hand, some assert that it owes its origin to the buckler shaped mould into which Aspic jelly was "set" by the cooks of a century or two ago. Be this as it may, my present care is to expound how to make Aspic or any other jelly—be it even Anaconda jelly—without the sacrifice of sundry fowls and joints of meat, as frequently set forth.

A jelly is only gelatine dissolved in water in such proportion that it will stand firm when cold, and the ordinary jelly of supper tables can be made by melting isinglass or gelatine in water, flavouring and colouring it with wine, essences, &c., then clearing it with whites of eggs, and putting it into a mould to set. A more delicate jelly can be obtained by boiling calves' feet, or even what are called "cow-heels," and using the liquor instead of a solution of gelatine or of isinglass.

Having got your unflavoured jelly or dissolved gelatine; if instead of flavouring it with wine and essences you flavour it so as to make it "savoury," by adding to, and boiling with it, some meat gravy, spices, &c., with a little *suc colorant* to give it a brown colour, you will have what is called an ASPIC JELLY.

A better way to produce an aspic, however, is to flavour it in the process of extracting the gelatine from the calves' feet or cow-heels, and this is how you should proceed, having still an eye to economy.

Put into a stewpan a couple of calves' feet chopped in pieces, a few slices of ham or bacon (a bone of ham broken up will do as well), any remains of game (not high) and poultry you may have, and also trimmings of cutlets or chops, and any odd bits of uncooked beef, mutton, or veal that are at hand, one or two onions, one or two carrots in slices, one clove, a clove of garlic, some spices, and sweet herbs in proportion, according to taste, and pepper and salt. Add a cup of cold water or broth, cover the stewpan, and put it on a brisk fire, shaking it occasionally. When the pieces of meat, &c., begin to take colour, put in another cup of hot water or hot broth, and in half an hour's time fill up the stewpan with either, or at any rate put as much in as you want jelly, adding, if necessary, a little *suc colorant* to give the jelly a good colour. After this, let the whole simmer for three or four hours, then strain through a fine strainer, and, when cold, carefully remove every particle of fat.

The *jus* (juice or gravy) thus obtained will be a firm jelly when cold, and will keep for several days. The next process is that of clarifying the jelly, which should be conducted as follows:

Beat up the whites of two eggs in a saucepan, half melt the jelly, pour it into the saucepan, and keep stirring on the fire till it boils. Let it boil a few minutes, then put in a wineglassful of white tarragon vinegar, and strain through a jelly bag. The simplest form, and I think, the best kind of jelly bag, consists of a

ASPIC JELLY.

chair put upside down on a table, with a square piece of flannel or a doubled napkin tied on the four feet thereof. Strain the jelly a second time if not quite clear the first time. The above process properly carried out ought to produce a jelly as clear as unclouded amber.

[If, by the nature of things, the scraps of fowls, game, and meat are not procurable, then I should substitute for them an entire fowl and a whole partridge, with a shin of beef or a knuckle of veal, or a rabbit may be used instead of fowls; or both fowls and game may be left out. Cow-heels, or even pigs' feet, in larger proportions, may be substituted for calves' feet. These are all matters of taste and expediency, the only one principle being to have enough animal matter to yield sufficient gelatine, and in such variety as to produce a pleasant flavour. If no calves' feet or other gelatine-yielding ingredients are procurable, a solution of gelatine or isinglass in water or broth may be used, in lieu of plain water or broth.]

Having thus got your jelly quite clear, the next step will be to dress your dish of aspic, and this will be found the most difficult, as well as the most expensive, part of the proceedings.

Take a jelly mould and pour into it a small quantity of half-melted jelly, let this set (on ice if necessary), and proceed to dispose upon it a layer of fillets of the breasts of fowls, game, or fillets of fish, sweetbreads, &c., all previously cooked, pickles, tarragon leaves, hard boiled eggs, &c., &c., all tastefully arranged; filling up the interstices with *pieces* of jelly, and then completing the filling up with half-melted jelly. Make another layer as before, or more, according to the size of the mould, let the whole set, and at the moment of serving turn out your aspic, which is done by immersing the mould in hot water for a few seconds. Great care is required in disposing the fillets, &c., in the mould, so as not to have too many pieces lying in one direction, which would have a tendency to split the jelly.

This dish is very effective for suppers, and if judiciously prepared, not so very expensive after all, for the same bipeds can be made to yield the fillets and flavour the jelly, only the fillets should be boiled by themselves. The addition of truffles is desirable, although those who either object to good things or to expense may leave them out without utterly spoiling the dish. If you can afford truffles; use the parings in making the jelly, and put in nice slices in building up the dish. A glass or two of Madeira, or even sherry, will do no harm, if thrown in during the process of clearing the jelly, but this is by no means a necessity.

A *fricassée de poulet*, or a salmis of game, served cold within a border of jelly, constitutes the simplest form of what in Gallic cookery is called a *Chaud-froid*. Some cookery books spell the name Chaufroix, on the assumption that the dish was invented in the last century by a cook so named.

The remains of fowl make but a tame sort of dish; whereas with what is left of partridges and pheasants, if there is only enough of it, a decent and toothsome supper dish can be produced by proceeding in this wise:

Cut off the wings, breasts, and legs, trim them neatly, and put them aside. Put the rest of the game into a saucepan, with a piece of ham, some strong stock or broth, a laurel leaf, some sweet herbs, pepper, salt, a few cloves, a small piece of garlic or some shallots, or both, truffles, and mushroom trimmings. Let the whole boil for some hours; then strain through a fine tammy. Skim off all fat, and let the sauce further reduce on the fire nearly to a glaze, when you work into it a glass of sherry. You now dip each piece of game into this sauce, and when the coating of sauce on each is cold repeat the operation. Dispose the pieces on a dish, and ornament with bits of aspic jelly. Or you may fill a border mould with aspic jelly, into which you place tiny fillets of truffles and breast of game alternately. When set, you turn out the border, and within it set up the pieces of game treated as above.

When the remains of game consist of a salmis, all that need be done is to pick out the best pieces, reduce the sauce of the salmis, and proceed as above.

To make an effective CHAUD-FROID of fowl you must first roast three or four fowls without allowing them to be browned, which is done by covering them over while roasting with a piece of paper well buttered. You then cut the breasts into neat thick fillets, and dispose them on end round a dish—what is called *en couronne*—placing a slice of truffle between each fillet. You then take some strong white stock, and in this boil down the bones of the fowls with mushroom and truffle trimmings, sweet herbs and spices to taste, and some shallots. When this sauce is well reduced, strain it and add a little white wine. In the mean time the flesh of the legs should be pounded to a pulp in a mortar, and this pulp passed through a sieve. To this you add sufficient sauce to make a thick *purée*, working into it also a small quantity of well-flavoured aspic jelly in a liquid state. When the *purée* begins to cool pour it in the middle of the fillets; then cover up the whole—"masking" is the technical word—with the sauce, and when quite cold ornament the dish with aspic jelly, truffles, &c.

Another form, which needs fewer fowls and less trouble, consists in cutting up the whole of one fowl into neat joints, covering each with the reduced sauce, and dressing them in pyramid shape, either within a border of aspic jelly, or simply with pieces of aspic around. Fowl can be combined with game by using fillets of fowl and a *purée* —either wholly made of game or of the flesh of the fowl's legs, flavoured by the addition of trimmings of game—in the middle.

When I speak of game, I mean game that is fit to eat, and not in that state of decomposition which by some is considered the chief attraction of game. In all cases the sauce is improved by the addition, off the fire, of the yolks of a couple of eggs beaten up with the wine and strained.

The one essential element to make a decent *Chaud-froid* is the truffle, without which a *Chaud-froid*, of fowl especially, would not be one at all. The conditions of success are, that the sauce be well flavoured and sufficiently reduced, and that the aspic lack neither flavour nor brilliancy.

VEGETABLES.

The English, as a rule, are essentially a carnivorous people. With the exception of those poetically sensitive persons who are called vegetarians, Englishmen seldom or never eat vegetables except as a vehicle for animal food. They are, perhaps, justified in this by the fact that, if there is a branch of cookery of which they are more ignorant than any other, it is the art of cooking vegetables. Those Englishmen, who by education, travel, and superior intelligence, have learned what to eat and how to eat, deplore that, in the bosoms of their families, they never can get those succulent leguminous preparations which are obtainable on the other side of the Channel, and, perhaps, at some select establishments, clubs, and hotels in town. Of course, I do not speak of the happy few whose means enable them to keep a true artist to direct their kitchen; I refer to those who must be content to leave the preparation of their food in the hands of the British female cook; whose modes of dressing vegetables—especially greens and the like—are as uninviting, not to use a stronger word, to the eye as they are insipid to the palate. Nevertheless, I have no doubt that there are people whose prejudice and ignorance are such that they would prefer a misshapen mass of vegetable matter, well squeezed together, to a dish of greens properly dressed; but as there may be others who would, if they could, have their vegetables decently

M

cooked, I will give my views on the subject of cooking most vegetables.

A superstition prevails that everybody knows how to boil a potato. Like the arts of gig-driving and leading article writing this faculty is assumed to be intuitive. Still many plain cooks may be found who cannot even perform this simple operation, although they would deem it *infra dig.* to black their master's boots.

The best way of boiling most vegetables is not to boil them in water at all, but in steam, using a contrivance which is called, I believe, a steamer; but, as was done in the case of the gigantic turbot spoken of by Brillat Savarin, any vessel which will stand the fire can be converted into a steamer; all that is required being that the thing to be cooked should be propped up above the boiling water. Vegetables so cooked or steamed, if intended to be eaten *au naturel* or *à l'Anglaise*, taste much better than if boiled in water.

POTATOES, whether steamed or boiled, are always best cooked without being peeled, except however in the case of very old potatoes, which should not only be peeled but should have every "eye" carefully scooped out, and then, before they are boiled, they should be soaked in salted water for some time. My favourite way of cooking potatoes is—after they have been washed quite clean—to put them unpeeled into a saucepan filled with cold water to the height of about an inch, then to sprinkle them with salt, and to place a wet cloth on the top of them. The saucepan is then put on the fire, and in about half an hour placed aside on the kitchener to remain until the potatoes are wanted.

One point always to bear in mind in the matter of plain boiling potatoes is to sort them as much as possible all of a size, for each batch of them which is about to be cooked.

Another way of boiling potatoes is to fill a saucepan with them peeled or unpeeled, then to add a due allowance of salt, and to fill up with cold water. When they have been on the fire about half an hour drain off all the water, place a wet cloth on the top of them, and set the saucepan by the side of the fire. No other covering should be put upon the saucepan but the wet cloth aforesaid. New potatoes should be well rubbed with a coarse cloth, and then cooked by either of the above methods, or steamed in a regular steamer. If they are very young they are all the better for lying in salt and water some time before they are cooked.

There are various ways of dressing new potatoes after they have been boiled. Tossing them in a saucepan with plenty of butter, and then adding a squeeze of lemon and some minced parsley produces what is called POTATOES À LA MAÎTRE D'HÔTEL, and this form is applicable to old potatoes as well, but these should first be cut into slices.

By omitting the lemon and tossing the potatoes in butter until they begin to brown, you will have what are called POTATOES SAUTÉES. If you fry some onions in butter until they begin to take colour and then add either new or old potatoes cut in slices (both being previously boiled) you will have POMMES DE TERRE À LA LYONNAISE. To this and the former a sprinkling of pepper should be added, but a delicious way of eating new potatoes is to put them raw into a saucepan with plenty of butter and to toss them until done, sprinkling with salt, and serving very hot.

A favourite way with me to dress potatoes is this: Cut them up into quarters; rub a saucepan with a piece of garlic, put into it a goodly piece of butter, and when it is melted throw in your potatoes (raw); add a very little water, pepper, salt, and a small quantity of grated nutmeg; let the whole simmer till done, and, before serving, add some minced parsley and a little lemon juice.

What are called baked potatoes—produced by putting them under a joint that is roasting—are simply an abomination, and the only greater one of which I know is when both meat and potatoes are put into the oven. It is not a bad way, however, to cook a potato to put it into an oven, or under hot ashes, in its skin or jacket, as it is called; but this method is hardly advisable for a dinner party, although to my mind, it is the only way to get the true flavour of the potato if you wish to have it *au naturel*.

When MASHED POTATOES are to be made it does not much matter how they are boiled, and indeed mashed potatoes can be made with potatoes left over from the dinner of the previous day; but, to be properly made, they should be passed through a hair sieve, and then worked in a saucepan with milk, butter, and salt; by this process you avoid coming upon pieces of hard potato, like flints in a chalk-pit.

Another form of serving them akin to the above, is POTATO SNOW: to make which, after being boiled, the potatoes should be passed through a hair sieve, and before they have time to cool, they should be put into a vegetable dish, with a lump of butter under them, and kept hot till the time of serving.

In their Gallic form mashed potatoes should be less stiff than in the English preparation of the same name: A slight flavour of garlic is added to them, they are diluted to the proper consistency by the addition of gravy or stock, as well as milk: some grated nutmeg, besides pepper, is usually added.

Another form which mashed potatoes take at the hands of French cooks, is that of DUCHESSES. The following is the recipe:

Pass half-a-dozen boiled potatoes through a sieve; work into them, in a bowl, one gill of cream, and the yolks of three eggs; add pepper, salt and nutmeg to taste, and some parsley chopped fine. When they are well mixed and smooth, take them up by tablespoonfuls, roll each into a ball, flatten it and flour it slightly; lay them all in a *sauté*-pan with plenty of butter melted. Cook them slowly. Turn them over when one side is coloured and serve hot when both sides are done. I also have the following recipe from an English friend:

POTATOES Á LA J'AIDIT: Take a large and rather over-boiled Spanish onion and beat it, hot, with from three to four times its bulk of boiled potato, also hot, a little salt, a little butter, and a good quantity of black pepper —through a fine sieve. Roll into balls, and brown them quickly in butter.

With some dishes FRIED POTATOES are *de rigueur*. To fry them well you must attend to the following points: Use plenty of fat: Wait till the fat is very hot before you throw them in: Let them be thoroughly dry, for, if at all damp, they will never be properly crisp. When they have got a fine golden tinge, take them out and lay them on a piece of blotting paper before the fire, giving them a good sprinkling of salt. Do not attempt to fry boiled potatoes; they must be raw, and you can cut them either in slices the thickness of a shilling, or in pieces about the size of a French bean and the length of the potato.

What are called POTATO CHIPS are simply potatoes cut in spiral parings, and fried *secundum artem*. The potato being of course properly peeled before the parings are cut.

The remains of boiled potatoes can be dressed in a variety of ways. Cut up into quarters, and with a white sauce, or plain melted butter with minced parsley put over them, they make a very nice dish.

Cold mashed potatoes *à l'Anglaise* may be used in the following way:

Stir an egg or two into your potatoes; add a few finely powdered spices, pepper and salt to taste, and some minced parsley; mix well, and roll the mixture into balls, or any shape you like; cover with fine bread crumbs, fry a nice golden colour, and serve garnished with fried parsley. This dish can be varied *ad infinitum*, by either inserting in the middle of each ball, or incorporating with the mixture, any of the following: The flesh of fowls or game, or of any kind of fish, lobsters, crabs, &c., all finely minced. If you have some very rich stock, moisten the minced meat or fish with it, and your dish will be improved; only, in that case, you must put a small portion of the mixture in each ball, and not mix it up with the potatoes.

The above combinations can be erected into a more imposing dish by placing the minced fish or meat in a pie dish, covering it over with potatoes, and then baking the same until the top is of the desired colour; in this case, however, a regular ragoût should be made for the animal part of the dish, and the potatoes play only second fiddle.

There are numerous other modes of treating potatoes, either alone or in combination with various meats and vegetables, but cookery—even of potatoes—has, like art, no end.

Before I proceed farther, I would wish to impress strongly upon the minds of operators that all vegetables cannot be too carefully cleaned and washed, and that every leaf or speck the least tainted or discoloured must be thrown aside.

It is better to steam greens, cabbages, and the like, for in that case the squeezing process is no longer necessary to free them from a superabundance of water, and this is a very great advantage for those who like their food to look nice, and who yet will have their cabbage plainly cooked without any further dressing. A fair sprinkling of salt should be applied to the vegetables before they are put into the steamer. Pepper, spices, sweet herbs, onions, &c., can be advantageously added to the water, thereby producing a savoury steam wherewith to cook the vegetables and improve their taste.

The form of dressing greens, however, which usually obtains, is that of boiling them in water; but, then those who know how to cook have various cunning ways of preparing them for the table after they have been boiled. Here are some of these:

1. Take a young CABBAGE or SAVOY, remove the outer leaves, and cut it in four or more "quarters." Lay them in cold water, with a good handful of salt, for two or three hours. Then throw them into boiling water to boil from fifteen to twenty minutes, after which put them on a sieve to drain thoroughly. Take a piece of the fat of bacon. Mince it very fine, adding to it the least bit of shallot or onion and sweet herbs, pepper and spices according to taste. Put it all in a saucepan, and as soon as the minced bacon is melted lay your pieces of cabbage in it, and add a sufficient quantity of hot stock or broth, or even plain water, to half cover them. Let the whole simmer till thoroughly done, when you carefully remove the pieces

of cabbage with a skimmer, and dispose them neatly on a dish. You then strain the liquor, thicken it with a little flour, skim off any superfluous fat, and pour it over the cabbage. If instead of this sauce you use a higher preparation, such as Spanish or any other brown sauce, or even add a few spoonfuls of this to the sauce made from the liquor aforesaid, your *entremet de légumes* will be all the more *recherché*.

2. Having cut a cabbage as above, remove the stalk and ribs of the larger leaves. Then proceed to cut each piece of cabbage crosswise into strips, a quarter of an inch wide. Parboil these, and put them into a saucepan with a good piece of butter, to which you add a small quantity of stock or broth, pepper, salt, and some powdered spices, according to taste. Let the minced cabbage simmer till done quite tender, adding a tablespoonful of vinegar or more at the time of serving.

Cabbages so dressed can be served by themselves, or as a *garniture* to boiled bacon or beef.

The RED CABBAGE, which is used only for making pickles in this country, when properly cooked produces a very nice dish, and on account of its colour a showy one withal. One mode of dressing it is identical with that described above for the common cabbage.

Red cabbages dressed in this way are better for lying in vinegar and water (equal parts) instead of water alone in the first stage of the process, described in No. 1. The salt should not be omitted. I have the following as a Dutch recipe for dressing red cabbages. The Gallic name would be CHOUX ROUGES À LA HOLLANDAISE, which sounds much grander than minced red cabbage; but with either name the dish has merits. This is it:

3. Prepare some minced red cabbage as in No. 2, only

do not soak it in vinegar and water, but in water alone and salt. Take an equal quantity of apples and onions, both minced fine, say for one cabbage a handful of each. Put them and the parboiled cabbage into a saucepan with a piece of butter, pepper, and salt *quantum sufficit*, and some parsley and sweet herbs tied up in a bundle, but judiciously proportioned. Let the whole simmer very gently for some hours, the longer the better. Then remove the bundle and throw in—at the time of serving— a gill of claret, in which you have dissolved a tablespoonful of sugar. A small pat of butter is then added, and your dish is ready for table.

There is yet another way of dressing very young cabbages, which is not to be despised.

4. Proceed as if you were going to dress your cabbage *à l'Anglaise*. When it is half-done drain it, and squeeze it dry if you like. Melt a piece of butter in a saucepan, add some flour to it, salt, pepper, some grated nutmeg or powdered mace, and enough cream to make a thick sauce. Place your pieces or quarters of cabbage in this to finish their cooking, and serve with the sauce over.

5. Take some savoys, cut them up small, and parboil them, as in recipe No. 2 ; take an equal quantity of parboiled rice ; put the two together into a saucepan full of plain broth or stock ; set it to simmer till both rice and cabbage are thoroughly done ; then serve. There should not be too much broth, for it is a soup to eat not to drink. Grated Parmesan cheese should be handed round with it. This is a very wholesome and nourishing dish, and as the cheese is not imperative it would be a great boon to some of our poor folks if they could be induced to try it. A piece of bacon, an onion, and some parsley would make an economical broth for this dish.

The following is an artistic way of dressing cabbages. Parboil them, just enough to make the leaves limp; which you separate and dry lightly with a cloth. Then take either sausage meat, or any forcemeat (*farce*) made with remains of cold meat, &c., nicely flavoured; place a tablespoonful of this upon a cabbage leaf, roll it up to the shape of a sausage, add three or four more leaves round it, and tie it up with thread. Having made a sufficient number of these rolls, line a saucepan at the bottom with bacon, lay your rolls upon this, and let the whole simmer on the fire a couple of hours, adding a small quantity of broth or stock, condiments according to taste, and salt if necessary. At the time of serving remove the threads and dispose the rolls on a dish. Strain the sauce. Remove the excess of fat. Thicken it with some butter and flour, and pour it over the dish.

Instead of making a number of rolls, as above, the cabbage can be dressed whole. When parboiled make a crucial incision on the top of it, open the leaves lightly, insert the meat between them, and tie up the cabbage with thread so as to preserve its shape. In this case, however, the parboiling and final cooking will take a longer time.

BRUSSELS SPROUTS can be cooked in the same way as described for cabbages in No. 4; here are various other modes of preparing them:

1. SAUTÉS AU BEURRE.—Trim neatly and wash them in several waters; put them to boil in plenty of salted water, and when almost done strain and dry them in a cloth; put them into a saucepan with a large piece of butter, pepper, salt, and grated nutmeg to taste; toss them gently on the fire until they are quite cooked.

2. AU JUS.—Parboil them only in salted water, then, having drained and dried them, put them to finish cooking in a saucepan with some well-flavoured clear gravy, adding pepper, salt, and grated nutmeg to taste.

3. A LA MAÎTRE D'HÔTEL.—Having boiled the sprouts as in No. 1, melt a piece of butter in a saucepan, toss them in this until done, adding some minced parsley, a sprinkling of pepper and salt, and the juice of a lemon.

4. A LA LYONNAISE.—Mince a small quantity of onions or shalots, fry them in butter to a light brown colour, then add the sprouts ready boiled, and pepper and salt to taste.

The proper way to cook common GREENS, BROCOLI SPROUTS, SCOTCH KALE, and the like, is to arrange them in nice little bundles like asparagus, and tie them with a string, then to put them into a saucepan with plenty of boiling water, salt *quantum suff.*, and a piece of soda. When cooked (let them not be overdone) take the bundles carefully out of the water, and put them to drain on a sieve near the fire, so as to keep them warm. At the time of serving remove the strings, send up your greens as you would asparagus, and if you have been in the habit of eating them *à l'Anglaise,* you will find that their appearance and taste are immensely improved. With them should be served, in a sauce-boat, either plain melted butter or any other sauce *ejusdem farinæ* which taste may suggest.

A cunningly devised salad sauce is no bad accompaniment to these kinds of greens, and, to my taste, even the simplest form of this, viz., oil, vinegar, pepper, and salt, is preferable to melted butter. One of my favourite ways, however, of dressing these greens, as well as cabbages, is the following:

GREENS ON TOAST: Cut some *croûtons* of bread in the shape of a cutlet, fry them in butter; having parboiled the cabbages or greens, arrange them in neat little pieces or heads to fit each piece of bread; stew them in some Spanish sauce, or in a well-devised brown sauce. When done lay each piece of greenmeat on its corresponding sippet of bread. Pour the sauce on the dish, and dispose the greens in a circle over it.

That most vulgar greenmeat TURNIP TOPS, can also be dressed as above, but these can be made to assume a more artistic appearance by being reduced to a *purée*, the process being this: Boil thoroughly, in plenty of water, with salt and soda in due proportions, drain, and pass through a hair sieve. Melt a piece of butter, to which add a little flour and the pulp of your turnip-tops; stir on the fire a few minutes, adding a little milk or cream and a little broth or stock, with pepper and grated nutmeg to taste. When of a nice consistency, not too thick, dress on a dish as you would spinach, and serve with fried sippets of bread round it. If properly cooked this dish has a better colour than spinach, and a very pleasant nutty bitter taste, which I sometimes think preferable to that of spinach for a change. The sieve to be used should be a strong horsehair one, as wire sieves are apt to impart a bad taste, especially in the case of vegetables containing strong acids, such as sorrel.

SORREL should be treated exactly as above, only it should not be so thick as spinach, but have the consistency more of a thick sauce or *purée*. It is generally not served by itself, but under a piece of stewed veal or veal cutlets. The pleasant acidity of a *purée* of sorrel goes very well with veal, and it is made more attractive by the addition of the yolks of one or more eggs stirred into it with the milk or cream; in this case, however, it is not necessary to put in any broth or stock.

A *purée* of sorrel, made rather thick, may be served by itself, with poached or fried eggs disposed upon it, or simply hard boiled eggs cut into quarters. By using spinach instead of sorrel you have another very good dish.

SPINACH is prepared by exactly the same process as turnip-tops, and there are several other vegetables which, similarly treated, are a very good substitute for it. The leaves of the white beet, and even those of the common beetroot, and also watercresses, make very good substitutes for spinach. The young shoots of nettles may also be used.

A skilful cook will produce very artistic *purées* or dishes of the nature of spinach by the judicious combination of spinach, sorrel, white-beet, water-cress, chervil, lettuce, and endive. A head of lettuce thrown in with spinach or sorrel, when it is put to boil in the first instance, is always an improvement.

With ENDIVE alone a very good *purée* can be made thus: Boil some endive in salted water, drain it and pass it through a hair sieve. Melt a piece of butter in a saucepan, add a little flour, then endive pulp, pepper, salt, and grated nutmeg to taste. Let the whole give a boil, then stir in off the fire the yolks of one or two eggs beaten up with a little milk and strained, as well as some parsley or some chervil finely minced. This *purée* may also be coloured with some

SPINACH GREENING.—This preparation can be bought cheaply enough of any Italian warehouseman, but if you wish to make it at home the proceeding is this: Pound a quantity of spinach in a mortar, put the pulp in a cloth, and, by twisting it at both ends, extract the juice, to which add a quarter of its weight of loaf sugar, and lay it in a *bain marie* to reduce to one half. When cold put it into a small bottle for use.

All these *purées*, when made of a thin consistency, are served as soups, with sippets of fried bread, and are called *Potage à la purée* of whatever it may be. And they are also served as a garniture to all sorts of meats; but for this purpose they must be made thicker. Lastly, in many cases they are made thicker still, and are eaten as vegetables by themselves.

When you use vegetables which do not contain much starch, this should be supplied by flour; otherwise, when the *purée* comes to be put into the soup plates, the vegetable fibres will separate from the liquid, and sink to the bottom of the plate. For the thicker forms of *purée* the addition of flour is not of so much importance.

The following may be taken as the common form to make all sorts of

Purées.—Boil the vegetables with salt, and, if they be green ones, with a little soda. When thoroughly done, drain them well and pass them through a hair sieve. Melt a piece of butter in a saucepan: Add a little flour: Mix it well, and throw in the vegetable pulp. Stir and proceed to flavour with pepper and powdered spices; or the spices, put in a muslin bag, may be boiled with the vegetables in the first instance. A piece of ham or bacon may also be boiled with them, and the flavour may be further modified by the addition of vegetables having a strong flavour, like onions, shallots, and garlic. The last part of the process consists in moistening the *purée* with broth, stock, milk, or cream, until it is of the required consistency; and then it is ready to be served. A *purée* for a soup is improved by having a small pat of fresh butter put into it at the time of serving. The inside of a French roll—soaked in milk or broth—added to the vegetables before they are passed through the sieve may be used instead of flour at the next stage of the process. A little sugar may be advantageously added to certain *purées*, such as peas, Jerusalem artichokes, and onions.

Purées can be made with the following vegetables besides those mentioned already, or with any combination of them: Asparagus, artichokes, broad beans, carrots, cabbage, celery, haricot beans, Jerusalem artichokes, mushrooms, onions, parsnips, peas, potatoes, tomatoes, turnips, vegetable marrow; and also with dried peas, beans, broad beans, lentils, and chestnuts.

Of possible combinations there is no end, and the skill and taste of the cook must in practice find them out. Likewise taste can best teach which *purées* will do only for soups, and which for both soup and to serve with meat, or for the latter purpose only.

In the case of artichokes, chestnuts, and mushrooms, the common form given above must be modified, as follows: When the ARTICHOKES have been boiled, the tender part of the leaves and the bottoms should be separated from the rest, and alone passed through the sieve (in this case a wire sieve would be fatal).

CHESTNUTS, stripped of their first or outer skin, should be boiled with salt, a bay leaf or two, and some coriander seeds. When they are done, remove the inner skin, and then proceed as usual.

MUSHROOMS should not be boiled at all, but should be cooked with butter and moistened with stock or broth, flavoured and floured before passing through the sieve.

It is very strange that a people like the English, who set so much importance upon the natural flavour of their greenmeat (and rightly, too, only they do not know how to preserve it) should in some cases, by their very plain boiling, all but destroy the flavour so much prized. It is the universal custom in England to slice or cut into fillets both FRENCH BEANS, and SCARLET RUNNERS, before cooking them. The result of such an operation is, that half the flavour goes to the water; and it is but natural that many people should say, as they do, that such vegetables have not much taste of their own, and are hardly worth eating. If they will take my advice, and boil beans and runners whole, they will come to a very different conclusion, and find out that beans have a flavour of their own, and a strong one, too. Runners and beans cannot be too young; directly the bean proper begins to form, and they have what is called a read, they are too old. There is, however, some difficulty in procuring at London shops beans of the proper age; but, like many other luxuries, this can always be secured by giving a little more money for the beans, which in that case the greengrocer will pick out for you, although he may have a strong objection to doing so. The fortunate possessors of kitchen gardens, however, can easily exercise the power of selection themselves.

Having secured beans of the right size, and nipped off the ends of each, you must boil them in plenty of water with a due quantity of salt and soda; and, like all other fresh vegetables to be boiled in water, they should not be thrown in until the water is boiling fast.

In France, to preserve the green colour of the beans, they tie up in a piece of cloth a small quantity of wood ashes as washerwomen tie up their blue or indigo, and put it into the saucepan while the water is getting up to boiling point; but I find soda answers quite as well, and with less trouble. The beans should be thrown into cold water after they are cooked; but this depends upon the way they are going to be dressed. The principal fashions after which I eat both French beans and runners are as follows:—

1. Incorporate with a piece of butter some parsley, garden cress, and chervil very finely minced, together with some pepper and a very little grated nutmeg; put the beans on a very hot dish, and the lump of butter thus prepared in their midst; the least bit of chives, chopped very small, may be added to the butter, and the cress or chervil, or both, may be omitted.

2. Make a sauce with butter, flour, water, salt, pepper, and nutmeg. The beans, which ought to have been thrown into a basin of cold water when a little more than half done, are well drained and put into this sauce to finish cooking. At the time of serving, the yolks of one or two eggs, with the juice of a lemon, are added.

3. A small quantity of fat bacon and a little shallot are chopped very fine and put into a saucepan; the beans, treated as in No. 2, are put in when the bacon is melted, and tossed in it till they are quite done. Pepper and other condiments to be added *ad lib.*, and a few drops of vinegar are not amiss.

4. One or two onions are sliced very thin, and put into a saucepan with plenty of butter; when they begin to take colour, put in the beans, first treated as in No. 2, and then proceed as in No. 3.

Previous boiling is by no means imperative in the last two formulæ, and I am not quite certain that a better dish is not produced if the beans are put raw into the bacon or into the butter and onions. Of course they will require a longer time to cook in this way.

Beans and runners are also very good if prepared as in No. 2, only with other sauces, such as tomato sauce or melted butter made with cream, or nobler sauces, like *Velouté, Béchamel,* &c.

Such beans as have passed the prescribed limit, if suffered to grow, will eventually produce haricots, which make most excellent dishes. It is hard to tell whether they are more delicious, fresh or dried. They are more delicate when they are fresh; but in this form they are a luxury which must be denied to the dwellers in cities, for, although all corn-chandlers keep some sort of dried haricot beans, and there are in London a few Italian warehouses where the superior kinds are to be got—fresh ones, I apprehend, are not procurable anywhere, as being, like many other good things, accounted unfit for human food by British cooks.

Fresh HARICOTS, or beans proper, are dressed in exactly the same way as French beans; the preliminary boiling, however, differs in this, that they should be boiled in plain water with neither salt nor soda, and that the former alone should be put in at the second stage of the proceedings with the other condiments.

The haricots, or beans proper, of scarlet runners, can be treated as those of French beans; some of them are of a very pretty pink colour, variegated with blue, but they lose their colours by boiling, and turn slate colour. If, however, the juice of a lemon be put in the water in which they are boiled, they will assume a whitish-pink hue. There are some kinds of runners which have a very thick tough skin to their beans, and these should be treated as follows: Boil with salt, and as soon as the skins begin to crack, throw the beans into cold water; then remove the skin of each, which will come off very easily, and proceed to dress your skinless beans in any of the forms already set forth.

BROAD BEANS should undergo a similar operation before

cooking, if their skin is at all tough; but it is always better to eat them young, when this process is not necessary. I have but one way, besides soups and *purées*, of cooking them. They should be gathered young, before the skin of the bean hardens, and then let them be boiled in water with a goodly piece of bacon and a sprig or two of savory. When they are done, put your piece of bacon in a dish, drain the beans, toss them for a minute in a saucepan, with plenty of parsley and melted butter made *sec. art.*, and fortify the bacon with a rampart of beans all round it. This is a sort of dish which is improved by the preliminary condiment of a walk of fifteen or twenty miles, and then it is good indeed.

Under certain circumstances I cut runners, and even French beans, in the green state, but then they are not filleted. I cut them diagonally, so as to form lozenges the size of a broad bean, and they are not cooked in water at all, but stewed with butter, onions, and condiments to taste.

PEAS are a more refined vegetable, and to be perfect they require the juices of three other leguminous productions, viz., onions, lettuce, and mint. The cook will exhibit her talent in the way she commingles these with peas. The way I do it is this: I tie up into a little bundle a head of lettuce and one or two onions, and throw them in with the peas into plenty of boiling water with salt. When cooked, I strain off all the water, remove the bundle, and serve the peas over a good-sized piece of butter, with which a very small quantity of mint, finely minced, has been mixed up. Sometimes I use parsley and mint in equal quantities.

When the peas are very young, they should not be cooked in water at all, but by the following process:

Melt a piece of butter in a saucepan, and in it place your peas raw, with some onion, lettuce, mint or parsley or both tied up in a bundle, pepper, salt, and the least bit of nutmeg (grated). Keep tossing the peas till quite done, when remove the bundle and add a small pat of butter; then serve. The yolk of one egg or more, according to the quantity of peas, beaten up with a little water and stirred into them just before serving, is an improvement, and so is a small quantity of sugar.

Another form, which is adapted for peas of all ages, consists in chopping some fat bacon very fine, with either onion or shallot in a small quantity and a little parsley. The raw peas are put with this into a saucepan, and—a due quantity of salt and pepper being added—they are tossed on the fire till done; I need hardly mention that the tossing is not to be continuous. Suppress the bundle and serve. Ham may be used instead of fat bacon, but in that case a little butter should be added. Savory (*sariette*) is a good herb to use with peas instead of mint or parsley.

The following is the most artistic way of preparing young peas, and what in England would be called the "richest."

Put the peas to cook in butter with a bundle as described above, pepper, salt, &c.; when they are done beat up some cream with a little sugar and the yolk of an egg. Stir this into the peas, and—after suppressing the bundle —serve, with sippets of bread fried in fresh butter.

Heads of ASPARAGUS cut up in small pieces as if to put into soup, can be dressed in the same way as peas. In its proper season, however, there is but one way of eating asparagus, and that is plainly boiled.

The proper way to prepare asparagus is to scrape each head with the back of a knife, then to tie it in small bundles of a dozen heads each, and to cut off the ends evenly; and it is best, if possible, to cut off all that part of the asparagus which cannot be eaten. Put it into a panful of fast boiling water with plenty of salt, and in about ten minutes it will be done. Practice can best teach the exact length of time required, and it must be borne in mind that of all vegetables asparagus can least bear being overdone. It should be well drained the instant it is done, and—the bundles being untied—served on a napkin. The usual practice of serving asparagus on toast is not nice, and as for eating the toast, as some do, that is less nice still. Plain melted butter, *sauce blanche*, or a simple salad sauce, are the best to eat with asparagus, but there is a form of sauce which fits asparagus very well I think, and this is butter liquefied and beaten up with pepper, salt, and the pounded yolks of hard boiled eggs.

Asparagus also makes very good fritters.

If SEAKALE is to be eaten in the plain English fashion it should be cooked in the same way as asparagus, only it requires to boil a little longer, and care must be taken that the water in which it is cooking boils evenly, for should the water stop boiling the seakale will be spoilt. It is well, when boiling seakale, to put a piece of butter in the water.

ARTICHOKES do not appear in a general way upon English tables. English cookery-books, with one or two exceptions, describe but one mode of cooking this vegetable—viz., plain boiling. Now, a plain boiled artichoke has merits when accompanied by a cunningly devised sauce, having just enough condiment to relieve without killing the flavour of the artichoke; but if the vegetable be young and fresh gathered, it is still better eaten raw with a *sauce poivrade*—*i.e.*, a judicious mixture of oil, vinegar, pepper, and salt, and perhaps a little mustard. However, the process of eating an artichoke, either raw or plainly boiled, is such that many people would think it tedious, and perhaps not very elegant; wherefore professors of cookery have invented other ways of dressing this vegetable, the chief point of which consists in dressing only the eatable part of each artichoke, so that it may be eaten with a fork, as are carrots or potatoes.

The process of removing from an artichoke the uneatable part is a very easy one when you know it; but the simple word "trim" is hardly sufficient to explain it to the uninitiated. What is meant by trimming an artichoke is this: Cut off the stalk close; turn the artichoke bottom upwards, and cut it in four, six, or eight "quarters," as you would an orange; take each quarter, and remove with a knife the embryo stamens which are at the core; then cut off all the leaves, leaving only an eighth of an inch of the outside one; this must be done in a slanting direction, for as the leaves approach the core there is more to eat on them. Lastly, pare the outside of each quarter neatly. All these operations must be done expeditiously; and as each quarter is done it must be put into a basin of cold water with the juice of a lemon squeezed in it.

When the artichokes are all trimmed they should be taken out of the basin and thrown into a saucepan full of boiling water, with salt and the juice of half a lemon; and when they are nearly cooked—say in fifteen or twenty minutes—they should be drained and put back again into the basin of cold water and lemon juice.

They are now ready for dressing; and ten minutes before serving, having drained and dried them in a cloth, you can proceed to dress them in any of the following forms:

1. Flour or dip each piece in batter, and fry it a light colour, serving it either alone or with other fried things.

2. Make a sauce with flour, butter, water, pepper, and salt; toss the pieces of artichokes in it till warmed, and add, just before sending up to table, the yolks of one or two eggs beaten up with the juice of a lemon.

3. Fry some chopped onions in butter, and put in the pieces of artichoke; toss them in the saucepan for ten minutes, and serve with the juice of a lemon, adding a little grated nutmeg, and salt and pepper if necessary. To be dressed in this way they should be boiled previously for ten minutes only.

4. Dispose the pieces of artichoke on a well-buttered silver dish. Strew plentifully over them a mixture of bread crumbs and finely-minced mushrooms and parsley, with a very little chopped shallot or garlic. Add pepper and salt, and a little more butter, and put the dish into the oven for ten minutes. Brown the top with a salamander, and serve. Previous boiling is not imperative; but when it is dispensed with the dish should remain longer in the oven, say about half an hour. Oil may be used instead of butter.

5. Artichokes are also used as *garnitures*, and to form with other vegetables the *ragoûts* called *jardinière*, &c.; and in order to have them all the year round for this purpose they can be preserved by the following process: Having "trimmed" them as above, boil them as for present dressing, but for five or ten minutes only. Drain and dry them in a cloth, then string them on twine, and hang them up in a free current of air to dry. The pieces of artichoke should not touch each other. When they are thoroughly dry they can be put away, and kept like dried mushrooms in jars or paper bags. But in the

present day these, as well as most vegetables, can be had in perfection preserved in tins and at a moderate expense.

It is better, when practicable, to avoid boiling artichokes in iron saucepans; and, indeed, this rule applies to all vegetables containing acids which will act upon iron. An earthen pot or a tinned copper pan should be used, or, if you *will* have iron saucepans they should be lined with white enamel.

CARDONS À LA MOËLLE is one of the standing dishes of the Paris restaurants. In England this vegetable is very little known. Cardoons are mentioned in seedsmen's prices current, but in greengrocer's shops they are seldom if ever seen. A very fair substitute for them, which, if it does not possess all the delicacy of taste of the real cardoon, has at all events the advantage of being very cheap—so cheap, in fact, that it is to be got for nothing—is to be found in the stalks of green artichokes, which often are sent to market with a foot or more of it attached to them—English-grown ones especially. Now these artichoke stalks can be made into a dish closely resembling cardoons—which are themselves a kind of artichoke—with this difference, that the leaves proper are very thick, and, being banked up like celery, grow very white and tender. The stalks or ribs (*côtes*) of these are eaten, and not the bud, so to speak, as with the green artichoke.

This is how to proceed with the stalks of these same English artichokes to make a very good dish of what most people would look upon as vegetable refuse. Cut the stalks in lengths of four or five inches, scrape off them—as you would off a carrot—their outer fibrous envelope, and as you finish each piece put it into a basin containing cold water and the juice of a lemon. When they are all ready, let them be boiled in water with salt and lemon juice for a few minutes. Then drain them again, and place them in cold water and lemon juice to wait till it is time to dress them for table. This process may be reversed, the parboiling taking place first, and the scraping afterwards. Cardoons are treated thus. But for artichoke stalks I prefer scraping them first.

The usual formula for the preparation of *cardons à la moëlle* is as follows; and artichoke stalks may be treated in the same way.

Put into a saucepan a few pieces of bacon cut small, as well as some carrots and onions, one bay leaf, a few sprigs of parsley, some whole pepper, and a few cloves. Add enough water to cover the pieces of bacon and vegetables, and set the saucepan to boil until the whole water is nearly evaporated, stirring the mixture at the latter stage of the process to prevent it "catching." Then add as much hot water as you put in at first; skim carefully, and strain through muslin. The liquor is called BLANC: it will keep several days, and is very useful to dress artistically many vegetables besides cardoons.

Having successfully prepared your *blanc*—lay your cardoons or artichoke stalks (previously scraped and parboiled) in a saucepan, with a few slices of lemon minus the pips and the peel; salt if necessary, and pour in a sufficient quantity of *blanc* to cover them, letting them simmer till done quite tender. Now set them up in a dish, and pour over them a well-reduced *sauce Espagnole* in which you have incorporated two or three ounces of beef marrow dissolved *au bain marie*—*i.e.*, in a vessel standing in another containing boiling water; then serve with bread sippets fried in butter.

Another way is to lay the marrow on the bread sippets

instead of putting it in the sauce. The Spanish sauce is not indispensable, for the *blanc* in which the cardoons have been cooked, if it be more highly flavoured and thickened with butter and flour, will do for a sauce, only the dish will not be, of course, so *distingué*.

With "tinned" cardoons the mode of proceeding is as follows:

Take a tin, open it, drain off the liquor, and lay the cardoons in a stewpan with enough well-flavoured stock to cover them. Let this remain on the fire just long enough to warm the cardoons through. Procure some large pieces of marrow by getting the butcher to break the bones for you, and lay the marrow in a saucepan with cold water and salt for about an hour; then pour off the water, replace it with fresh salted water, and put the saucepan on the fire. As soon as the water boils, take the saucepan off the fire, and let the marrow remain in the water till wanted. Fry in butter some well-shaped sippets of bread; cut up the marrow, and place a piece of it on each sippet. Dispose these round a dish; pour some brown sauce, reduced almost to a glaze, in the middle; lay the cardoons on it, and serve.

Seakale and CELERY, likewise, can be cooked as are cardoons; but the former is best plainly boiled, as described before. Some fine heads of celery, or cardoons, stewed in a *blanc*, as above, then served with a well-flavoured, clear gravy, constitute the dish called CELERI, or CARDONS AU JUS; and, if served with a well-made white sauce, you have CELERI, or CARDONS À LA CRÊME.

A simpler mode of dressing all these things is to let them simmer, after they have been duly parboiled, in any stock or broth there may be in the kitchen, and when they are cooked to thicken and flavour the liquor, which forms the sauce. Tomato sauce goes very well with them also, as it does with almost everything eatable; but it must be proper tomato sauce, not an infusion of capsicum in vinegar with some tomato pulp floating in it. Lastly, they may be eaten with melted butter made with egg-yolks and lemon juice; and this form more nearly approaches the English fashion of eating vegetables.

One of the prettiest dishes of vegetables I know of consists of a CAULIFLOWER of ivory whiteness resting upon a bed of well-made tomato sauce. To boil a cauliflower: after it has been trimmed and soaked in salted water for some time, it should be put in plenty of fast boiling water, with a due quantity of salt. Care should be taken not to overboil it. Try the stem with a thin iron skewer, and the moment it is soft remove the saucepan from the fire, and put the cauliflower to drain on a hair sieve. When two or more cauliflowers are used, they should be moulded into one for serving. To do this; when they are boiled cut off the stalk, and dispose the pieces of cauliflower head downwards in a basin; press them gently together, turn them out dexterously on a dish, and two or three small cauliflowers will by this means present the appearance of one large one. Care must be taken to have the basin quite hot, and to operate quickly. This cannot very well be done with the small purple cauliflower or brocoli; but all the formulæ given for cauliflowers proper may be applied to BROCOLI likewise.

Instead of tomato sauce, the following sauces may be used: Caper sauce, gherkin sauce, *sauce piquante, sauce blanche, Béchamel*, or *maître d'hôtel*. The sauce should be put into the dish, and the cauliflowers laid upon it; but if the moulding process has not been successful, or if the cauliflowers are not very nice-looking, then pour the sauce over them so as to hide their deformity.

The very best way, however, to treat cauliflowers is *au*

gratin, and this has the advantage that it may be applied to the remains of cauliflowers served at the dinner of the day before. This is the simplest form of it: Dispose the pieces of cauliflowers on a dish, pour a good supply of liquefied butter over them, and plenty of grated Parmesan cheese, with a judicious admixture of powdered white pepper, salt, and nutmeg. Put the dish into the oven for a few minutes, or brown with a red-hot salamander, and then serve.

Here are other modes of proceeding: Rub the dish very slightly with garlic or shallot, mould your cauliflowers in a basin, and pour over them—before turning them out—some melted butter, into which you have dissolved a good allowance of Parmesan cheese; turn them out on the dish, strew plentifully with grated Parmesan, a few baked bread crumbs, pepper and salt *quant. suff.*, pouring the remainder of the sauce over; brown and serve.

Instead of moulding the cauliflowers: dip each piece in the sauce and dispose them flat on the dish, filling up the interstices with bread crumbs and Parmesan cheese in equal parts; add pepper and salt according to taste; brown, and serve.

The great thing to be avoided is not to make these preparations too dry, and yet there should not be over much butter. The browning must be carefully done, so as to produce a surface of a uniform golden colour—not in patches, some burnt black, and others not browned at all.

To those who may object to cheese, I can recommend the following recipe, which has great merit of its own:

Dispose your pieces of boiled cauliflower upon a dish well rubbed with garlic; over them strew a mixture of bread crumbs and anchovies, capers and olives minced fine, pepper and salt; over all pour a judicious quantity of fine salad oil; bake for about ten minutes, and serve.

VEGETABLE MARROWS plainly boiled first, as well as celery, and even seakale if you choose, can be dressed according to the forms above given for cauliflowers—indeed, one of them, *au gratin*, suits most vegetables.

LETTUCE and ENDIVE are often served in a cooked form on the continent; and, although I think that, unless made into a *purée*, their proper place is in a salad, I will describe the way to cook them.

Remove all or most of the green leaves, and parboil your endives in fast boiling water, containing a sufficient quantity of salt, till they are quite limp. Take them out and throw them into cold water, then drain and wipe them dry in a cloth. Now mince them moderately small, and finish cooking them in a saucepan containing some butter, a little flour, pepper, and nutmeg according to taste. The saucepan may be previously rubbed with garlic; and in the process of cooking they should be moistened with a little stock or broth, or even water. In this latter case a *liaison*—*i.e.*, the yolk of an egg, with a squeeze of lemon—may be stirred in at the time of serving.

This is another way : Having thoroughly picked and cleansed the endives tie them up with string, and parboil them as described above ; then line a saucepan with slices of bacon, lay your endives on this, with a small bundle of sweet herbs, onions, &c., and pepper and other spices to taste; moisten with stock, and when they are quite done dispose them neatly upon a dish—having removed the strings—and serve with a Spanish sauce over them, or a sauce made from the liquor left in the saucepan, well freed from superfluous fat.

A well made *farce*, or simply some sausage meat, may

be put after the parboiling process inside each endive. Then having tied them up again very carefully, proceed as above.

The way to dress LETTUCES is the same as for endives, with the only difference that the parboiling takes much less time.

Both may also be served on bread sippets fried in butter, as mentioned for cabbages and greens.

Many other vegetables may be stewed with advantage, for being thus *cuits dans leur jus* they lose none of their flavour. Vegetable marrows, turnips, carrots, beetroots (previously baked), potatoes, Jerusalem artichokes, parsnips, cucumbers and onions make capital dishes when properly cooked, without the agency of water. In the course of my experiments I have never tried a fresh combination for making a stew of the above but it has proved successful. It would be too long to describe them all, and I shall, therefore, content myself with setting forth those which have found the most favour with my friends.

1. Take some vegetable marrows, not too old (what this vegetable gains in size by age it loses in flavour), cut them up in pieces the size of a small egg, having first peeled them. Rub a saucepan with garlic, put a goodly piece of butter and a little flour in it, and throw in your pieces of vegetable marrow when the butter is melted, adding pepper, salt, and grated nutmeg. Take care they do not catch or burn, which is avoided by tossing and adding more butter if necessary. In about a quarter of an hour throw in a handful or two of grated Parmesan cheese, according to the quantity. If they look too dry add a small quantity of milk, and let the stew simmer till the marrows are quite done, when you serve with or without *croûtons* (sippets) round the dish.

The foregoing recipe is applicable to all the vegetables mentioned above, with the exception of onions.

2. Chop half an onion very small, and put it in a saucepan with a lump of butter; when it begins to brown throw in your vegetables (cut in pieces) pepper, salt, and a little grated nutmeg; moisten with a little broth or stock, and let them simmer till done.

3. Put the vegetables, cut up as before, into a saucepan with pepper, salt, nutmeg (grated), chopped parsley, and a large piece of butter; toss them for a few minutes in the saucepan, and add a small quantity of hot water—just enough to prevent their catching. When done, stir with them the yolk of an egg beaten up with the juice of a lemon.

A combination of several vegetables, such as beetroot and potatoes, or carrots, turnips, and potatoes, or parsnips and turnips, &c., treated by any of the above methods, will produce very nice *entremets de légumes*. In most cases of stewing vegetables the least bit of sugar will be an improvement, but it must be used as carefully as if it were Cayenne pepper, under pain of spoiling the dish.

Another very good way of dressing those vegetables, which the French call *racines*, mostly mentioned above, and also potatoes, is to cut them with a vegetable scoop, into the shape of one ounce bullets, and to toss them in plenty of butter till quite done, adding during the process salt, pepper, and a very little powdered sugar.

Small new CARROTS are excellent cooked in this way, and when they are done the addition of some chopped parsley and a squeeze of lemon is an improvement.

By a somewhat similar process, turnips are glorified into the dish called NAVETS GLACÉS. The process is this: Cut some turnips all to a uniform shape, either like small pears or like orange quarters. Parboil them for five minutes in salted water. Drain them thoroughly, then place them in a well buttered saucepan, sprinkle them with plenty of powdered loaf sugar, put the saucepan on the fire, and, as soon as they begin to colour, moisten with a small quantity of clear stock ; add a pinch of powdered cinnamon, and pepper and salt; let them stew gently until done, and serve with the sauce over them.

The following is another recipe :

Having cut the turnips as above, put them in a *sauté*-pan, sprinkle them freely with powdered loaf sugar, and toss them on the fire until they begin to take colour, and the sugar forms a kind of caramel. Then take them out, put them into a saucepan, wash out the *sauté*-pan with a little stock, pour this over the turnips, add pepper and salt to taste, and let them stew gently till done.

PARSNIPS can be cooked in exactly the same manner, and so can the SMALL WHITE ONIONS used for pickling, either as a dish to be eaten by itself, or to be used as a garniture for stewed beef, mutton cutlets, &c.; and this reminds me of an excellent good soup which was invented by a noble French *gastronome* of the old school, the Marquis de Cussy. It is very easily prepared, is by no means expensive, and will be appreciated by the most fastidious.

SOUPE À LA CUSSY.—Pick and clean a dozen or more small white onions, such as are used for pickling ; cut them in the very thinnest slices you can, and put them into an enamelled saucepan with a tablespoonful of powdered loaf sugar and a goodly lump of fresh butter; keep shaking the saucepan until the onions are a fine golden colour ; then add to them as much hot water as you want soup. Let it give one boil, add one or two liqueur glasses of the best French brandy, pepper and salt judiciously, and pour into the soup tureen over a small quantity of bread, cut in the shape of small dice and previously fried in butter until they also have a golden hue. I have grated Parmesan cheese served with this soup, for those who like it. It is an improvement, if it is possible to improve one of the simplest and most agreeable combinations in the way of *soupe maigre* that ever was invented.

The larger onions, which are called Spanish, I much like to eat simply boiled in water, with a *vinaigrette* sauce—*i. e.*, oil, vinegar, pepper, and salt. It is not everybody, however, who likes onions as much as I do. I, in common with the ancient Egyptians, have the greatest veneration for these bulbs, without which no cookery worth the name would be possible. The following will be found a more elaborate way of dressing SPANISH ONIONS:

They should first be parboiled in water and salt for about ten minutes; then the core, or centre, of each onion should be removed with the same instrument as is used in coring apples, to wit, a tin cylinder, half an inch in diameter—care being taken to leave the bottom part intact. This done,

1. Arrange the onions in a saucepan, in which you have previously melted a piece of butter, and mixed with it a tablespoonful of flour. Fill up the cavity of each onion with a mixture of bread crumbs, anchovies (well washed and cut up small), capers, pepper and salt; add a mixture of half stock or broth, and half claret made hot; put in, tied up in a bundle, some parsley, sweet herbs, and a few cloves, and set your saucepan on the fire to simmer gently, until the onions are thoroughly done, when remove the bundle of herbs, and dispose the onions carefully on a dish. Pour the sauce under them and serve.

o

2. Fill up the interior of each onion with some nicely-flavoured forcemeat; dispose them in a well-buttered saucepan, add a bundle of herbs, &c., as before, and cover the whole with slices of bacon. When the onions are done, remove them into a dish. Make a sauce of what is left in the saucepan by adding some flour to it, and, if necessary, some other condiments, and some stock or broth. Skim off superfluous fat, strain and pour the sauce over the onions, and serve.

3. Another way is, instead of making a sauce of what is left in the saucepan, to use some Spanish or Italian sauce.

4. Tomato sauce goes very well with stewed onions, either stuffed or not. This is the formula which I prefer to most. Make a mixture of bread crumbs, pure tomato sauce, a small quantity of ham finely minced, and one or two raw eggs, with pepper, salt, and powdered spices. Stuff the onions with this, and put them to stew, with a bundle of sweet herbs, in a saucepan well lined with bacon; moisten with some well-flavoured tomato sauce, and when done serve with the sauce over, having previously removed the superfluous fat from it.

Bread sippets fried in butter should almost invariably be served with all the above dishes of onions.

Vegetable marrows, cucumbers, and tomatoes make very nice dishes if treated by stuffing. It is a very good way of utilising those scraps of meat which are always going begging, so to speak, in most kitchens. Of course all depends upon the making of the stuffing, call it *chair à quenelles, farce,* forcemeat, or what not. The following will be found a good common form :

Remove every particle of fat, skin, and gristle from the scraps of meat to be used; then pound the meat in a mortar and force it through a wire sieve; pound again what will not go through, until you have thus sifted nearly all your meat. Have ready some fine bread crumbs, and to two parts of meat add one part of bread crumbs and one part of butter; mix the whole thoroughly in a mortar, flavour it according to taste with salt, pepper, spices, and sweet herbs (all finely powdered), and moisten it with milk or cream, adding the yolks of one or more eggs according to quantity. When the mixture is of the consistency of a smooth thick paste it is ready for use. All sorts of meat, poultry, game, or fish may be used either alone, or in combination, according to the purpose the *farce* is wanted for. The introduction of some lean ham will not be amiss in certain cases.

When trouble is an object, an easy and coarser substitute will be found in sausage meat.

To stuff VEGETABLE MARROWS or CUCUMBERS, they should be cut in halves lengthways, and when you have scooped out the inside, they should be filled with the above meat, and baked in a well-buttered dish, to be served with Spanish sauce or tomato sauce over them.

Another way consists in laying the stuffed marrows in a saucepan previously buttered, with a bundle of sweet herbs, and a small piece of garlic or shallot, moistening with tomato sauce, or simply broth. When they have simmered sufficiently to be quite done, remove them on to a dish very carefully, strain the sauce, flavour and thicken it if necessary, pour it over the dish, and serve. Lastly; not a bad form of dressing marrows, cucumbers, celery, seakale, &c., is to lay them in a well-flavoured tomato sauce, and let them simmer until quite done; or Spanish, Italian, or any other high flavoured sauce, may be used instead.

In point of flavour, wholesomeness, colour—in fact, on all points—there is no vegetable to be compared to a tomato. Truffles may be the diamonds of the kitchen, as some writer calls them; and I am not prepared to deny the fact, for they are very expensive, and they are passing good to eat. Everybody's purse, however, is not equal to truffles as a regular article of food, nor will truffles go well with all and every dish. Tomatoes, on the contrary, are cheap enough; they can be preserved even in this country at small cost, so as to be available all the year round, and, barring white soups and sauces, there is not a savoury dish to which the judicious addition of their flavour is not a considerable improvement.

What is called tomato sauce in this country is only a libel on the real article. Vinegar, in quantities more or less large, and cayenne pepper are used in the preparation of it, and, as might be expected, these things overpower completely and kill that pleasant acid taste, quite *sui generis*, to which is mainly due the great charm of the tomato.

In some shops you can buy preserved tomato sauce made in France, and this will be found very good if it is really of Gallic origin, a fact easily ascertained by opening a bottle and tasting it. If it tastes of tomatoes it is good French tomato sauce; if the compound is very acid and hot to the mouth—in other words, if vinegar and cayenne predominate—then it is the British form— to be avoided.

Good French TOMATO SAUCE, however, is not very cheap; and as tomatoes can be bought in London—at a certain season of the year—at a very moderate rate, those who choose to take the trouble can provide themselves with a sufficient stock of good wholesome tomato sauce, if they will attend to the following directions. To ensure perfect success the tomatoes should be gathered quite ripe on a bright sunny day, about one or two o'clock in the afternoon. Those who have no garden to grow tomatoes in, or, having a garden, look out in vain for a bright sunny day, must manage as best they can. Cut up the tomatoes into quarters, and put them into a saucepan with salt *quant. suff.*, a good handful of basil, and three or four cloves of garlic. A little water should be put into the saucepan to prevent the tomatoes catching. When they are thoroughly done, turn them out upon a hair sieve, and wait till all the water has drained from them. Throw away this water, and proceed to pass the tomatoes through the sieve. The pulp thus obtained is put into a saucepan to boil for about half an hour, and a moderate quantity of black pepper may be added to it according to taste. When the sauce is quite cold put it into widemouthed bottles, cork tightly, and tie up each cork with string or wire; dip the neck of each bottle into melted rosin, and you may then put them away to be used when required. The bottles should be of moderate size, for, once opened, the sauce will no longer keep good.

If, before putting on the wire, the bottles of sauce are placed upright in a large vessel full of cold water, and this is put on the fire until the water boils, the preservation will be more certain still, and the sauce will keep good any length of time. Care must be taken, however, not to remove the bottles from this *bain-marie* until the water has become perfectly cold.

Another way consists in letting the tomato pulp reduce in a saucepan until it assumes the appearance of a very thick paste—care being taken to stir it constantly; when cool it is put away like jam in pots, and will keep any length of time. This is what is called *conserva* in Italy, only in that country the tomato pulp is reduced to the consistency of a thick paste by the action of the sun instead of that of the fire. To use the *conserva*, a small quantity is dissolved in water. It makes very good sauce, but the taste is different from that of the fresh tomato, or of the preserved sauce, described above.

Another way of preserving tomatoes in countries where the heat of the sun is strong consists in splitting them in halves and exposing them to the sun, taking care to take them in at night, and to turn over each individual half at least once a day, until they are quite dry. To make the sauce from these they should be soaked in cold water for six or seven hours; then boiled and passed through the sieve. The sauce thus obtained is slightly different in flavour from that made with *conserva*, or with the fresh fruit.

To make sauce for present use the process is nearly the same as that for preserving; but there are many varieties, and these are some of them :

1. Cut up the tomatoes and put them into a saucepan containing a little water, with some parsley, basil, marjoram, and thyme in judicious proportions, a clove of garlic, a laurel leaf or two, a few cloves, some salt, and some whole pepper; when thoroughly done strain all the water off and pass through a hair sieve : put a piece of butter into a saucepan; add to it, when melted, a spoonful of flour and the tomato pulp; mix thoroughly, and when warm the sauce is ready for use.

Sauce for preserving may be flavoured as is the above, instead of in the simpler manner which I have given before.

2. Cut up and remove from each tomato the pips and watery substance they contain; put them into a saucepan with plenty of butter, pepper, salt, a laurel leaf, and some thyme; add a few spoonfuls of either stock, gravy or Spanish sauce; keep stirring on the fire until they are

reduced to a pulp, when you pass them through a sieve, and your sauce is made.

3. Mince a small quantity of bacon and put it into a saucepan with sweet herbs, salt, pepper, a few cloves, some minced parsley, and a shallot; when these ingredients are quite warm, put in the tomatoes, cut up and bereft of their inside and pips; let the whole simmer, stirring frequently, for half an hour or more; when the tomatoes are quite dissolved, pass them through the sieve and serve.

STUFFED TOMATOES make an excellent *entremet de légumes*. They may be stuffed with boiled rice or mashed potatoes, or with any *farce* of meat, fish, or poultry. The way to do it is this. Cut each tomato in halves, so as to cut across all the divisions there are in it; empty it of the pips, &c., and fill up each half with the stuffing. Lay them in a buttered dish and bake. Another way consists in making an incision in each tomato, so as to be able to empty it; you then fill it with the *farce*, put it together again, and bake.

Or they may be laid in a stewpan over slices of bacon, and stewed till done; some stock and parsley, sweet herbs, &c., being added. The tomatoes are then carefully taken out, and disposed on a dish; and the sauce they have stewed in, being strained and freed from superfluous fat, is poured over them. It must be borne in mind that either to bake or to stew tomatoes as above takes very little time—ten minutes at most.

Here is yet another form: Empty the tomatoes as best you can without cutting them open too much and stuff them with the following composition: To some well-flavoured tomato sauce add bread crumbs until you bring it to a moderate consistency; beat up some eggs, one for every three tomatoes to be stuffed; mix the whole well together, add more condiments, if necessary, stuff the tomatoes with this, bake for a few minutes on a buttered dish, and serve.

This is an Italian recipe: Peel your tomatoes, cut them in halves, empty them, and place them on a dish that will stand the fire, and in which you have poured a small quantity of olive oil; make a mixture of bread crumbs, ham, parsley, basil, marjoram, thyme, some garlic (all very finely minced), pepper, and salt. The bread crumbs should be in the proportion of two to one with the ham; the other things should be in such proportions as the talent of the cook can devise. This mixture should be strewed over the tomatoes so as to almost cover them; a moderate quantity of salad oil should be poured over the top, and a few minutes' baking will produce a dish of the most toothsome description. Anchovies, olives, capers, mushrooms, and even truffles, chopped up small, may be used, either in addition to, or instead of the ham; and, lastly, those who do not like oil may use butter instead.

There now remain two vegetables yet to be dealt with, which if they be among the lowest in the classification of naturalists, are the very highest in that of cooks. MUSHROOMS and TRUFFLES, without doubt, are of the greatest help to professors by the matchless flavour they impart to the preparations in which they are used. They are, however, often eaten alone, and I will describe some approved ways of preparing them for that purpose, although I think that, especially in the case of truffles—unfortunately expensive things—they are best used in flavouring sauces and *ragoûts* and in stuffing turkeys and pheasants.

The primitive or English fashion of cooking mushrooms consists in broiling them on a gridiron, or frying them with a little butter; but both these methods are capable of considerable improvement, and this is how to proceed.

Having picked and cleaned the mushrooms, make a mixture of pepper, salt, minced parsley, and a little minced shallot, sprinkle each mushroom with this, and wrap it up in a piece of paper plentifully oiled or buttered. Broil on a gentle clear fire, and serve paper and all. It is not necessary to wrap up each mushroom separately, but two or more, according to size, may be put into the same piece of paper, only in that case, besides buttering the paper, a small piece of butter should be put between the mushrooms.

Another way consists in making small paper cases, into which you put the mushrooms, cut up in small pieces, with pepper, salt, shallot, and parsley minced small, and a piece of butter. The cases (previously oiled) are then put on the gridiron, or they may be baked in the oven, which must not be too hot. A squeeze of lemon added at the moment of serving is an improvement. Serve in the cases.

A very excellent way of preparing mushrooms consists in stewing them according to the following directions. They may then be eaten alone or with plain cutlets, steaks, &c.

Parboil your mushrooms for a minute or two, having first cut them in convenient pieces, if they be very large ones; throw them in cold water, with the juice of a lemon or some vinegar; melt a piece of butter in a saucepan with flour, pepper, and salt, as if to make a *sauce blanche*; take the mushrooms out of the water, dry them in a cloth, and toss them in the saucepan, with the butter, &c.; moisten with stock or broth, add a little grated nutmeg and a few dried sweet herbs in fine powder. In less than ten minutes' stewing the mushrooms will be done; at the time of serving, and off the fire, stir in the yolk of an egg beaten up with the juice of a lemon; the saucepan may be rubbed slightly with garlic before commencing operations, and minced parsley may be used instead of sweet herbs; if served alone, there should be round the mushrooms a circle of bread sippets fried in butter.

Here is another mode :

Mince some shallots and parsley as finely as you can; put them into a saucepan with a piece of butter and some flour, pepper, salt, and nutmeg; stir this mixture on the fire, and before it acquires too dark a colour throw in the mushrooms (parboiled as above), and at the same time moisten with a mixture of half white wine and half stock or broth; let the whole simmer a quarter of an hour, and serve. By using oil instead of butter, and putting in some garlic as well as shallots, you will produce a dish of MUSHROOMS À LA PROVENÇALE. In either case the squeeze of lemon, and even a few drops of vinegar, are not amiss.

Truffles if they are to be eaten as a separate dish, cannot be too simply cooked, and a very good formula is the following :

TRUFFES À LA SERVIETTE.—Carefully wash and brush the truffles quite clean, then wrap them up in wet paper, bury them in hot wood ashes for an hour or so; remove the paper and serve in a napkin.

Another simple mode of dressing truffles is to steam them as follows : Fill the bottom part of what is called a steamer in kitchen parlance, with a mixture of sherry and water in the proportion of two to one; put the truffles in the upper compartment and let them steam for about an hour; serve under a napkin.

There are, however, more elaborate modes of dressing truffles, viz. :

TRUFFES SAUTÉES.—Put some butter in a saucepan and

some truffles cut in slices; toss them for five minutes, then moisten with a glass of sherry, and add pepper, salt, a little powdered nutmeg, and a small piece of glaze; let them stew gently till done. Serve with sippets of bread fried in butter.

TRUFFES À L'ITALIENNE.—Lay some truffles cut in slices in a dish that will stand the fire, strew over them some parsley and shallot finely minced, some pepper and a little salt; pour some olive oil over them, put them in the oven (covered closely) for a quarter of an hour or twenty minutes, and when done squeeze the juice of a lemon over them and serve.

TRUFFES À LA PÉRIGUEUX.—Cut the truffles in slices, and make as many bread sippets fried in butter as you have slices of truffles; fry these in plenty of butter for a few minutes with a little salt and some powdered spices; dispose them on a dish with a sippet between each slice of truffle; take some Spanish sauce, to which you add a couple of glasses of sherry and a pat of fresh butter; let it boil once or twice; pour over the truffles and serve.

The standard dish of TRUFFES AU VIN DE CHAMPAGNE is produced in this way: Put into a saucepan some slices of ham, so as to cover the bottom of it; lay your truffles on this with some slices of onions, whole pepper, salt, and a few cloves; add a bottle of champagne, and simmer for an hour or more. Remove the truffles carefully and serve under a napkin. I must confess, however, that lilies can be painted even in cookery, and that for my part I should prefer the truffles inside of a turkey or pheasant, and the champagne in a glass by my side.

I will conclude with a classical recipe combining both truffles and mushrooms, and which I extract from the appendix of a late edition of "La Physiologie du Goût.' I can recommend it as first-rate.

Cut some truffles and mushrooms in moderately small slices; put them in a saucepan with a goodly piece of butter, and a little garlic finely minced; or, better still, rub the saucepan freely with garlic. When the butter is melted squeeze in the juice of one or two lemons. Leave your mushrooms and truffles for a little while in this; add pepper and salt in due proportion, and a little grated nutmeg; then put in a sufficient quantity of good Spanish sauce to make a nice *ragoût*, which must simmer for about half an hour. Five minutes before serving add a glass or two of sherry, and you will have produced a noble dish.

DRIED BEANS.

It is strange that the only dried *légume* which is used to any extent in England, should be one of the most indigestible of them all. With the rare exception of a few haricot beans, peas are the only dried vegetables admitted into English cookery, of which pea soup and pease pudding are well-known institutions. I have seen it stated as a fact, and no doubt with truth, in a standard work on matters domestic, that lentils were not used as an article of human food in this country. Now, although these do not much differ from dried peas in their composition, yet they contain a certain aromatic principle which, while it renders them easier of digestion, imparts to them a very agreeable taste. One of the best of thick soups, the *potage à la Conti*, is naught else but a *purée* of lentils, and the *potage à la Condé*, another very good soup, is simply a *purée* of a particular kind of haricot beans. These, of which there are numerous varieties, are unquestionably the most nutritious of all dried vegetables. They only contain about eight per cent. less of starch, dextrine, and sugar than wheat, while of azotised substances they contain over four per cent. more. But, apart from any considerations of digestibility and of nutritiveness, these dried vegetables are the foundation of many agreeable dishes, besides soups; and as variety of food is one of the great essentials of good health, many people would gladly use these things if they knew how to prepare them, and this is what I will endeavour to explain.

The first step is to boil them, and, unlike fresh vegetables, which should always be thrown into boiling water, these must be put to cook in cold water. I have seen in a cookery book (not Irish) directions to "boil beans in cold water"—a difficult process, I imagine, to carry out. The point to be obtained is that the beans should be thoroughly done and floury, and yet that each should remain whole without the skin being cracked. To insure this, after having been picked out clean and washed, the beans before being put to cook should be allowed to soak in cold water for at least twelve hours. No salt should be put into the water until they are almost done; and during the process of boiling small quantities of cold water should be put at intervals into the saucepan, and the addition of an onion stuck with cloves, some whole pepper, and a bay leaf will be an improvement. When dried vegetables are intended for a *purée* the process of boiling is somewhat different, for it is obviously of no consequence that the skin should split.

The principal varieties of DRIED HARICOTS are the *Soissons*, the *Flageolets*, both green and white, and the red and the speckled haricots, all of which can be had in perfection at good Italian warehouses in town. Of LENTILS there are two kinds—the small (called *à la reine*), and the large; the former are the darkest, and best adapted for *purées*, hence some cooks call the *potage à la Conti*—*potage à la reine*.

PEAS are well enough known, both whole and split, and are fit for *purées* only; but there is a kind called Spanish peas, which make a very good dish of themselves; and then there are peas dried green, wherewith green pea soup can be made at all times. Lastly, DRIED BROAD BEANS are to be got, and they make a very fair purée of its kind for a change. I now proceed to set forth the various ways of dressing these dried vegetables after they have been boiled in the manner just described, taking haricot beans as a type.

1. A LA MAÎTRE D'HÔTEL.—Put a large piece of butter in a saucepan, and, when it is melted, drain the beans quite dry, do not allow them to cool, put them in with pepper and salt to taste, some minced parsley, and the juice of half a lemon, or more, according to quantity; toss them on the fire for a few minutes, and serve.

2. AU LARD.—Cut up a small quantity of bacon into very small dice, put it in a saucepan on the fire, and, after the lapse of a few minutes, toss in the beans; add pepper and salt to taste; give them a turn or two, and serve.

3. AU JAMBON.—Use ham instead of bacon.

4. A LA LYONNAISE.—Mince an onion very small, and fry it in plenty of butter till it assumes a pale straw colour; then put in the beans, with pepper and salt to taste; toss them a short time, and serve.

5. AUX TOMATES.—Toss the beans in a saucepan with a due quantity of well-flavoured tomato sauce.

6. A LA SAUCE BLANCHE.—Melt a piece of butter in a saucepan, add a pinch of flour, then the beans, and pepper and salt to taste; after a turn or two on the fire, stir in the yolk of an egg beaten up with the juice of half a lemon and strained.

7. AU JUS.—Melt a piece of butter in a saucepan, add the beans, moisten with as much well-flavoured beef gravy as may be necessary; season with pepper, salt, a little grated nutmeg, and a dash of tarragon vinegar; toss them for a few minutes, and serve.

8. EN SALADE.—Place the boiled beans in a vegetable dish. Mix the following sauce: Three parts of olive oil and one of tarragon vinegar, pepper and salt *quant. suff.*,

some chervil, parsley, and a few chives finely minced. Pour this over the beans, turn them over quickly, and serve. Of course this formula is only one of many, and the composition of the sauce can be varied *ad lib*. In this form the beans may be eaten either hot or cold.

Haricot beans, as wells as lentils, peas, or broad beans, can be made into *purées* to be used as a garnish for poultry, a dish of cutlets, or a piece of stewed meat. When it is to be so used, the purée should be thicker than when it is intended for a soup; it should be, in fact, of the consistency of the well-known pease pudding. A common formula to make such a *purée* is the following:

Set the pulse to boil, putting into the saucepan with it some whole pepper, a few cloves, an onion, a head of celery, and some parsley; when quite done, add salt, and pass it through a hair sieve; then work into the *purée* a certain quantity of butter. If intended for soup, the *purée* should be diluted with either meat stock or vegetable stock, according as it is wished to have a soup *au gras* or *au maigre;* and the *purée* should be finished by the addition (off the fire) of the yolks of one or more eggs beaten with some milk or cream, or simply a little water.

I shall conclude this paper with a few dishes, the foundation of which is dried vegetables of various kinds; and, although they are but the bill of fare of Continental peasants, I can assert that—if the great condiment of good appetite be added to them—they can be relished even by ladies and gentlemen.

1. Boil a quantity of haricot beans, lentils, or Spanish peas; when half done strain off the water, and replace it with fresh boiling water, but in lesser quantity; add one or two onions stuck with cloves, a good-sized piece of bacon, some powdered black pepper, and a little salt to taste. Let the whole boil till the bacon is cooked.

2. Having half-boiled some beans as above, add in changing the water a couple of heads of celery cut in pieces, a clove or two of garlic, pepper and salt to taste, and a certain* quantity of olive oil. Serve, over slices of stale bread, when the haricots are done.

3. Boil some Spanish peas; when nearly done, change the water replacing it by boiling water and throw in some maccaroni with salt to taste. When these are done, strain off the water, turn the whole out into a basin with a large lump of butter; add pepper and grated cheese (it need not be Parmesan), or oil in which a piece of garlic has been boiled may be used.

4. Put your beans, peas, or lentils to boil with the scrag-end of a neck of mutton, or with a piece of pickled pork, or even with some sheep's or pigs' trotters only; add one or two onions stuck with cloves, whole pepper, salt to taste, and some celery if you have it, and serve when done.

SALADS.

Every household presided over by a thrifty housewife, boasts of some mysterious preparation with which the mistress of the house compels reluctant housemaids to rub the furniture at stated periods. The object of this operation is to keep the polish bright, and I believe it answers the purpose very well. I could not give the recipe of this wonderful compound, for I do not know it, but I could not better describe it than by saying that in appearance, smell, and peradventure taste also, it closely resembles that other mysterious composition which will be produced in a pyramidal and circumvoluted bottle if you ask for salad-dressing at an hotel or eating-house. In most private houses the same oddly-shaped bottle is the only source whence the salad-dressing is obtained. Now, the great charm of a good salad is not only that the greenmeat part of it shall be fresh and newly gathered, but that the dressing or sauce shall be also fresh and newly mixed. The art, however, of mixing a salad-dressing is all but unknown in this country; the operation entails too much trouble, and requires too great a nicety in the apportionment of the condiments, for the broad mind of the British cook to be troubled about it; ask her to mix a salad, and she simply pours out a good allowance of the contents of the queer-shaped bottle over a lot of lettuce, endive, and water-cress chopped up more or less small, and imagines the product to be a salad. Yet salads are appreciated by Britons, for it stands on record that a noble Gaul—having fled the guillotine at the end of the last century, and, finding himself without cash in this country—contrived to pick up not only a living but a competency by taking to salad-making as a profession. This is how it came to pass: I abridge from Brillat-Savarin.

A French *émigré*, named D'Albignac, was dining at one of the most fashionable taverns in London, when he was addressed by a party of dandies who occupied the table next to him, with a request to mix a salad for them, coupled with a polite compliment upon the proficiency of the French in this art. D'Albignac, with some hesitation, consented and, being supplied with the best ingredients at hand, was very successful. In the course of the proceedings he entered into conversation with the dandies, and in answer to their questions he frankly avowed his position; consequently they felt justified in insisting upon his acceptance of a five-pound note, which he took without much pressing. The dandies asked for his address, and a few days after he received a request to go and mix a salad at one of the largest mansions in Grosvenor-square. D'Albignac saw his opportunity, and was not slow in availing himself of it. Providing himself with some choice condiments, and having ample time to think over his task, he went, and was triumphant. He was paid in proportion to his success. In a short time his reputation began to spread, and all the people of fashion in the capital of the three kingdoms were dying to have a salad mixed by the French gentleman—the fashionable salad-maker, as he was called. He soon set up his carriage and kept a footman to carry a mahogany case containing choice ingredients to mix salads withal, such as vinegars of various flavours, oil with or without the taste of olive, &c. Later, he supplied similar cases ready fitted with ingredients, and sold them by hundreds. In the end he amassed some eighty thousand francs, with which—the guillotine having been superseded—he retired to his native country, where he lived happy ever after.

An English wit and divine—Sydney Smith—says of salads :

> Oh, great and glorious and herbaceous treat!
> 'Twould tempt the dying anchorite to eat,
> Back to the world he'd turn his weary soul,
> And plunge his fingers in the salad bowl.

But my object is neither to prove that salads are very good things, nor that English cooks do not know how to prepare them. Few will venture to deny either of these propositions. My purpose is to expound the art and mystery of dressing salads, as practiced by those who are masters of the subject.

The consideration of salads may be divided under three heads—the vegetable part, or foundation; the dressing, or sauce; and the accessories. One of the chief requisites of a good salad is that it should be newly gathered, and, if you can get it free from mould and gravel, it is better not to wash it at all; but if—as is more often the case—you must wash your salad, you cannot be too careful in draining all the water from it; for every drop of water left in a salad tends to spoil it, no matter what amount of talent has been bestowed upon the dressing. Great care is also necessary in picking the salad, so as to exclude every leaf in the least tainted or discoloured. It is a great mistake to cut up lettuce and endive, *more Anglico*, into fine shreds; this operation at once destroys the freshness, taste, and character of the dish. Of course I do not mean that Cos lettuces simply split in two should be made into a salad; but there is a happy medium, which is always best in most things. Besides, it is by no means the largest lettuces which make the best salads; the Cos lettuce, *Gallicè "Romaine,"* is all very well in its way, but the cabbage lettuce, the *laitue pommée*, when it is well *pommée*, is by far preferable. This should be cut into quarters like an orange, but when the exigences of ornamentation do not demand shapely pieces, the lettuce should not be outraged by the contact of steel. The leaves should be torn asunder by the agency of the fingers alone, the rent fragments can then be perfectly dried by being shaken in several napkins (a dry one being substituted for each as it become saturated) until each individual leaf is perfectly dry. The same remark will apply to endive, but this can better bear cutting up than lettuce, and may be treated accordingly; but it is a mistake to put endive and lettuce in the same salad bowl. What is called corn salad goes better with endive, although 1 think that it is wrong to put too many herbs into one salad—as a salad; as a condiment it is a different matter. As such, water-cresses, tarragon, burnet, garden-cress, American, and Australian cress, chervil, parsley, basil, mint, balm, marjoram, &c., may be used, but they must be used with discretion. Likewise beetroot, cucumber, onions, celery, radishes, chives, and garlic, can be put into a salad with success if you know how to use them.

That artificial herb, mustard and cress, which is always associated with all salads by the British greengrocer, should never be used if it can be avoided. The American and Australian curled and perennial cresses are much preferable in point of taste and appearance. These, as well as water-cress, tarragon, and burnet, must not be cut up too small, but the leaves only, especially in the case of water-cress, must be used, and not the stalks as well.

They must be well washed, and the water may be got rid of by drying them in a cloth, without injury to the freshness of the salad. Other herbs must be minced quite fine, and a pinch or two will be about the proportion of them for an ordinary salad. Chives and onions must also be minced small; but in some special cases onions in slices are used; otherwise spring onions are best. Garlic is only to be used with an endive salad, and the proportion of it must be regulated according to taste. It need not, however, appear in the salad at all; a crust of bread slightly rubbed with it will convey a sufficient amount of flavour if it is only put into the bowl while the operation of turning the salad is going on. By a similar contrivance a slight flavour of onion may be given to a lettuce salad. Celery chopped up small may be used as a condiment, or it may of itself form the staple of the salad. Potatoes (boiled, of course), make a very good salad, either of themselves, or associated with celery, beetroot, and other things; they are also sometimes used as part of the dressing. Slices of cucumber are never amiss in certain salads; radishes, whole or sliced, and slices of beetroot, help the ornamentation if not the taste of a green salad.

Another sort of salad is what the French call *Barbe de Capucin*—I do not know the English name; it is a sort of endive.

Dandelion, especially if it be cultivated, makes a very good salad, either alone or with lettuce.

The leaves and flowers of nasturtium, as condiments as well as ornament, are often added to a salad. In Italy and the south of France they have a way of making a salad with unripe tomatoes, gathered just as they begin to show the least red.

I cannot call to mind at the moment any other greenmeat which is eaten as a salad. But I may say generally that any vegetable which is not positively unwholesome when uncooked may form the foundation of a salad. I have eaten delicious salads in Italy composed entirely of dandelions and other wild herbs gathered by the road and the river side. There is no lack of dandelions in the rural lanes of this country, and I believe burnet grows wild; but I should be puzzled to find the dozen and more different herbs which composed my wild salads, and I have not sufficient confidence in my botanical knowledge to try the experiment.

Potatoes and beetroot are by no means the only vegetables which can be made into a salad when cooked. Dried or fresh haricot beans, French beans, asparagus, Jerusalem artichokes, cauliflowers, brocoli sprouts, turnip-tops, &c., make very good salads. They should be plainly boiled in salt and water, and well drained. When they are quite cold, then make your salad.

I now come to speak of the ingredients which are used to make the dressing or sauce of the salad. It is in the proportion of these that the great difficulty lies. A Spanish proverb says that, to make a good salad, a miser should pour out the vinegar, a spendthrift the oil, a wise man the pepper and salt, and a madman should turn it— *travailler* is the technical expression. This may give some idea of the principles of salad mixing; but oil, vinegar, pepper, and salt are not the only things which are used to produce what I should call a good salad-dressing, and to make this it will take not only a wise man but a practical one as well, with plenty of experience in his business. What I have often said before of cooking applies still more forcibly to salad making; for in this you have no action of the fire, which sometimes corrects the mistakes of the operator; it is as in fresco-painting—once you have mixed your salad, there it is, for better or for worse. A sauce or a *ragoût* you may modify, correct, and alter in many ways as you go on; a salad you cannot, without making a mess of the whole thing, when once you have mixed the greenmeat with the dressing. Practice is the only master of whom to learn salad-making. I do not pretend to teach anyone how to make salads; all I can do is to point out, to those who wish to become adepts in the art, how to set about it.

Oil, which plays the most important part in the business, should be of the very finest quality, but it ought by no means to be the almost colourless and insipid liquid which is, I believe, called Jew's oil. There should be a taste of olive in it, but not so strong as to be disagreeable. It is a *quasi* nutty flavour that it should have, and the colour should be golden.

The artistic salad-maker cannot be too particular in the choice of the vinegar to be used in his preparations. The British vinegar of commerce may be all very well for cooking purposes, pickling, &c.; but, for salads, vinegar made from wine should be used, and it should be clarified until it is almost as clear as water. The stronger the vinegar is, the better.

At some first-class Italian warehouses good French vinegar is procurable; but it may not here be out of place if I describe the process by which a constant supply of WINE VINEGAR, after the Gallic fashion, can be obtained.

Get a small oaken cask, which has once contained wine. Heat to boiling point half a gallon of the best French vinegar, pour it into the cask, and roll it about in all directions; after which half fill your cask with some good white wine. Place it by the side of the kitchen fire, or, if in summer, in the open air, in a place well exposed to the sun. At the end of a week or so throw in another half-gallon of boiling vinegar, and nearly fill up the cask with white wine. Leave the bung partially open, and in six weeks you can begin to draw as good vinegar as can be wished for. If every time any vinegar is drawn it is replaced by an equal quantity of white wine, the supply will never fail; and if at the outset a certain quantity of brandy be put into the cask, the quality and strength of the vinegar will be improved thereby.

Vinegar greatly improves by age, especially when a vinegar plant—or " mother "—forms in the cask; but this can be insured ·by procuring a vinegar plant and putting it into the cask. None but wooden taps should be used to a vinegar cask, and the bung-hole should be covered with a piece of muslin or may be stopped up, and an air-hole made in the head of the cask and covered with muslin; for, in spite of the proverb, flies will be caught by vinegar.

When the acidification is complete, and the vinegar ready for use, the cask should be kept in a warm and dry spot, never in a cellar.

To clarify vinegar, mix a wine-glassful of milk with a bottle of vinegar; then make a cone or filter of filtering paper, which you place in a glass funnel; pour the mixture into this very carefully, and in due course the vinegar will come through as clear as can be desired.

For purposes of salad-making and cooking generally, vinegar is flavoured in a variety of ways. This is done by putting some strong wine vinegar into a wide-mouthed bottle, and adding to it any of the following:

1. A couple of handfuls of tarragon leaves, gathered the day before.

2. Twenty or thirty green capsicums, previously bruised.

3. Four or five cloves of garlic, also bruised.

4. A cupful of celery seed, or more, well crushed in a mortar.

5. The same quantity of cress seed, similarly treated.

The above proportions are for one quart of vinegar. The bottle should be corked up and exposed to the sun, or kept in a very warm place, for two or three weeks, when the vinegar should be strained and filtered. By a similar process vinegar is flavoured with mint, horseradish, cucumber, &c. The following are more elaborate forms of aromatised vinegar.

TARRAGON VINEGAR.—Fill up a stone jar or widemouthed glass bottle with as many tarragon leaves (not newly gathered) as it will contain without pressing them down. Add a small quantity of cloves, and the thin rind of two or three lemons. Fill up with vinegar, cork well, and expose to the sun for at least a fortnight. At the end of that time, strain the vinegar, squeezing it well out of the leaves, and filter (twice if necessary) through paper.

"FINES HERBES" VINEGAR.—Take equal parts of tarragon, garden cress, chervil, and burnet (all gathered the day before), one green chili, and a couple of cloves of garlic. Fill your bottle or jar with these, and treat as above.

Another form is this : Equal parts of tarragon, burnet, and chives, the thin rind of one or two lemons and a few cloves and proceed as above. Some people add to this a handful of fresh elder flowers. It is better, in making these vinegars, not to make too much of them, but just enough to last the season.

Although plain English mustard is often used in making salads, French mustard is undoubtedly better. The *moutarde de Maille, à l'estragon* or *à la ravigotte* is the best. The following recipe is the homely Gallic form of mixing MUSTARD, which produces not a bad imitation of the celebrated *moutarde de Maille*.

Take about a quart of brown mustard seed, and mix with it the following ingredients : Parsley, chervil, tarragon, burnet—about a handful of each finely minced; some celery seed, cloves, mace, nutmeg, garlic, and salt in such proportions as taste may suggest. Put the whole in a basin, with enough vinegar just to cover the mixture. In twenty-four hours' time proceed to pound it in a mortar. When thoroughly pounded pass through a fine hair sieve; add enough vinegar to make the mustard of the proper consistency; and proceed to fill up, cork, and seal your pots or bottles.

The pepper and the salt used for salad-making should be in the finest powder. All kinds of sauce, such as Worcester, Harvey, anchovy, catsup, soy, &c., are used in salads, but they are dangerous things in the hands of novices.

Eggs, either raw or hard-boiled. should nearly always enter into the composition of a salad-dressing. In the former case the yolks alone are used; in the latter the yolks are applied to the same purpose, and the whites are put into the salad, or on the top of it, either chopped up small or cut in rounds. In some cases, besides the yolks which go in the dressing, whole hard-boiled eggs, cut into quarters or rounds, are used in the ornamentation of the salad.

As a general rule I may say that the proportion of the oil to the vinegar should be—supposing the latter to be of average strength—as three to one; but due regard must also be had to the mustard and strong sauces, such as Worcester, which may be used. The yolks of two eggs, either raw or hard-boiled, will be enough for an ordinary salad. The proportions of the other ingredients are a matter of taste, which cannot be defined.

Lastly, the proportion of the dressing to the salad must be such, that when the two have been thoroughly mixed together no dressing shall remain at the bottom of the bowl. This will never be the case when there is too much dressing in proportion to the salad, when the salad has not been properly freed from water, when too much vinegar has been put into the dressing, or when the ingredients have not been properly and artistically mixed. Therefore will it always be an indication of failure.

It takes from forty to fifty minutes to mix a salad *secundum artem*; and although it is better to eat it as soon as the dressing and the greenmeat have been "worked" together, still it will keep good for an hour or so; after that it will rapidly deteriorate.

The following may be taken as the common form for mixing together the ingredients which compose a SALAD DRESSING:

Put the hard-boiled yolks of eggs into a bowl, and smash them with a wooden spoon; add the mustard, pepper, and salt, and thoroughly mix them; then proceed to put in the oil a little at a time, never adding more until you have so rubbed what is in the bowl that it presents an uniform texture. When you have put in all the oil, add any sauce (such as Worcester, &c.) which you may wish to use; but be careful not to put in too much. Last of all, pour in the vinegar little by little, and keep on rather beating than stirring the mixture for about five minutes. At this stage of the proceedings you may taste the dressing, and make any alteration which you think necessary; but it ought to require none. You now put in all the herbs, onions, &c., which you may wish to use as condiments, *i.e.*, chopped up small; mix them thoroughly with the dressing, and then put in the salad proper, which you mix or "work," as the Spanish proverb implies, like mad; and, after ornamenting the top as I shall explain farther on, you can send your salad to table.

When raw yolks of egg are used, the *modus operandi* is as follows: Beat up the yolks slightly, and strain them through a small colander into a bowl; put in the pepper and salt; mix well, and pour in the oil very gradually, never ceasing to stir all the time. When you have used half the oil, have the vinegar ready in a cup, with the mustard, sauces, &c., mixed with it, and proceed to pour this in, in small quantities alternately with the rest of the oil, stirring vigorously to the end. Finish the operation as above.

A salad dressing, made with raw eggs, is in the nature of what is called a *mayonnaise*. In fact, the *mayonnaise* proper is nothing more than the above salad-dressing with a larger allowance of yolks of egg, which have the effect of making the sauce firmer; and it is used to serve up fowls, fish, and crustacea with salad.

There are, however, many elaborate recipes for making a MAYONNAISE, and this is one of them:

Pound in a mortar the yolks of four hard-boiled eggs, add to them a tablespoonful of aspic jelly or calves'-foot jelly just sufficiently warmed to make it liquid; strain this into a bowl; add two more tablespoonfuls of jelly and the same quantity of oil, some pepper, salt, mustard, and other condiments to taste; mix thoroughly; then add, a little at a time, rather more than one tablespoonful of very strong tarragon vinegar. Continue to stir until all the vinegar is incorporated. If the weather is hot, the bowl should be placed on ice until the sauce is wanted.

Raw yolks of egg may be used instead of hard-boiled

yolks for the above, or you may use both raw and boiled yolks, half of each.

The following are other forms of MAYONNAISE.

1. Beat up the yolks raw, strain, and mix with them the pepper, salt, and (gradually) the oil and vinegar, with mustard, &c.; then add equal parts of cream and calves'-foot jelly, about one tablespoonful of each, if four tablespoonfuls of oil have been used. Set on ice till wanted, if in summer.

2. Make a custard with four eggs, half a pint of milk, and a little gelatine. When cold add a gill of cream, and (a little at a time) about one and a half tablespoonfuls of salad oil, and the same quantity of tarragon vinegar in which has been dissolved as much salt as may be necessary.

3. Strain the yolks of four eggs into a basin, which you place in a cool place, or, if necessary, in water or on ice; then proceed to pour in—a few drops at a time—some salad oil without ceasing to stir the mixture. When about one tablespoonful of oil is well incorporated with the yolks of egg, put in, in the same manner, a teaspoonful of French vinegar. Keep on adding oil and vinegar in these proportions until you get a sauce the consistency of very thick cream. You then add salt and white pepper to taste, and mix them well.

4. Add to the above, to give it a green colour, a sufficient quantity of the following herbs, very finely minced, tarragon, chervil, and garden cress in about equal proportions.

Another variety of *mayonnaise* consists in using lemon juice as well as aromatised vinegar, of course in proper proportion. The great secret of success in a *mayonnaise* consists in the operation of mixing, and patience and hard work go a good way towards it. Some cookery books tell you that you should always turn one way in mixing a *mayonnaise*—this is by no means necessary; neither is the addition of cold water, as sometimes recommended. Spinach greening may be used to colour a *mayonnaise*.

Tartare sauce, as well as *remoulade*, *ravigotte* and *poivrade*, in their cold forms are only elaborate salad-dressings.

The first is only a *mayonnaise* with a good allowance of mustard—English as well as French. Garlic vinegar, as well as Chili and tarragon vinegar, should enter into its composition.

The following is my usual formula for making

SAUCE À LA TARTARE.—Strain the yolks of four eggs, put them into a basin, and stir olive oil into them—one tablespoonful at a time; after each tablespoonful of oil put in one teaspoonful of tarragon vinegar. Keep on doing this until the sauce is of the desired consistency; then add pepper, salt, a good allowance of mustard (English), the least bit of cayenne, and a couple of shallots minced very fine.

REMOULADE is also a *mayonnaise* into which, when it is made, you mix equal parts of tarragon, chervil, olives, parsley, and capers, all finely minced.

A RAVIGOTTE is made by adding to a plain *mayonnaise* the following herbs and ingredients chopped up very small: Shallots, capers, anchovies, a very little garlic, garden cress, burnet, tarragon, basil, and celery, all in the proportions which taste may suggest.

This sauce is also made as follows : Pound the above ingredients in a mortar, adding chervil, parsley, and any other sweet herbs you may have at hand, all in due proportions; add one or two yolks of hard-boiled eggs and the same number raw, with pepper and salt; strain through a colander, and then stir in the oil and vinegar in the same manner as for *mayonnaise ;* mustard may be added.

SAUCE POIVRADE is simply a plain salad dressing.

All the above sauces and salad-dressings, except *mayonnaise,* can be made without eggs; and in that case a small quantity of mashed or even plainly boiled potatoes will be found a very good substitute if introduced and treated as directed for hard-boiled yolks of egg. I sometimes use both potato and eggs.

As I have said before, it is imperative that the oil used for dressing a salad should be of the best quality, and it is better to mix your salad without oil if what you have is not first-rate. A ready substitute for oil is found in cream, and this is how to proceed :

Mix the yolks of two eggs, hard-boiled or raw, with pepper, salt, mustard, and any other condiments you may wish. Stir the cream into this gradually, then the vinegar, and proceed as for an ordinary salad. A simpler form consists in mixing the cream with pepper and salt only, and then either putting in the vinegar and then the greenmeat, or mixing the greenmeat with the cream, and pouring the exact quantity of vinegar over it. When dressed with cream, it is better that the salad proper should consist of lettuce only. CREAM DRESSING does not go very well with endive ; but this is a matter of taste. Lemon juice may be substituted for vinegar in this dressing. The salad should be "worked" with the cream and pepper and salt, and the lemon juice should be squeezed over it.

Bacon or ham is also by no means a bad substitute for oil, and it is best used with a salad of lettuce only. Cut the ham or bacon into small dice, each of which should consist of two-thirds fat and one lean ; fry these for ten minutes or so, and then add a good allowance of vinegar, into which you have put pepper, salt, mustard, &c., in due proportion. Pour the mixture, as soon as it boils, over the salad, which must be put into a warmed salad bowl and eaten without delay. This is, of course, a homely dish, but it has merits nevertheless. Another way of dispensing with oil is to heat some butter until it gets a deep brown colour; then to add to it vinegar, pepper, salt, mustard, &c., and, when the mixture boils, to mix the salad, which must be eaten immediately. Hard-boiled eggs, minced more or less small, should be put into this salad.

Here is another form : Melt a large piece of butter, and add to it pepper, salt *quant. suff.*, and a very little flour ; then pour some boiling water to it, just enough to make a sufficient quantity of dressing; stir the mixture on the fire till it boils, when you take it off, and stir into it the yolks of two eggs beaten up with the juice of a lemon. When your sauce is quite cold, strain it through a colander, and add to it vinegar, mustard, and any other seasonings which taste may suggest.

A richer form of the above consists in making what is called a cup-custard, into which you put pepper and salt instead of sugar. When the custard is cold strain it, and use it instead of oil to mix your salad.

The accessories of a salad may be described as everything which is good to eat cold. All kinds of pickles, olives, capers, anchovies, sardines, herrings, prawns, shrimps, crabs, lobsters, Italian and German sausages, ham, all sorts of cold meat, fowl, fish, and game, can be advantageously introduced in a salad, and it is simply a matter of taste which and how many of these things are to be associated together with the greenmeat in the same salad bowl or dish.

Olives should be well washed before using them, and the stone should be neatly removed, so as not to spoil the shape of the fruit. There is a kind of olives, which are sold ready stoned, with a small piece of anchovy inserted in each of them in place of the stone; these are not so good for dessert as the plain olives, but for salad purposes they are capital.

Anchovies require even more washing than olives, and if they be not first-rate, and neatly filleted and cleaned, they will assuredly spoil your salad. Sardines, herrings, other fish and crustacea, should be very carefully picked, and cut up in neat fillets or pieces. Meat should be cut up in fillets, and all "outside" parts — *i.e.*, those browned by the operation of roasting — removed. In the case of fowls and game, the most economical way is, of course, to cut them up in small neat "joints"; but the most artistic way is to cut out "fillets" of the meat only, so as to have no bones in the salad.

Although all kinds of greenmeat are used in these compound salads, lettuce with a few aromatic herbs is preferable to any other. The proper sort of dressing is a *mayonnaise*, a *tartare*, or a *ravigotte*. In cookery books these salads are usually called *mayonnaise* of fowls or fish, as the case may be, and they include that well-known British institution, the lobster salad of ball suppers and picnics.

To prepare one of these salads in an artistic way, the lettuce and what *fines herbes* you may wish to use should be dressed with a plain salad sauce without eggs, and the fish, flesh, or fowl fillets should be steeped for an hour or so in a similar sauce. You then dispose your materials neatly on a dish, and cover up the whole with a well-made *mayonnaise, tartare,* or *ravigotte*, finishing by ornamenting your dish as will be explained farther on.

Endive and mixed salads are not so well fitted for a lobster or a meat salad, but small and judicious proportions of pickles, anchovies, olives, ham, Bologna sausage (minced small), add considerably to the merit of a salad of endive or of celery and water-cress. Of course when Bologna sausage is used there is no need of a piece of bread rubbed with garlic.

These compound salads are a capital way—especially in summer—of disposing of the remains of meat, fowls, &c.; and, as there is no end to the combinations which can be produced, I will not attempt to give a list of them.

The ornamentation of salads is the next thing to consider. On supper tables more particularly, very pretty effects are produced by tastefully-ornamented salads, and to do this properly no small amount of taste and trouble is required.

The readiest mode of ornamenting a salad is by disposing, on the top of it, all or a portion of the following things, in some sort of pattern—viz., hard-boiled eggs, cut into rounds or quarters; slices of beetroot, truffles, and cucumber, cut into shapes; radishes, pickled gherkins, cut in some fanciful way, fillets of anchovies, &c. The flowers of borage, nasturtium, &c., can also be used; and in large dishes, according to the nature of the salad, crayfish, and prawns can be introduced—whole as ornaments, and likewise pieces of aspic jelly.

Another way, which may be called the geometrical form, well repays by its effect the trouble it entails.

Begin by preparing your colours, so to speak, each in a separate saucer. These are (black) truffles minced very small, also caviar; (two dark greens) watercress or parsley, minced fine; (three lighter greens) capers, gherkins, garden cress, all finely minced; (purple) minced beetroot; (red) lobster spawn; (orange) yolks of hard-boiled egg, rubbed through a fine colander; (white) whites of hard-boiled egg minced small.

Having dressed your salad, and arranged it neatly in a bowl or on a dish, as the case may be, proceed to dispose on the top of it, with a teaspoon, the above minced materials, so as to form a tasteful pattern. A little practice will soon enable you to do this neatly, so that the colours do not run into one another; and in the variety of designs which can be produced with eggs, beetroot, and cress alone, there is ample room for the display of considerable taste and ingenuity.

Several other things can be used in a minced form to ornament salads as above, such as ham (lean) anchovies, aspic jelly, olives, &c., but, of course, due regard must be had in the selection of these to the nature of the salads for which they are used; as, when it comes to be eaten, they form an integral part of the dish, and are eaten with it.

A very elegant form of serving a compound salad is to enclose it within a moulded border of aspic jelly; thus the ordinary lobster salad, for instance, is made to assume a much more *distinguée* appearance. This is a simple way of producing this very handsome dish.

SALADE DE HOMARD EN ASPIC.—Cut a number of pieces of lobster into convenient sizes. Have some well flavoured aspic jelly, just melt it and pour a layer of it a quarter of an inch thick into a border mould; when it begins to set, arrange the pieces of lobster—reserving two or three of the best—in the mould with leaves of tarragon; fill up with jelly and lay the mould on ice for the jelly to set. Cut the remainder of the lobster and dress it—with some sauce—with an ordinary salad dressing. Turn out the border on a dish, fill the inside with salad heaped up, lay the reserved pieces of lobster on the top, and ornament with minced white and yolk of eggs, truffles, and aspic jelly, in any design you may fancy.

The following is one of my formulæ for what is called a Russian salad, susceptible, like similar preparations, of endless variations.

SALADE RUSSE.—Cut, with a vegetable scoop, some pieces of carrots and of turnips, to the size of an olive; boil them in salted water, with a piece of butter, but do not let them be overdone ; lay them out on a sieve to drain and get cold : cut some beetroot in the same way, and likewise some truffles. Take equal parts—say a cupful—of each of the above, a similar quantity of preserved fresh (not dried) haricot beans ready cooked, and of asparagus points preserved in the same way. Take also two table spoonfuls respectively of capers, of French pickled gherkins (which you cut into the shape of capers), and of anchovies perfectly cleaned and cut into small pieces ; a couple of dozen or more of olives (stoned), one table-spoonful of tarragon and chervil minced fine, and half that quantity of chives also minced. Mix all the above in a rich salad sauce. Dress within a plain border of aspic, and ornament with hard boiled eggs, caviar, lobster spawn, olives, pickles, truffles, &c. The Spanish preserved sweet capsicums (*Pimientos dulces*) are a great addition to a salad like this, not only for their exquisite taste, but on account of their brilliant colour.

FARINACEOUS FOOD.

MACCARONI, which in many parts of Italy forms the staple food of the population, is in England very little appreciated, and still less understood. This may possibly arise not so much from want of taste in the consumer as from want of skill on the part of the cook. In the first place, maccaroni is accepted as the name of only one form of a comestible which in Italy assumes countless agreeable shapes, and which, although all made from the same material—*i.e.*, "hard wheat," with very slight modifications—are very different in taste, and if cooked in the proper manner will produce many very good dishes, which only require to be known to be appreciated. In the next place, English cooks are ignorant of the very first principles of cooking maccaroni, the chief of which is that it should be thrown into boiling water. Instead of this, their practice is to put it into cold water, and some in their ignorance go the length of washing it, and even of putting it to soak before cooking. Washing maccaroni is unnecessary, putting it to cook in cold water is a blunder, soaking it is a crime. Before proceeding to describe the correct way of boiling maccaroni, and the different forms in which to dress it, I will set forth a catalogue of its principal varieties.

Maccaroni may be divided into two classes: the maccaroni proper, or *paste lunghe*, and the *paste tagliate*, known in France as *pâtes d'Italie*, and scarcely known at all in this country. They are also to be divided into two great categories, which I may call the northern—of which Genoa maccaroni may be taken as the type; and the southern—represented by the manufacture of Naples. Genoa maccaroni is considered by many better than the Neapolitan, and so it is as far as the coarser kinds (some of which are of the colour of brown bread) are concerned, but the best qualities prepared at Naples are quite as good and better than those made in the northern city. And so, in the words of Leporello, *" Madamina, il catalogo è questo."*

MACCARONI PROPER, OR PASTE LUNGHE.

Naples.

1. *Maccaroni di Zita.*—Bridal maccaroni, the same, only larger than the following.

2. *Maccaroni.*—Maccaroni proper, such as is used in England for making maccaroni cheese, &c.

3. *Maccaroncini.*—Half the thickness of the above, and with a very minute perforation.

4. *Vermicelli.*—Thinner still, and solid.

5. *Spaghetti.*—What are called (wrongly) vermicelli in this country.

6. *Fidelini.*—The same, only rolled up in knots or bunches; also called vermicelli in England.

7. *Lasagne.* — Thick ribbons, 1½in. wide, the same length as maccaroni proper; usually serrated at the edges.

8. *Tagliarelle.*—Narrower and thinner than the above, and with smooth edges.

9. *Tagliarini.*—Narrower still.

Genoa.

10. *Maccheroni grandi.*—Resembling No. 1.
11. *Maccheroni piccoli.*—Resembling No. 2.

12. *Maccheroni rigati.*—The same as the above, but fluted spirally.

13. *Maccheroncini.*—Resembling No. 3.

14. *Cannelli.*—A very large but thin tube.

15. *Cannelli rigati.*—Fluted *cannelli.*

16. *Selleri.*—Resembling in form perforated colt's foot rock.

17. *Spaghetti.*—The same as Neapolitan *vermicelli.*

18. *Fedelini.*—The same as the Neapolitan *spaghetti.*

19. *Lasagnoni.*—A ribbon 1½in. wide, with one frilled edge.

20. *Lasagne.*—Narrower and thinner than the above.

21. *Lasagnette.*—Narrower and thinner still.

22. *Bavette.*—And

23. *Bavettini.*— Correspond to the *Tagliarelle* and *Tagliarini* of Naples. An intermediate size is also called

24. *Fettuccie.*—Ribbons.

Several kinds of the above, notably Nos. 13, 17, 18, and 23, are also dried in knots or bunches.

PASTE TAGLIATE.

25. *Recch'i Prevete.*—(Priest's ears), the shape of half a mussel shell.

26. *Cannarune.*—Like sections of a pig's windpipe.

27. *Mostacciuoli*, also called *Penne.*—Piping, smooth or ribbed, about the size of the largest maccaroni, cut diagonally in pieces about 1½ inches long.

28. *Paternostri.*—Beads, cut from tubing, resembling "bugles" of different sizes.

29. *Cappelletti.*—Little caps.

30. *Anelletti.*—Small plain rings of various sizes.

31. *Stelloni.*—(Large stars), more like cog-wheels.

32. *Anellini ricci.*—Smaller than the above.

33. *Stelle.*—(Stars) of various sizes, like the heraldic "mullet"; but with more than five points.

34. *Occhi di Pernice.*—(Partridge eyes), small discs with a hole in the centre.

35. *Gnioccoli.*—Resembling finely twisted "chitterlings."

36. *Scorze di Nocelle.*—Like bits of Barcelona nut-shells.

37. *Semenze di Mellone.*—Melon seeds.

38. *Semenze di Peperoli.*—Capsicum seeds.

39. *Acini di Pepe.*—Pepper corns.

40. *Peperini.*—A smaller size.

41. *Avena.*—Oats.

42. *Punte d'aghe.*—(Needle points), like good stout tacks with the heads off.

43. *Semenze di Cicoria.*—Chicory seed.

44. *Stivaletti.*—Resembling bilberries.

45. *Croci di Malta.*—Tiny Maltese crosses.

46. *Ancore.*—Grapnels.

47. *Pesci.*—(Fish), very small fry indeed.

But there is no end to these minor varieties; among them may be found hearts and diamonds, clubs and spades, trumpets and quatrefoils, the Arabic numerals, and all the letters of the Roman alphabet.

The cardinal rule for cooking maccaroni is to throw it into BOILING water; then add salt, *q. s.*, and keep stirring now and then : have ready a jug of cold water to throw into the pot or saucepan the moment you find that the maccaroni is done, which can only be ascertained by tasting. Each kind of maccaroni or *paste* takes more or less time to cook, according to its shape; and then some people like it more done than others. It should have a certain amount of crispness, if I may so express it; the Neapolitan word is "*vierde,*" which means the freshness of a freshly gathered vegetable, and expresses it perfectly. The object of pouring in the jug of cold water is to obtain that freshness by stopping the ebullition. The next step is to strain the maccaroni thoroughly (When used with soup, I prefer it boiled in the soup itself—omitting the dash of cold water—but it may also be boiled in water first, and then put into the soup.) Care should be taken always to boil maccaroni in plenty of water, the large sorts especially; for the *paste* it is not of so much consequence.

Now, having boiled your maccaroni, proceed to dress it:

Put a goodly piece of butter in a hot dish or bowl, and throw the maccaroni on the top of it, with plenty of grated Parmesan; mix as you would a salad, and serve. Every sort can be dressed in this way, and it is a very good breakfast, luncheon, or supper dish. For children the smaller kinds of paste, with the omission of the cheese, are very wholesome food.

The smaller kinds of long maccaroni are dressed as follows, in Naples, during Lent:

Cut up a clove or two of garlic, wash and cut up two or three anchovies, and do the same to a few olives; throw the whole into some fine salad oil, which you let boil until the slices of garlic begin to take colour, and then pour over your maccaroni. This is a peculiar dish, not bad for those who like it, but it is an acquired taste.

When fresh tomatoes are procurable, both maccaroni and *paste* are delicious dressed with them. This is the process:

Remove the stalks of the tomatoes, cut them up into quarters, and put them into a saucepan with a little water, pepper, salt, a bay leaf, and a good sprig of fresh or dried basil; boil till thoroughly done, then empty upon a hair sieve, throw away all the water that comes through of itself, and pass the tomatoes through the sieve with a wooden spoon; the pulp thus obtained is then made very hot with a lump of butter, and the maccaroni is dressed with it, and plenty of grated Parmesan. When tomatoes are plentiful a better sauce is obtained by carefully emptying each tomato of its seeds, after it has been cut up into quarters.

The Neapolitans prepare the *raù* (ragoût) which, with maccaroni, is the Sunday dinner of all who can afford it, with *Conserva di pomi d'oro* (described elsewhere). The only difference between rich and poor being that the quality of the maccaroni and of the meat used by the former is better; the process is the same—viz.:

Take a piece of fillet of beef, or of silver side; make a hole in it lengthways, and insert a long piece of bacon, half fat and half lean, previously rolled in sweet herbs and ground pepper; then tie up your piece of meat carefully. Take a good-sized piece of the fat of bacon, and mince it very finely with a meat chopper, adding to it garlic, onions, basil, thyme, and marjoram in due proportions; when the whole is well amalgamated, put it in a saucepan, and place the meat over it, turning it till it gets a nice brown all over; then add pepper, salt and the tomato *conserva*, diluted in water till it is of the consistency of thin pea soup, and let the whole simmer till dinner time; three or four hours are required to cook the meat. At the time of serving strain the sauce, and dress the maccaroni with it and Parmesan cheese. The large kinds only are dressed in this way. The meat is sent up with some of the sauce round it, and very good eating it is; cold it is still better. A few small potatoes put to cook in the sauce with the meat are a good *garniture* for the meat.

The usual way of serving maccaroni in England is that called in French *au gratin*. It ought to be done in this way:

Having boiled your maccaroni, place it on a dish with plenty of butter and grated Parmesan cheese, add a little pepper, and sprinkle the top freely with Parmesan, so as to cover the maccaroni completely; brown with a salamander, and serve very hot. Where no salamander is obtainable, judicious exposure to the fire will produce the desired effect; but in any case, care should be taken not to dry up the maccaroni too much, but just to brown the cheese on the top of it. For this dish the maccaroni may be boiled in milk instead of water, and the result will be still more satisfactory.

The following is a recipe more suitable to the English taste:—Take two ounces of boiled maccaroni and drain it well; put into a saucepan one ounce of butter, mix it well with one tablespoonful of flour, moisten with four tablespoonfuls of veal stock and a gill of cream; add two ounces of grated Parmesan, one tablespoonful of mustard, salt and cayenne to taste; put in the maccaroni, and serve as soon as it is well mixed with the sauce, and quite hot.

Any kind of maccaroni may be served with curries instead of rice; it is also a good *garniture* for hashed mutton and kindred dishes.

The introduction of maccaroni in meat and chicken pies is a great improvement to them, but the king of maccaroni pies is as yet unknown in England, and is thus made:

MACCARONI PIE.—Make a short crust with flour, eggs, butter, sugar, and a little salt, roll it to the thickness of the eighth of an inch, and line with it a plain shape previously buttered. Have some large maccaroni boiled and dressed with *raû* as described above, some balls of well devised forcemeat, and of sausage meat; some yolks of hard boiled eggs, mushrooms, truffles, and cockscombs, previously cooked. Fill up the shape with all these things judiciously arranged, the maccaroni predominating, then add a due quantity of the sauce of the *raù* and grated Parmesan cheese. Cover the whole with a disc of crust, and bake it in a quick oven just long enough to cook the crust. This pie may be eaten hot or cold.

A very nice simple pudding may be made of maccaroni as follows : Boil some *spaghetti* or *fidelini* in milk with some sugar, and let them be very much overdone ; strain, and add to them the yolks of three or more eggs, according to quantity; put in a little powdered cinnamon, mix well, and pour into a shape, previously buttered and bread-crumbed; then bake, in a quick oven, just long enough to colour the outside.

Semolina, and a coarser sort called *semola*, are prepared from the same kind of wheat as is maccaroni, and are in effect very much the same thing excepting that they are coarsely ground into a kind of meal instead of being wrought into fanciful shapes. Homely puddings and a sort of porridge can be made with them, either in conjunction with milk or stock.

Indian corn (*granone*) is grown extensively in Italy, where it is used, unground, to fatten poultry and pigs, and when made into flour it forms an article of daily food for people of all classes. It is cooked in a variety of ways, some of which, such as the *polenta alla Milanese*, are not devoid of merit.

Before the grains begin to harden, the ears—bereft of their green leaves and their " beards "—are often eaten broiled' or roasted; and at a more advanced state of maturity they are eaten boiled in water. These are both very primitive forms ; but the first is not without a certain degree of delicacy.

Polenta is a sort of *bouillie* or porridge made of Indian corn flour, water and salt. The proper way to make it is to take a handful of the flour, and let it drop gradually into a saucepan containing boiling water and salt, stirring all the time, and continuing to stir until the flour is cooked, and the polenta acquires the consistency of thick pea-soup. You must not, however, keep on dropping the flour in; a very small quantity is sufficient to make very thick polenta—certainly not more than one handful or less to a pint of water.

This preparation is very good food for children, and it is made more attractive by a large piece of butter being put into the water when making the polenta, and grated Parmesan cheese being either incorporated in it or served over it. The addition of butter and cheese, however, is seldom resorted to by the poorer classes, for in the south of Italy, at any rate, butter is to a poor man as are truffles unto a London "cabby." Some season it occasionally with a cheese of the country, which quite belies the saying "as different as chalk from cheese." It is strange that the same country should produce the very best cheese, at least for cooking purposes, and also the very worst in existence.

The poor people make a paste with the flour, hot water, and a little salt; they fashion it into small loaves, in which they stick a few raisins, and then bake them in the oven, if they have one, or under hot wood ashes. These loaves will keep for a week or ten days, and are very eatable—if you have nothing else to eat.

A more artistic form of this species of food is this:

Make a good thick polenta, adding butter and cheese to it in the process of making. Pour it into a dish, or on a marble slab, and when cold it will be of the consistency of blancmange; you then cut it in small pieces of any shape you like, and fry them in boiling oil or lard. Raisins or currants may be put in when making the polenta.

The MILANESE POLENTA is made somewhat after this fashion; and is a highly commendable preparation:

Make some polenta, not too thick, with plenty of butter. When cold, cut out of it such shaped pieces as will line a plain mould, previously buttered. The mould being lined, sprinkle the inside freely with grated Parmesan, then proceed to fill up the mould with pieces of polenta, slices of Parmesan cheese, and balls of sausage meat, or any other kind of forcemeat—cockscombs, livers, &c., of poultry, all previously cooked, a few bits of butter, and a little pepper, all in due proportions; lastly, cover the whole with a disc of polenta, which, as well as the lining, should not be more than a quarter of an inch thick. Bake for an hour and serve.

The experienced cook will be able to make several puddings with Indian corn flour by using it instead of flour proper or semolina.

FÉCULE DE POMMES DE TERRE—potato flour or starch—is an improvement upon corn flour for thickening gravies and sauces.

This is how to make it.

Wash thoroughly a bushel of potatoes, so as to free them entirely from dirt; then proceed to grate them on a coarse cheese-grater, and place the potato pulp thus obtained in large deep dishes, with plenty of water; let it stand about twelve hours, then pour off the water, which will carry away with it a portion of the fibrous matter; refill the dishes with water, stir, and pour it off again, as before, after the same lapse of time. When this has been done three or four times, a white sediment only will be found to remain at the bottom of the dish; keep changing the water and stirring till the sediment is quite free from any fibrous particles, when you may let it dry, to be collected when quite so, passed through a fine hair sieve, and bottled for use. It is best to do this in summer, when the dishes can be exposed to the sun. Heat, however, is only necessary towards the later stages of the process, and that of the fire will do quite as well.

A more expeditious way is to scrub the potatoes clean, and grate them on a sieve, pour plenty of water over them, receive it in a pan at the bottom of which in a short time the starch of the potato will be deposited.

This *fécule*, mixed with cold water (a couple of tablespoonfuls to a pint) and a little sugar, and then stirred on the fire till it thickens, makes a delicious pap for infants, infinitely preferable to tapioca, arrowroot, &c., if I may trust to the recollections of my youthful days.

Rice plainly boiled in water is often served on English tables, but not always is it well cooked, even in so simple a form. If properly dressed no two grains should stick together, and each grain should be just sufficiently cooked to assume a corkscrew or spiral appearance. To produce a creditable dish of PLAIN BOILED RICE you should proceed in this wise:

Get the best rice that can be bought, and carefully pick it grain by grain, excluding all bad and broken grains and impurities; wash it in cold water two or three times, rubbing it between the palms of the hands during the process; then put it into a saucepan with enough cold water to cover the rice, and set it on the fire, to be removed as soon as the grains begin to burst, and the water is nearly all absorbed. This will take twenty minutes or so. Turn out the rice on a dish or a sieve, place it in front of the fire to dry, and in ten minutes it is ready for table.

Another way is as follows:

Wash half-a-pound of rice in salt and water, put it into four pints of boiling water if Patna rice—if Carolina into five pints. Boil it twenty minutes, drain it in a colander, and set it near the fire to dry. Shake it into a dish without touching it.

Here is yet another way. Take half-a-pound of Patna rice, wash it well in two or three changes of water, and let it stand for half an hour or less in cold water. Pour off the water and put the rice into a saucepan with sufficient fresh cold water to cover it by two or three inches, adding a little salt; then put it on a brisk fire till the rice be soft, when take it off and throw in a large cupful of cold water, which at once stops the boiling; shake the saucepan well, strain off the water and place the saucepan on the hob with a dry towel over the rice: there must be no other cover.

The best form, however, of preparing rice as a dish of itself is the following:

RIZ À LA TURQUE.—Put into a saucepan six cupfuls of stock or broth into which you have previously dissolved a good allowance either of tomato paste, French tomato sauce, or the pulp of fresh tomatoes passed through a sieve; pepper and salt according to taste. When it boils, throw in, for every cupful of stock, half a cupful of fine rice well washed and dried before the fire. Let the whole remain on the fire until the rice has absorbed all the stock, then melt a goodly piece of butter and pour it over the rice. At the time of serving, and not before, stir lightly to separate the grains, but do this off the fire.

What is called RISOTTO in Upper Italy is prepared in

this way: Fry in a saucepan, with butter, an onion finely minced, and when it is of a golden colour put in your rice and keep adding stock or broth as fast as the rice will absorb it, and throw in a pinch of saffron. When the grains begin to burst remove from the fire, add plenty of grated Parmesan, a little salt, pepper, nutmeg, and a piece of butter. Stir well and serve.

In the matter of cooking rice it is imperative to remember that it should never be stirred while cooking, for if this be done it will "catch" at the bottom of the saucepan, and acquire a burnt or smoky taste.

A very nice dish can be made by adding to some plainly boiled rice some ham and some parsley chopped very small, with pepper, salt, and a little spice, forming, by the addition of several eggs worked into the mixture, a thick sort of paste. Fashion this into balls or any other shape you like; egg and bread-crumb them twice; then fry them in plenty of hot lard and serve on a napkin with a few sprigs of fried parsley.

A border of rice is no bad addition to a mince or to some *ragoûts*; but it should not be plain rice. A good way is to mix into some plain boiled rice a certain quantity of tomato sauce and the yolks of one or two eggs, adding grated Parmesan or not as you may fancy; or the rice may be dressed with butter and cheese alone.

Rice boiled in milk and sugar is a very nice and wholesome dish. In France they generally flavour it with cinnamon, but I think the Turkish fashion of flavouring rice with rose water or essence of roses preferable. To our Western palates it is a new flavour, and in my opinion a very pleasant one. It has been objected to me that rice thus flavoured had too great an affinity to the wares of the perfumer I think that the perfume and flavour of the rose are too beautiful to be rejected in cookery because they are used in perfumery.

The British form of rice pudding is very excellent for young children I have no doubt; but for such as know how to eat, this is how a RICE PUDDING should be made.

Having boiled your rice in milk with plenty of sugar and the thin outer rind of two lemons, pour it into a basin to cool, and when cold stir into it several eggs; add a small quantity of candied citron cut up small, and pour the whole into a mould previously buttered and breadcrumbed. Bake half an hour and serve. This is very good cold, and may be served with custard or jam as a sauce.

Rice so prepared can be used as a border for stewed fruit, as can also rice plainly boiled in milk or in water. Or again, the border may be made of a *bouillie* (porridge) of ground rice and milk; and this latter is as pleasant an adjunct to a dish of stewed fruit as any I know of. But the best of all sweets made with rice is what is known as RIZ À L'IMPERATRICE, of which the following is the recipe:

Boil three tablespoonfuls of rice picked and washed clean, in a pint of milk with sugar to taste and a piece of vanilla; when quite done put it into a basin to get cold. Make a custard with a gill of milk and the yolks of four eggs; when cold mix it with the rice. Beat up into a froth a gill of cream with some sugar and a pinch of isinglass dissolved in a little water; mix this very lightly with the rice and custard. Fill a mould with the mixture and set it on ice; when sufficiently iced, turn it out and serve with any cold jam sauce or a salad of fruit—such as strawberries—round it. This latter is simply the fruit freed from stalks and tossed in plenty of powdered loaf sugar and a small quantity of pale brandy.

EGGS.

THERE is nothing on which tastes differ so much as on matters of food, and on matters of food so much as about breakfast. Some people eat none; others make it their principal meal. Englishmen mostly breakfast the moment they get up; Frenchmen do not breakfast till some hours after the work or pleasure of the day has begun. I will not pretend to decide which is the pleasanter or the more wholesome course to pursue. My own device is that, considering the shortness of life and the charm of variety, we should each be allowed to please ourselves so long as no excess be committed. But there are those in this world whose mission is not so much to please themselves as to please others; and the woman—be she wife or housekeeper—who has to provide breakfast for her lord and master, has no easy task before her should he be at all of a critical turn of mind and fastidious about his food. Some there are who are easily pleased; others who hate to-day what pleased them yesterday. Now with such a one for whom to cater, this matter of breakfast becomes a serious puzzle.

Nothing is more palatable as a breakfast dish than a well-made omelet or a couple of well-fried eggs; but the generality of English cooks can only boil or poach eggs, and what they call an omelet is only a cross between a pancake and a piece of washleather. Now, no great amount of talent is required to cook eggs in a variety of charming ways, and the process is so simple, in most instances, that I hope some of my fair readers will successfully instruct their cooks from the directions that I am about to set forth.

Given the ordinary British cook, this is how I should gradually train her up to the preparation of an omelet. By dint of great perseverance, I should endeavour to make her keep her omelet-pan perfectly clean and bright; that is a great step. Next, I should teach her how to fry a couple of eggs, thus:

Melt a piece of butter in an omelet pan, and then break two eggs into it carefully so as not to break the yolks; let them set nicely over the fire, and when nearly set slip them out on to a hot dish. The butter should not be allowed to get too hot, but as soon as it is melted the eggs should be thrown in, and not more than two should be fried at a time. The butter which is left in the omelet-pan should be poured over the eggs when serving, or it may be left on the fire till it is nearly black, and then poured over the eggs with the addition of the least drop of tarragon vinegar (*un filet de vinaigre*), and a little minced parsley. Eggs cooked in this way are called ŒUFS AU BEURRE NOIR, and when the butter is not made black they are called ŒUFS SUR LE PLAT or AU MIROIR.

A nice way of cooking eggs is AU FROMAGE, which is done thus: Put a couple of slices of Gruyère cheese (or any other kindred sort) with a small piece of butter in the omelet-pan; break two eggs over them, add a very little salt and some pepper, and let the whole remain on a gentle fire until the whites are set: then serve.

Other forms in which to serve fried eggs are to dish them over a *purée* of spinach, sorrel, endive, or celery. They may also be served with some tomato sauce, Italian sauce, *sauce piquante*, *sauce Périgueux*, &c., under them. But care must be taken not to put too great a quantity of *purée* or sauce in the dish.

Eggs neatly fried as above, and daintily placed on a slice of well-broiled ham or bacon are perhaps an improvement on the poached eggs usually served in this way, and are certainly preferable to eggs which have been fried with the bacon.

Fried eggs laid on a slice of buttered toast, covered with a little anchovy paste, are an appetizing dish.

When more than two eggs are to be served at one time, and especially if they are to be served over a *purée* or sauce, it is best to fry them one by one, and to trim the white round each egg : this adds to the appearance of the dish. All the above can be cooked just as well in a metal dish on the hot plate, and served on it, or they may be cooked in the oven.

When you have got your cook to dress and send up fried eggs decently, then you may advance her to the next stage, which is scrambled eggs (ŒUFS BROUILLÉS).

The proceeding is this: Having melted a piece of butter in a *sauté*-pan, or in an omelet-pan, break into it the eggs, and stir them up with a spoon on one side of it until nearly set, then turn them out neatly into a dish and serve. A small quantity of tomato sauce may be scrambled in the pan with them, or some finely minced shallots, ham, sausage (Bologna), remains of fish (such as salmon), or sardines, anchovies, preserved tunny, mushrooms, truffles, &c., always finely minced; also asparagus points, young peas, &c. One thing to be remembered is not to put in too much of these things, and to put them in at the same time as the eggs, so that they may be set in with them.

But the great point to be observed is not to overcook scrambled eggs in any form, and to this end it must be borne in mind that eggs do not cease cooking, and consequently hardening, for some minutes after they have been put into the dish in which they are to be served, and that therefore allowance must be made for this in judging the time that they are to remain in the omelet or sauté-pan. This is a point of the greatest importance, particularly in cooking omelets; and cooking scrambled eggs—which are in truth but an omelet with no outside or shape—is very good practice for learning to judge time in the more difficult process of producing an omelet which, while retaining the soft nature of scrambled eggs inside, must have both shape and colour.

The production of an omelet may be divided into two operations—the mixing and the cooking. The first can easily be described in words, and is capable of numerous variations. The second is the most difficult to describe and to carry out—although simple enough when once you know it. I must again repeat that the omelet-pan should be perfectly clean; this is indispensable. The fire should be bright. These conditions being fulfilled, put a piece of butter the size of an egg into the pan, let it melt without browning, and as soon as it is melted and hot pour in your omelet mixture, and, holding the handle of the pan with one hand, stir the omelet with the other by means of a flat spoon. The moment it begins to set cease stirring, but keep shaking the pan for a minute or so; then with the ladle or spoon double up your omelet, and keep on shaking the pan until one side of the omelet has become a golden colour, when you dexterously turn it out on a hot dish, the coloured side uppermost. After the omelet is doubled up, the insertion of a little piece of butter under it facilitates operations. Two points to be observed are, that the coloured side of the omelet should be like gold, and that this result should be attained without the inside becoming too firmly set.

The mode of cooking omelets varies according to their

composition. The above hints refer particularly to the simplest form of omelet.

In mixing omelets two general rules should never be forgotten. One is not to use more than eight eggs for any one omelet. Some cookery books fix the limit at twelve, but that is too many, especially if the operator be new at her work. To my mind two omelets of six eggs each are far preferable, for many reasons, to one of twelve. Still keeping in view the unschooled British cook referred to at the beginning of this paper, I should let her only use two eggs at first, the number to be increased as she becomes proficient. The other rule is not to beat up the eggs too much; the object of beating them is simply to mix the whites and the yolks well together, and this should be done only just before the mixture is put into the omelet-pan.

The simplest form of mixing an omelet consists in beating up two eggs in a basin, with salt and pepper to taste, and a pinch of minced parsley. There are people who add pieces of bread crumb and a few morsels of butter. To this I see no objection; but the admixture of water or milk with the eggs is much to be deprecated, although mentioned in some cookery books which are accounted authorities.

From this very simple dish, which I may call a PLAIN OMELET, spring many varieties. Here are some of them.

1. OMELETTE AUX FINES HERBES.—Three eggs and one dessert spoonful of the following mixture: Parsley, chervil, garden cress, and chives, all finely minced, pepper and salt to taste. This may be varied in many ways, by using shallots or onions instead of chives, and by omitting some of the other herbs; and by introducing the least bit of powdered spices.

2. OMELETTE AU JAMBON.—Three eggs, with pepper and

salt to taste, a pinch of minced parsley, and as much ham (cut up into very small dice) as will fill a tablespoon. A little shallot finely minced may be added.

3. OMELETTE AU LARD.—Use bacon instead of ham.

4. OMELETTE AU PARMESAN.—Three eggs, a tablespoonful or more of grated Parmesan cheese, pepper and salt to taste, beaten up together, fried a light colour, and served with grated Parmesan strewed over it.

5. OMELETTE AUX TOMATES.—Three eggs beaten up with a tablespoonful of tomato sauce, pepper and salt to taste, and a little minced parsley. A small quantity of grated Parmesan may be added.

6. ——— Peel and remove the inside of a large tomato, cut it in small pieces, and mix it with three eggs, minced parsley, pepper and salt to taste, and, if you like, a suspicion of shallot.

7. ——— Lay a plain omelette over some well-made tomato sauce.

8. OMELETTE AUX TRUFFES.—Add to a plain omelet mixture a small quantity of cooked truffles minced fine.

9. ——— Mince or slice some cooked truffles, not too finely, dress them with just enough well-flavoured brown sauce (*sauce Espagnole*) to keep them together, and insert them at the time of serving in the fold of the omelet; or they may be served round it.

10. OMELETTE AUX CHAMPIGNONS.—Parboil some mushrooms, and use them instead of truffles, as in either of the above recipes. A white sauce may be used with them instead of *sauce Espagnole*.

A combination of these last forms of omelets constitutes a dish much in vogue at the crack restaurants in New York, where it goes by the name of

11. OMELETTE À L'ESPAGNOLE.—With four eggs beat up a judicious mixture of ham, tomatoes, mushrooms,

and truffles, prepared as in the above recipes, a few minced shallots, some parsley, and pepper and salt to taste. Fry *secundum artem* and serve hot.

Asparagus heads or young peas can be introduced into an omelet as they are introduced into scrambled eggs, or they may be dressed with a plain white sauce, and served round or inside the omelet, and so you will have

12. OMELETTE AUX POINTES D'ASPERGES, and
13. OMELETTE AU POIS.

By using kidneys on the same principle another form of omelet will be produced. The proceeding is this: Parboil some sheep's kidneys—a process, by the way, which should always precede the dressing of that article of diet in any form whatsoever. Cut them up in moderate-sized pieces, and toss them in a saucepan with a little butter. Add some pepper and salt to taste, some minced parsley, and, if you like, some minced truffles and mushrooms. Then incorporate in a saucepan a small quantity of flour with a piece of butter, add equal parts of white wine and stock in proportionate quantity to that of the kidneys, which you transfer into this second saucepan and toss on the fire until done, when you add to them a squeeze of lemon. Being served alone, kidneys so prepared constitute the well-known dish ROGNONS AU VIN DE CHAMPAGNE. You may use champagne if you choose, but this is by no means necessary. If a proper quantity of this *ragoût* of kidneys be served round an omelet, or some of it be inserted in the fold thereof you will have what is called an (14) OMELETTE AUX ROGNONS.

Numerous other vareties of omelets may be produced by introducing into a plain omelet mixture pieces of anchovy, sardines, herrings, or preserved fish of various kinds, all being of course carefully cleaned, and —in the case of some—cooked by broiling or otherwise.

Omelets can also be compounded with prawns, shrimps or oysters, all of which should be parboiled and then dressed with a little white sauce, and the *ragoût* thus prepared should be served either within or round the omelet. The following is my formula for preparing oysters either for the above purpose, or to put into small bread *croustades* :

Parboil a quantity of oysters in their own liquor, remove the beards, cut each oyster into four or six pieces. Melt a piece of butter in a saucepan, add to it a pinch of flour, the liquor of the oysters, a little cream, salt, pepper, nutmeg, the least bit of cayenne, and some finely minced parsley. Put in the oysters and toss them in this sauce just long enough to make them quite hot. Stir into them (off the fire) the yolk of an egg beaten up with the juice of half a lemon and strained. With the remains of fish—of salmon or trout especially, from the previous day's dinner—a very neat omelet can be produced in the fashion following :

Beat up three fresh eggs with a quantity equal to an egg in bulk of the flesh of boiled salmon shredded fine with a fork, a pinch of minced parsley, pepper, salt, and half a dozen bits of butter the size of a pea. Cooked according to art this mixture will produce a noble omelet.

To conclude this matter of omelets I will give a modified formula of the celebrated OMELETTE AU THON, which graced the table of Brillat-Savarin's *curé*. I say modified, because fresh tunny fish, which is occasionally procurable in Paris, is not, I believe, to be had in London.

Get some tunny fish preserved in oil, and mince half a slice of it very finely; do the same to a couple of fresh soft roes of carp previously parboiled ; rub a frying-pan with a piece of shallot; put into it a goodly piece of butter, and toss your mince in this for a minute, then put it into a basin containing six fresh eggs; beat the mixture well, add salt and pepper, and proceed to make the omelet. The dish which is to receive it should be prepared beforehand in this wise : Mince some parsley and a few chives, incorporate with them a piece of fresh butter, put it on the dish, which should be hot enough to melt it, and squeeze the juice of a lemon over. On this you place the omelet when cooked. Brillat-Savarin remarks on this dish, that it is to be reserved for connoisseurs, who know what they are about, and eat composedly.

Hard boiled eggs, besides being one of the essentials of salads and kindred preparations, form the foundation of some excellent dishes.

To boil an egg hard requires no great skill, all that need be done being to let it boil a sufficient time. This done they should be cut up in slices, or into quarters, and they make a very effective garnish to a *purée* of sorrel or of spinach, in addition to, or instead of bread sippets. But here are more elaborate ways of serving them :

STEWED EGGS.—Cut some Spanish onions in slices and fry them in plenty of butter, till they are thoroughly done. Add a small quantity of flour to them, and when this is amalgamated with the butter moisten with a due quantity of cream or simply milk, then put in some pepper and salt to taste, a little grated nutmeg, and a quantity—equal in bulk to that of the onions—of hard boiled eggs cut in slices. Let the whole simmer gently till quite hot, and serve with bread sippets fried in butter.

ŒUFS AU GRATIN.—Dispose a number of slices of hard boiled eggs on a well buttered dish, strew over them a moderate quantity of grated Parmesan cheese, with pepper and salt to taste, and the least bit of grated nutmeg, sprinkle a few baked bread crumbs on the top, and put the dish into the oven, serving as soon as the top takes colour. Rubbing the dish slightly with garlic or shallot before commencing operations is accounted by some an improvement.

ŒUFS FARÇIS.—Cut some hard boiled eggs in halves. Mince the yolks with olives, capers, anchovies, and truffles, a little tarragon and chervil, and add pepper and salt. Fill each half egg with this mixture, pour some liquefied butter over, warm them in the oven and serve each half egg on a bread sippet, cut with a fluted cutter and fried in butter. I need hardly remark that this dish can be varied in many ways.

Hard boiled eggs may also be served *à la maître d'hôtel* or with a *Béchamel*, or with a *Soubise* sauce. The first form consists in tossing them till warm in some butter—after having cut them in pieces—and then adding pepper, salt, minced parsley, and a few drops of lemon juice. For the others they need only be warmed in a sufficient quantity of the respective sauces.

I would observe in conclusion, that I by no means pretend to have exhausted all the forms that eggs may be made to assume as a savoury dish; but I have described I think a sufficient number for my present purpose.

Of eggs made into sweet dishes I treat elsewhere.

COOKING CHEESE.

ONE of the best examples of cooked cheese is the Fondue. In its original form this ancient dish is very simple indeed. I will first transcribe the recipe given by Brillat-Savarin, who says that the Fondue was invented in Switzerland, and consists principally of eggs and cheese in such proportions as time and experience have revealed. This is it:

"Recipe for the FONDUE extracted from the papers of Mr. Trollet, Bailli of Mondon, in the canton of Berne.

"Weigh as many eggs as there are guests, and take a piece of Gruyère cheese weighing the third, and a piece of butter weighing the sixth of the weight of the eggs; break the eggs into a saucepan and beat them well; then put in the butter and the cheese grated or sliced. Place the saucepan on a brisk fire, and stir its contents with a wooden spoon until the mixture is properly set, but not too hard. Put into it a little or no salt, according as the cheese is more or less old, and a good allowance of pepper, which is one of the positive characteristics of this classical dish. Serve on a slightly warmed plate, call for the best wine, which will be drunk freely, and you shall see marvels."

Modern professors have improved a good deal upon the above formula, and although it is by no means bad as it is (provided the saucepan be removed from the fire at the right moment), the modern form is much better, and amply repays by its superior excellence the greater trouble and care required to prepare it. I will endeavour to describe as fully as I can the way I proceed in the operation of making a Fondue; and if any who may work from my recipe should fail, let them not be disheartened, but try again and again, and they will be rewarded.

Melt an ounce of butter in an enamelled saucepan, and stir into it a tablespoonful of flour. When the two are well amalgamated put in a small quantity of milk and about three ounces of grated Parmesan cheese. Stir the mixture on a very slow fire till it assumes the appearance of thick cream, but beware of its becoming too hot or boiling, for that would be fatal. Now put in one clove of garlic, a small quantity of flour of mustard, a dash of powdered nutmeg, and some finely powdered white pepper. Mix thoroughly, and, if upon tasting you find that it is required, add a little salt. Keep on stirring the mixture at a very moderate heat for a good ten minutes, then remove the clove of garlic, take the saucepan off the fire, stirring occasionally until the contents are nearly cold, and then stir in the yolks of three eggs beaten up with the least drop of milk and strained. Mix well; then incorporate swiftly with the mixture the whites of five eggs beaten up into a stiff froth. Pour into a deep round tin, and put it into the oven, which must not be too hot. From twenty to thirty minutes baking will make the Fondue ready for table, to which it must be quickly sent in the tin, with a napkin pinned round it.

The sign of success in this dish is that it should not be greasy to the taste, but rather dry, although each mouthful of the inside portion of it should melt like a piece of ice pudding upon being pressed between the tongue and the palate.

Pepper should predominate, but moderately so, and

above all the flavour of garlic should be properly regulated, and should not be too strong. If the proportions of the various ingredients are in the least degree altered from the right point, or if the mixture be allowed to get too hot in the preliminary manipulations, or if the Fondue is baked too little or too much, all hope of success is at an end. In short, to attain even moderate perfection in the preparation of this dish a great amount of care and perseverance are required.

Parmesan is the only cheese which can be used for the above dish. With English cheeses, such as Cheshire or Gloucester, and even the American imitations of these, other dishes may be prepared in the nature of a Fondue, but by no means so delicate. These are some of them :

1. Make a thickish paste in a saucepan with milk and flour, taking care that it is quite smooth; add to and thoroughly mix with it as much grated cheese (Cheshire, &c.) as you have used flour and a little over, a small quantity of salt, a little flour of mustard, and some pepper. Beat up, say for every pint of milk used, three eggs. Incorporate these with the paste, then fill a dish, or a number of patty pans, with this paste. Bake a nice brown colour, and serve quickly.

2. Take equal parts of any of the above cheeses, of butter, and of bread crumbs (the inside of a French roll is best). Soak the bread crumbs in milk, and pound them in a mortar with the cheese and butter until the whole is well amalgamated, adding during the process, pepper and salt in due proportion, a little flour of mustard, and the yolks of four eggs—supposing the whole of the above mixture to weigh about three-quarters of a pound. Beat up the whites of the eggs to a stiff froth, quickly mix the two together, fill some patty pans or some

paper cases with the mixture; bake in a quick oven —a longer or shorter time, according as you use patty pans or paper cases—say from ten to twenty minutes. These are called RAMEQUINS (ramakins) in cookery books. Their Gallic form is as follows :

3. Into a saucepan containing about a pint of hot water put three ounces of grated Gruyère cheese, and the same quantity of butter, and pepper and salt *quant. suff.* Let the water boil until the cheese is dissolved, then incorporate with it as much flour as will make a very stiff paste, which you may touch without its sticking to the fingers. Work it well with a wooden spoon, and be careful to leave no knots in it. You now remove the saucepan from the fire, and work into it at least four eggs, one by one. Let the paste get quite cold, and then dispose it in little balls, a size bigger than a walnut, on a baking sheet. Bake a light brown colour, and serve. Or, instead of baking them, they may be fried in plenty of lard.

What are called TALMOUSES À LA ST. DENIS are not unlike ramakins, except that Brie cheese is used instead of Gruyère. This, however, is a better way of preparing them :

Take equal parts of Brie and of butter, and, having removed with great care all the rind from the cheese, make a paste by working some eggs and flour with the cheese and butter, a little salt, and a very little pepper. Roll out your paste to the thickness of two half-crowns, cut it out in triangles, brush the top with egg, and bake till done.

Some English soft cheeses may be used instead of Brie, but I am afraid the result would only be a bad imitation of the real *Talmouses*.

SIMPLE SWEETS.

The last dish of a good dinner should be light and elegant, and convey the greatest amount of pleasure to the taste with the least possible nourishment.

First-rate artists can supply a never-ending variety of *entremets sucrés* suited to the taste of the most fastidious. These, however, are often expensive, and require a first-rate artist to produce them. On the other hand, there are numbers of simple and inexpensive preparations, within reach of anyone who chooses to take a little trouble. Some of these I will describe, beginning with a very good way of disposing of jam—a modification of the well-known croûtes of the Paris restaurants.

Cut some slices of bread the same thickness as for sippets to put round spinach, &c.; cut off the crust and shape them with paste-cutters into elegant forms, such as a trefoil, a Maltese cross, &c.; then proceed to fry them in plenty of fresh butter till they assume on both sides a light golden colour; let them drain and cool. Now each piece is to be spread over with jam, but not too much of it, and it should be done very evenly. Apricot jam is about the best, but others will do as well, or two kinds of jam may be used, half the pieces being spread with one and half with another. This done, dispose your pieces round a dish, making one overlay the other in a circle. Sift some very finely-powdered sugar over them, and in the middle pour a sauce made by dissolving some of the jam in a couple of glasses of sherry and a liqueur-glass of brandy. At the time of serving place the dish in the oven for a few minutes, pass a red-hot salamander over the *croûtons*, and send them up to table. A very pleasant combination of flavours is obtained by using apple-jam to spread over the *croûtons*, and black currant-jelly for the sauce. When apricot-jam is used, a few almonds, finely minced and spread over the jam, are an improvement. Another form of this dish is the following:

Use slices of sponge-cake instead of *croûtons*, but cut thicker, and let the sauce be a well-flavoured custard. This makes a cold dish, and if each piece of sponge-cake is dipped in sherry after the jam is put over it, that operation will add considerably to its merit. In all cases the great thing to be avoided is the using of too much jam, and more particularly with sponge-cake.

A sponge-cake, well soaked in sherry, stuck all over with almonds, and covered with cream, sweetened and whipped to a froth, is a common dish enough. There are, however, numerous modifications of this simple dish, which are quite as simple, although possessed of a good deal of merit. In the first place, some of the cream can be coloured with cochineal, spinach greening, caramel, &c., and you can thereby produce a parti-coloured dish, which will be more effective than one entirely white. Then the cream can be both coloured and flavoured with a variety of things—viz.:

1. Coffee; this is done by making a very strong infusion of coffee, and adding some of it to the cream after it is whipped.

2. Chocolate; dissolve a sufficient quantity in hot water, strain it, and when cold add to the whipped cream.

3. The juice of any kind of fruit, such as raspberries, currants, strawberries, &c., can be added to the cream always after whipping.

4. Various kinds of jam strained through muslin, with a little cold water added to them if they are too thick. Some cochineal should be added when the juice of fruit or jam is used.

5. A small quantity of liqueur (such as maraschino).

6. The thin rind of lemons or oranges, scraped and added to the whipped cream.

7. Orange flower-water or rose-water, or the least drop of essence of roses or vanilla, will produce other varieties of flavours.

8. The juice of good orange marmalade will give both flavour and colour to the cream. Soaking the sponge-cake in sherry will not do with all and everyone of these flavourings, nor is a sponge-cake *de rigueur*. What are called Savoy or finger biscuits piled up on a dish will do just as well, and in some cases better.

Now, if you line a mould with these biscuits, fill the inside with whipped cream and ice it, you will produce what is called a CHARLOTTE RUSSE. The proceeding is this: Line the bottom and sides of a plain mould with finger-biscuits, which you trim for the purpose. Beat up into a froth one pint of double cream, sweetened to taste with pounded lump sugar; add one ounce of the finest isinglass dissolved in a gill of milk with a liqueur glass of maraschino. Pour this mixture into the mould, set it on ice for a couple of hours, then turn it out and serve.

The French form of apple pudding is also called a Charlotte, and is made in this way:

CHARLOTTE DE POMMES.—Line a pie dish with thin slices of bread buttered on both sides, fill it with layers of apples cut up very small, placing a little apricot jam between each layer, some grated lemon rind, and plenty of sugar; cover the top with slices of bread buttered in the same way, and bake till the bread is well browned.

Here is a more elaborate form:

Cut from a loaf of household bread a number of slices of uniform thickness (about a quarter or three-eighths of an inch), butter a plain mould and all the slices of bread, shape one of them round to fit the bottom of the mould and another one for the top, cut the rest in pieces an inch wide and the height of the mould in length, lay one of the round pieces at the bottom of the mould, and line the sides with the small pieces, carefully coating their edges with white of egg so as to make them hold well together; stew a quantity of apples with a proper allowance of sugar, a little water, the juice and the thin rind of a lemon, and a piece of cinnamon; when thoroughly done pass them through a hair sieve, fill the mould with this *purée,* put on the other round slice of bread for the cover, and bake in a quick oven for about an hour and a half.

Another very good sweet is made with apples in combination with rice and eggs in the following fashion :

POMMES AU RIZ MERINGUÉES: Peel six apples, core them, cut them in half, and place them in a flat stewpan with half a pint of water, four ounces of loaf sugar, a few cloves, and a little cinnamon; let them boil gently till they become quite soft, then remove them and let the syrup boil away till reduced to a couple of tablespoonfuls when you strain it over the apples. Put into a saucepan half a pound of Patna rice and a quart of water, leave it on the fire till the water boils, drain off the water, add one pint of milk, four ounces of white sugar, and the thin rind of a lemon; when the rice is thoroughly cooked and has absorbed all the milk let it get cold, then remove the lemon rind and work into it the yolks of three or four eggs. Then lay it out on the dish in which it is to be served, place the apples on the top, and cover the whole thoroughly with the whites of the eggs beaten up into a stiff froth with a tablespoonful of powdered lump sugar, sprinkle powdered sugar over, and bake about twenty minutes in a slack oven.

The above dish can be varied by using, instead of apples cooked as above, a *purée* or marmalade of apples or of any other fruit, and likewise oranges treated in the manner following :

ORANGES AU RIZ MERINGUÉES.—Peel off the thin rind of a number of oranges, make a thick syrup by boiling some loaf sugar in a little water, and let the orange rind infuse in this for a little time, but not boil in it. With a sharp knife remove from the oranges every vestige of the remainder or white part of the rind ; core them as you would apples, so as to get rid of the pips, cut them in half, dispose them on the rice, pour some of the above syrup over them, and then finish the dish as in the foregoing recipe.

The custard pudding of the nursery is also a very simple dish, which can be set before grown-up people if prepared after the following fashion :

CARAMEL PUDDING : Put a handful of loaf sugar to boil with a very little water until the syrup becomes a deep brown ; warm a small basin, pour the syrup in it, and keep turning the basin in your hand until the inside is completely coated with the syrup or caramel, which will by that time have set. Strain the yolks of eight eggs from the whites, and mix them gradually and effectually with one pint of milk. Pour this mixture (which may be left plain, or may be flavoured with orange flower water, essence of vanilla, or of lemon, &c.) into the prepared mould, lay a piece of paper on the top, set it in a saucepan full of cold water—taking care that the water does not come over the top of the mould—put on the cover, and set the saucepan by the side of the fire to boil gently for one hour. Then remove the saucepan to a cool place, and when the water is quite cold take out the mould, wipe it dry, and turn out the pudding very carefully.

It is indispensable, to insure success, that the basin and the saucepan be covered while boiling as described above; and I would advise beginners not to be disheartened if they do not succeed at first, for they will have many failures before they are able to turn out this pudding whole. It requires great care. If you use whole eggs instead of yolks alone, you will make success certain; this, however, will be at the expense of the delicacy of the dish. The caramel forms a kind of brown syrup which goes round the pudding; but, by way of variety, a sweet sauce made with jam may be substituted. I ought also to mention that in making the caramel care should be taken not to make it too brown, for in that case it would impart a bitter taste to the pudding.

The next simple sweet which occurs to me is the well-known OMELETTE SUCRÉE, which is made by beating up eggs and sugar with a very little powdered cinnamon or any flavouring essence, cooking in the usual way, and serving with powdered sugar. If one white of egg be beaten up into a froth and well mixed with the rest, it will improve the omelet, as will also the keeping some of the whites back—mixing, say, six yolks and four whites, one of them beaten up into a froth. By holding a red-hot poker over the sugar at the moment of serving, so as to form a pattern, both the appearance and the taste of a plain sweet omelet are improved.

An OMELETTE AU RHUM is produced by pouring a certain quantity of rum over an omelet made as above, and the usual practice is to set it alight as it is about to be placed on the table. What is called an OMELETTE AUX CONFITURES, is accomplished by inserting, at the moment of serving, in the fold of the omelet any kind of jam or jelly; but in this case no essence or spice should be used, as it would kill the flavour of the jam.

An OMELETTE SOUFFLÉE is not quite in the nature of an omelet, for it is not fried but baked, and the way to make it is this:

Beat up the yolks of three eggs with some pounded loaf sugar, and any flavouring essence, such as lemon, vanilla, &c.; whisk the whites into a stiff froth, mix the two together quickly and thoroughly. Lay the mixture in a heap on a silver dish, put it into a brisk oven, and the moment it is done send it up to table very swiftly. The above preparation is not an easy one to accomplish successfully, and a great deal of practice will be required to arrive at anything like perfection. And from this I am naturally led to describe that very delectable compound, a SOUFFLÉ.

The same ingredients which go to make the homely batter pudding of English nurseries, manipulated in the proper manner, and flavoured as taste may suggest, become glorified into what is called a *soufflé*. The manipulation is simple enough, but the cooking, which is done in the oven, requires a certain degree of skill, although it merely consists in knowing when the oven is at the right temperature; for if this be either too high or two low, the *soufflé* will not be fit to eat, much less to look at.

Soufflés are usually served in the tin or dish in which they are baked. To pin a napkin round the tin when the *soufflé* is cooked, and to send it up to table, are operations which must be performed swiftly. A large paper case may also be used to bake a *soufflé*, and some cooks will fix a band of paper round the tin when this is not deep enough to allow of the *soufflé* rising. The best way, however, is to have a tin sufficiently deep, and, if within the resources of the establishment, when the *soufflé* is ready, it should be put, tin and all, into what is called a *soufflé* case, just as flower pots are slipped into elegant vases to be placed on the dining table.

Another point to be borne in mind is that the moment a *soufflé* is done, and has attained, so to speak, its bloom or fulness, it must be served; for when once a soufflé ceases to go up it begins to go down, either in or out of the oven. In fact, like time and tide, *soufflés* wait for no man: to be sure of success the cook must be well acquainted with the habits of her company, so as to be able to judge the time of putting the *soufflé* into the oven. For this reason a *soufflé* is not a safe dish to have for a dinner party. The best of cooks will at times fail in a *soufflé*, for no particular reason or fault of their own. My plan is always to have another dish in readiness to take the place of the *soufflé*, should it prove a failure.

Some kinds of *soufflés*, however, can stand a little waiting better than others, which must not wait at all. A Fondue—which is nothing else but a savoury *soufflé*—a rice or a potato *soufflé*, may be kept waiting a minute or two; but to an *omelette soufflée* or a coffee *soufflé* for example, waiting is fatal. The liability of a *soufflé* to fall can always be lessened by increasing the proportion of flour used in making it; but this is done at the expense of the delicacy of the dish, and indeed some *soufflés* should contain no flour at all.

I will now proceed to explain how the different kinds of *soufflés* are compounded, and describe the simplest one, which only differs from a batter pudding in the manipulation of the ingredients, and the absence of that eminently British institution, the currants.

Mix together in a saucepan one tablespoonful of flour, a small piece of fresh butter, half a pint of milk, and some powdered lump sugar to taste. Stir this on the fire for a few minutes, then put it by to cool, and keep stirring it now and then to prevent a skin forming on the top. When cold work into the mixture the yolks of four eggs; add any flavouring you like; mix it well for some minutes; then have ready the whites of six eggs beaten up into a stiff froth, mix the two effectually and quickly together, pour into a tin, and put into the oven at once. Some cooks always put a very small pinch of salt in their *soufflé* mixture, others do not use any butter, and others again put in some cream instead. The readiest mode of flavouring is by using the essences sold by all grocers in little bottles; but it can also be done by boiling a piece of vanilla in the mixture in the first instance, or a stick of cinnamon, or the rind of a couple of lemons or oranges. They may also be flavoured with liqueurs, such as maraschino, noyeau, &c., but these should be put in the last thing before the whites of eggs. The above is, so to speak, the common form of all *soufflés* which take their name from the particular flavour put into them. A more delicate form of *soufflé* is produced by using potato flour instead of wheat flour. In this case no butter should be used, and the mode of operation is somewhat different. The potato flour should be mixed with a little of the milk, and when quite smooth the rest of the milk should be added with the sugar, and the mixture stirred over the fire until it thickens. Rice flour, or arrowroot, may also be used instead of corn flour. Then, again, *soufflés* are made absolutely of rice, potatoes, chestnuts, &c., in the manner following :

RICE SOUFFLÉ.—Boil a handful of rice in a pint of sweetened milk, with a stick of cinnamon, a piece of vanilla, or the thin peel of an orange or lemon, until the rice has absorbed all the milk. Put it by to get cold, remove the substance used for flavouring, work in the yolks of six eggs, then (as explained above) the whites of eight eggs whipped into a stiff froth.

POTATO SOUFFLÉ.—Boil a couple of large potatoes. Pass them through a sieve. Mix in the yolks of six eggs beaten up with pounded lump sugar to taste. Add a few drops of essence of vanilla or lemon, then the whites of eight eggs as above. If a larger proportion of potatoes be used, then the *soufflé* becomes a GÂTEAU DE POMMES DE TERRE, in which form it will fall little or not at all, and with a jam sauce round it will make an agreeable and wholesome sweet.

The shape or mould in which a *gâteau de pommes de terre* is baked, should be buttered and bread crumbed; it will require to bake longer than a *soufflé*, and when done it should be turned out of the mould on to a dish.

CHESTNUT SOUFFLÉ.—Peel the outer skin from a quantity of chestnuts, and boil them in plenty of water with a bay leaf and a pinch of salt; when quite done remove the inner skin, and pound them in a mortar, with sugar to taste, and some almond flavouring. When reduced to a perfectly smooth paste, incorporate with them half an ounce of very fresh butter, then as many yolks of eggs as will make the mixture of the proper consistency. Add an equal number of whites of egg, and one or two over, whisked stiff as usual.

MACCARONI SOUFFLÉ.—Proceed as with the rice soufflé, taking care to break up the maccaroni into small pieces. The finest vermicelli is the best kind to use.

Another description of *soufflé* is that which is made with fruit, of which I will take as an example an

APPLE SOUFFLÉ.—Boil some apples with very little water, plenty of lump sugar, and a few cloves or a little cinnamon, until you get a well-reduced marmalade, which you pass through a hair sieve. Mix a very little potato flour with a gill of milk; stir it over the fire until it thickens; add the yolks of four eggs, and as much apple marmalade as will give you a mixture of the proper consistency; work it well so as to get it of a uniform smoothness, then add the whites of six eggs in the usual way. A little fresh butter may be added to this form of *soufflé*, but it is by no means necessary.

By a somewhat similar process *soufflés* of apricots, strawberries, plums, greengages, &c., may be produced.

Another form consists in working into a plain *soufflé* mixture a small quantity of any sort of ready-made jam or marmalade. When some fruit (such as strawberries), is used, a little cochineal should be added, to give the compound a nice colour.

To flavour *soufflés* with lemon or oranges when no essence is used, the juice of two lemons or of two oranges, and their thin rind chopped up small or grated, should be added to a plain *soufflé* mixture when cold, and then the eggs should be worked in as explained above.

The last kind of *soufflé* I have to describe is that which is flavoured with coffee, tea, or chocolate. Using essence of coffee is not satisfactory for *soufflés*. My notion of a COFFEE SOUFFLÉ is this:

Take a couple of ounces of good coffee newly roasted, grind it and pour over it half a pint of boiling milk, stir it well and let it stand in a covered vessel for at least an hour, then strain it; mix a couple of teaspoonfuls of potato flour with a little drop of the coffee till quite smooth, then add the rest of the coffee, and stir on the fire until it begins to thicken, adding pounded loaf sugar to taste. When the mixture is cold, put in a liqueur glass of pale brandy, the yolks of four and the whites of six eggs in the usual way. Another way is to use water instead of milk, and again another is to omit the brandy. A TEA SOUFFLÉ is made by using a strong infusion of orange-flavoured Pekoe either in milk or in water. To make a CHOCOLATE SOUFFLÉ, a couple of ounces of chocolate flavoured with vanilla should be grated, and then boiled, until quite dissolved, in half a pint of milk, with the addition of a little potato flour and sugar to taste; when the mixture is cold, the yolks of four eggs and the whites of six are added in the usual way.

Another form of chocolate *soufflé* is this:

Two ounces or more of chocolate are scraped fine, and made into a paste in a mortar by the addition of a little cream, then the yolks of four eggs at least are added, with some essence of vanilla and sugar to taste; when the mixture is worked quite smooth, the whites of six eggs are added as before. All *soufflés* should be sprinkled with finely powdered lump sugar when they are put into the oven, and again when being sent up to table.

A very simple, cheap, and yet effective sweet dish is that known in France by the name of ŒUFS À LA NEIGE, which are prepared thus:

Beat up a quantity of white of egg into a froth with a little sugar. Have some milk, previously sweetened, in a saucepan on the fire, and when it boils throw in your egg froth in separate tablespoonfuls. A few seconds will cook each on one side; then turn it over, and, when cooked on the other side, place it in a glass dish. When all your egg froth is cooked, strain the milk from the bits of eggs that are in it, and make a custard with it and the yolks of the eggs, flavouring it as you like. When cold pour it into the glass dish, but not over the boiled whites, which will float on the top of the custard. Sprinkle a few nonpareil ("hundreds and thousands") over the whites, and serve. Before pouring the custard into the glass dish, any milk that may have drained from the boiled whites should be removed.

But the simplest of all sweets is the following pudding, which is composed of white of egg and sugar only.

EGG SNOW PUDDING.—Prepare a small basin with a coating of caramel as described above for caramel pudding. Whisk the whites of half a dozen eggs to a stiff froth, then place them into the prepared basin, which they should only half fill. Tie a piece of paper over the top of the basin, and place it in a large pan containing a sufficient quantity of hot water to float the basin; cover the pan, and so place it on the range as to keep the water very hot without letting it boil. After the lapse of three-quarters of an hour turn out the pudding on a dish with the caramel syrup, which will come out of the basin round it.

This dish will not always succeed, but when it does it eminently fulfils the conditions of what a sweet should be, although it cannot lay claim to any fantastic deliciousness of flavour.

ON A SCOTTISH CUSTOM.

KEEPING New Year's Eve is a Scotch custom much in vogue in France; and as I am very fond of old customs, Scotch or otherwise, I never fail to see the old year out and the new year in in a fit and proper manner. This means, *inter alia*, that a festive drink or cup is elaborately prepared by the present writer, and at the orthodox moment of twelve p.m. the household, barring children in arms, partake of it and wish each other all that is usual on such occasions.

There are many drinks suitable for this celebration, but still their number has a limit, and besides, a change is always welcome, although there is an interval of twelve months between each potation. On the 31st of December last, therefore, I resolved to invent something new, and the company assembled were rather disgusted when they were told that the festive cup would consist of wine and jam. When, however,

I showed them the stuff and they twigged it,

they all declared, and some I dare say " swore," as in the song, that there was nothing like my new drink. I confess I rather liked it myself, and, in common with others, wished when it was all gone, that I had made more of it. The ladies of the party were so pleased with it that encouraged by their approbation, I will describe the whole process.

The jam I used was made of black currants in this way: Extract the juice and pulp from the fruit by passing it through a sieve—then put into a preserving pan 2½lb. of crystallised sugar and a little more than half a pint of water; let the syrup boil for about half an hour, then add to it 3lb. of the pulp and juice of the currants; let the whole boil until the jam sets firmly, which you ascertain by pouring a few drops of it on a cold plate, and then proceed to fill your pots, to be tied up, &c., when cold.

Now for the drink—Into a saucepan containing rather less than one quart of water put half an ordinary-sized pot of the jam, a small handful of cloves, a stick of cinnamon a foot long, broken in small pieces, the rind of two or three oranges, and the same quantity of lemon rind, with sugar à discrétion, but not too much. Set the saucepan to boil with the lid on for an hour and a half or more. While this is going on have four bottles of claret (it need not be Château Lafitte), which you place inside the fender so as to warm the wine as much as possible; then pour it into a large saucepan, add the third of a bottle of Cognac, and set it on the fire to get as hot as possible without boiling. As soon as the requisite temperature is attained, pour in the liquor from the other saucepan through a fine strainer, give the whole a stir for luck, fill your glasses, put a little grated nutmeg on the top of each, and "you shall see marvels."

I have given the proportions I used as nearly as possible; but frequent tasting during the process, and the quality of the ingredients used, must also guide those who have not sufficient experience in these matters to hit off the right quantity in each particular case.

The black currant jam of commerce would, I believe, do quite as well as that made in my way; and the nutmeg might be put in to boil with the other spices.

In conclusion, I would observe that, to the best of my

belief, this drink is new; but of one thing at least I am certain—that it is excellent, and my parting wish to my readers is that they may never have a worse drink wherewith to keep the old Scotch custom of seeing the old year out.

BILLS OF FARE.

JANUARY.

1.
Potage au pauvre homme.
Raie au beurre noir.
Côtelettes de mouton à l'Anglaise.
Purée de pommes de terre.
Omelette au Parmesan.
Tartelettes de pommes.

2.
Oysters.
Consommé de volaille aux quenelles.
Chartreuse de perdrix.
Grenadins de bœuf à l'Espagnole.
Petits soufflés au Parmesan.
Salade d'oranges.

3.
Potage à la Condé.
Sole à la Normande.
Civet de lièvre à la Française.
Roast pheasant.
Salade Russe.
Cheese straws.
Gâteau de pommes de terre.   Beignets d'oranges.

4.
Bisque aux écrevisses.
Turbot, sauce aux câpres.
Croquettes de volaille.   Alouettes en caisses.
Carré de veau à la Macédoine.
Sarcelles rôties.
Cardons au jus.
Maccaroni au gratin.
Marrow pudding.
Noyeau jelly.
Pain d'honneur.   Bouchées aux confitures.

FEBRUARY.

1.
Purée de céleri.
Fried smelts.
Lark, steak, and kidney pudding.   Mashed potatoes.
Stuffed Spanish Onions.   Cheese.
Ginger pudding.

2.
Potage aux Ravioli.
Torbay whitings à la maître d'hôtel.
Filets de pluviers aux truffes.
Rump steak, potatoes sautées.
Seakale à la sauce blanche.
Watercress-butter and cheese.
Beignets d'oranges.   Caramel pudding.

3.
Purée de lentilles.
Brill à la Hollandaise.
Côtelettes de mouton à la Maintenon.
Braised fowl à la jardinière.
Golden plovers.
Epinards à la crème.
Rhubarb tart.   Vanilla custard.

4.
Crécy au riz.
Brandade de morue.
Fried fillets of sole.
Filets de Lapereau à la Périgord.   Salmis de bécassines.
Escaloppes de veau à la Milanaise.
Entrecôte de bœuf braisée à la mode.
Purée de pommes de terre.   Céleri au jus.
Roast wild duck à la bigarade.
Chouxfleur au gratin.
Biscuit au chocolat.   Crème Garibaldi.
Boudins à la Romaine.   Mirlitons aux confitures.'

MARCH.

1.
Croûte au pot.
Sole aux fines herbes.
Fricandeau aux épinards.
Fondue au Parmesan.
Compôte d'oranges.

2.
Julienne.
Turbot au gratin. Alouettes en caisses.
Stewed beef, with mushrooms and potato croquettes.
Cauliflower salad. Gruyère cheese.
Barcelona-nut cream. Apple jelly.

3.
Consommé au céleri.
Saumon grillé à la maître d'hôtel.
Croquettes de volaille. Paupiettes de bœuf à l'Espagnole.
Pintade rôtie au cresson.
New potatoes sautées au beurre. Asperges, sauce poivrade.
Omelette au Parmesan.
Bouchées aux confitures. Nougats à la crème.

4.
Consommé à la royale.
Saumon, sauce au fenouil.
Epigrammes d'agneau aux épinards. Suprême de volaille.
Filet de bœuf à la jardinière.
Roast curlews.
Cardons à la moëlle. Petits soufflés au Parmesan.
Crème à l'orange en Chartreuse.
Soufflé à l'ananas.
Tartelettes de pêches.
Génoises au chocolat.

APRIL.

1.
Brunoise.
Soles en caisses aux champignons
Bifteck à la Béarnaise.   Pommes de terre frites
Epinards au jus.
Maccaroni au gratin.

2.
Consommé aux pointes d'asperges.
Rougets en papillotes.
Cassolettes de pommes de terre au Salpicon.
Côtelettes de mouton, oignons glacés.
Salad of new potatoes.
Œufs au gratin.

3.
Consommé aux pâtes d'Italie.
Maquereaux, sauce au fenouil.
Roast leg of lamb, mint sauce.   New potatoes.
Roast wood pigeons.
Russian salad.   Tartelettes Piémontaises.
Œufs à la neige.

4.
Potage à la reine.
Saumon, sauce Hollandaise.
Filets de Maquereau à l'Italienne.
Crème de veau à la Périgueux.
Côtelettes d'agneau aux concombres.
Entrecôte de bœuf à la Napolitaine.
Poulets rôtis au cresson.
Asperges, sauce blanche.   Fondue au Parmesan.
Chartreuse d'oranges.
Crème au café.
Mirlitons au marasquin.
Gelée à la Russe.

MAY.

1.
Potage à la Nivernaise.
Whitebait.
Hashed mutton.   New Potatoes.
Stewed summer cabbage on toast.
Cream cheese.
Gooseberry tart.

2.
Potage à la purée d'asperges.
Dorade au Madère.
Côtelettes de mouton grillées.   Carottes à la maître d'hôtel.
Lasagnes aux tomates.
Salade d'oranges.

3.
Potage printanier.
Soles aux fines herbes.
Ris de veau piqués au jus.
Poulardes braisées à la jardinière.
Parmesan, watercress-butter.
Crème Garibaldi.   Soufflé de riz à la vanille.

4.
Potage à la jardinière.
Darne de saumon au gratin.
Timbales de veau aux truffes.   Côtelettes d'agneau à la Macédoine.
Filet de bœuf aux olives.
Mayonnaise de homard en aspic.
Fondue au Parmesan.
Gelée au marasquin.   Gâteau Savarin au rhum.
Meringues à la crème.   Bouchées aux confitures.

JUNE.

1.

Potage à la crème d'orge.
Escalloppes d'agneau au gratin.
Mayonnaise de poulet.
Beignets au Parmesan.
Riz à l'Impératrice.

2.

Soupe à l'oseille.
Truite grillée à la maître d'hôtel.
Filet de bœuf rôti.   Pommes de terre.
Salade de laitue.
Cream cheese.   Omelette aux confitures.

3.

Potage aux pâtes d'Italie.
Saumon, sauce aux câpres.
Kromeskys de volaille.   Tendrons de veau aux petits pois.
Filets de Bœuf à la Béarnaise.
Cailles rôties.   Haricots verts à la crème.
Petits soufflés au Parmesan.
Salade de fraises aux oranges.   Boudin glacé à la vanille.

4.

Consommé de volaille.
Côtelettes de saumon aux concombres.
Whitebait.
Poulets sautés à l'estragon.
Grenadins de bœuf à la Macédoine.
Quartier d'agneau rôti.
Petits pois à l'Anglaise.   Pommes de terre.
Asperges, sauce poivrade.
Tartelettes Piémontaises.
Croûtes à l'ananas.   Bouchées aux abricots.
Boudin glacé au café.

JULY.

1.
Potage à la purée de pois verts.
Truite à la maître d'hôtel.
Côtelettes de veau à la Milanaise.
Salade de homard.
Cream cheese.   Soufflé au chocolat.

2.
Consommé au riz.
Filets de maquereau à l'Italienne.
Ris de veau piqués aux champignons.
Escalloppes de mouton aux haricots verts.
Omelette aux Parmesan.
Crème de fraises.

3.
Consommé à l'estragon.
Sole à la maître d'hôtel.
Rissoles de volaille.
Côtelettes de mouton sautées aux pommes de terre.
Cailles rôties.
Artichauts à la sauce blanche.
Ramequins.
Tourte de cerises.
Glace au café.

4.
Consommé de soles.
Filets de saumon, sauce piquante.
Whitebait.
Timbales de ris de veau aux truffes.
Escaloppes de levraut à l'Italienne.
Roast quarter of lamb.   Peas.   Pommes de terre sautées.
Tomates au gratin.
Gruyère sandwiches.
Salade de fruits.   Omelette soufflée.
Nesselrode pudding.

AUGUST.

1.

Potage à la bonne femme.
Rougets en papillotes.
Poulet rôti au cresson.
Pois à la Française.   Œufs au gratin.
Compôte de prunes.

2.

Tomato soup.
Croquettes de homard.
Côtelettes de mouton braisées aux choux.
Cailles rôties.
Fondue au Parmesan.   Gâteau Napolitain.

3.

Crème de riz aux pois.
Soles frites à la Colbert.
Filets de veau à l'Italienne.   Pommes de terre frites.
Haricots verts à la maître d'hôtel.
Roast grouse.
Cream cheese.   Raspberry and currant tart.

4.

Consommé aux quenelles.
Truite grillée à la tartare.
Suprême de volaille.   Paupiettes de bœuf à l'Espagnole.
Roast haunch of venison.
Haricot verts au beurre.
Tomates au gratin.
Petits soufflés au Parmesan.
Boudin glacé aux fruits.
Gâteau Napolitain.

SEPTEMBER.

1.
Potage à la jardinière.
Dublin Bay haddock and egg sauce
Bifteck aux olives.
Vegetable marrow aux tomates.
Maccaroni au gratin.
Tartelettes de prunes.

2.
Potage à la purée de laitue.
Vol au vent of codfish.
Epigrammes de mouton aux tomates.
Chartreuse de perdrix.
Scotch woodcock.
Biscuit au café.

3.
Potage à la Sévigné.
Grey mullet à la maître d'hôtel.
Kromeskys aux huîtres. Côtelettes de mouton aux haricots verts.
Roast goose.
Salade de laitue et cresson.
Fondue au Parmesan.
Greengage tart.
Soufflé à la vanille.

4.
Bouillabaisse.
Escaloppes de turbot à la Périgord.
Salmis de perdreaux. Timbales de veau en Chartreuse.
Braised saddle of mutton, à la jardinière.
Roast Blackcock.
Vegetable marrow au fromage.
Omelette au jambon.
Charlotte Russe.
Tartelettes de pêches.
Nougats à la crème.
Gâteau de pistaches.

OCTOBER.

1.
Potage au maccaroni.
Baked John Dory.
Mutton cutlets en papillotes.
Roast woodcock.
Cauliflower salad.   Pommes à la Condé.

2.
Purée of endive.
Matelotte de harengs aux champignons.
Croustades de volaille.
Grenadins de veau à la Macédoine.
Filet de Bœuf rôti à la Française.
Salade de cresson.
Vegetable marrow au gratin.
Charlotte de pommes.   Omelette au rhum.

3.
Consommé de gibier aux quenelles.
Brill au Madère.
Soles au gratin.
Côtelettes de mouton à la Réforme.
Chartreuse de perdrix.
Faisan truffé.
Salade Russe.   Fondue.
Œufs à la neige.   Bouchées aux confitures.

4.
Consommé aux œufs pochés.
Fried whitings.
Matelotte d'anguilles.
Quenelles de veau aux épinards.   Canard aux olives.
Aloyau braisé à la Nivernaise.   Duchesses.
Roast snipes.
Fried vegetable marrow.
Aspic de homard.
Cheese straws.
Pine apple cream.   Apple soufflé.
Caramel pudding.   Gelée au Curaçao.

NOVEMBER.

1.
Oyster soup.
Soles à la ravigotte.
Filets de bœuf à la jardinière.
Croustades aux huîtres.
Beignets soufflés.

2.
Purée de gibier.
Cabillaud à la crème.
Roast sirloin of beef.
Choux de Bruxelles au jus.   Mashed potatoes.
Maccaroni au gratin.
Beignets de pommes.

3.
Clear ox tail soup.
Stewed red mullets.
Lobster Kromeskys.   Quenelles of veal with mushrooms.
Braised loin of mutton.
Pommes de terre sautées.   Céleri au jus.
Roast pheasant.
Parmesan cheese.   Watercress salad.
Pine apple jelly.   Chocolate blancmange with whipped cream.

4.
Hare soup.
Baked gurnet.   Soles aux champignons.
Veal cutlets aux épinards.   Quenelles of rabbit, tomato sauce.
Braised ribs of beef.
Golden plovers.
Topinambours à la crème.   Œufs au gratin.
Tartelettes piémontaises.
Mousseline pudding.   Punch jelly.
Mirlitons aux confitures.   Génoises au chocolat.

DECEMBER.

1.
Palestine soup.
Fried whitings.
Croquettes of beef.   Brussels sprouts à la crème.
Roast partridges.
Scolloped Oysters.
Sweet omelet.

2.
Onion soup.
Cod au gratin.
Stewed steak.   Haricot beans à la Lyonnaise.
Roast teal.
Omelette au Parmesan.
Chartreuse d'oranges.

3.
Consommé à la royale.
Boiled turbot, tartare sauce.
Merlans au gratin.
Timbales de foies gras aux truffes.   Pork cutlets à la Robert.
Braised turkey stuffed with chestnuts.
Roast sirloin of beef.
Fried potatoes.   Brussels sprouts au jus.   Cauliflowers au gratin
Plum pudding.
Mince pies.
Meringues à la crème.   Maraschino jelly.

4.
Consommé de volaille.
Boiled cod and oyster sauce.
Croustades of lobster.
Salmis de faisan aux truffes.   Grenadins de bœuf aux olives.
Boiled ham.   Roast turkey.
Roast woodcocks.   Cardons à la moëlle.
Œufs farcis à la royale.
Fondue au Parmesan.
Plum pudding.
Mince pies.
Lemon cheesecakes.   Chocolate cream.

INDEX.

Acini di pepe	*page* 233
Alouettes en caisses	118
Ancient food, On some	62
Ancore	233
Anelletti	232
Anellini ricci	232
Apple fritters	80
soufflé	267
Apricot fritters	81
Artichokes	181
to preserve	183
stalks	184
Asparagus	180
Aspic jelly	155
to dress	157
Attendance	15
Australian beef	95
Avena	233
Barbe de Capucin	214
Barde	144
Batter	78
Bavette	232
Bavettini	232
Beans, French	176
haricot	178
broad	179
dried	206
Beans (dried)	205

Beans (dried) à la maître d'hôtel.	page 207
à la Lyonnaise	207
à la sauce blanche	207
au jambon	207
au jus	207
au lard	207
aux tomates	207
recipes for	208, 209
en salade	207
purées of	208
Beef, Australian	95
fillet of	150
On a tin of	95
steak	121
à la Parisienne	122
tea	47
Beignets soufflés	77
Bills of fare	275
Bisque aux écrevisses	31
de Homard	31
Blanc	185
Boiling fowls	92
ham	93
meat	90
Boning fowls	133
Bouillabaisse	69
Bouillon	41
Brillat-Savarin	2, 7, 11, &c.
Broad beans	178
dried	206
Brocoli	187
Broths for the sick	45
Brunoise	42
Brussels sprouts	170
à la Lyonnaise	171
à la maître d'hôtel	171
au jus	171
sautés au beurre	170
Butter à la maître d'hôtel	54
melted	54

Cabbage, to steam	page 167
to boil	167, 171
red	168
red, à la Hollandaise.	168
Caisses, alouettes en	118
soles en	119
Calamari	72
Cannarune	232
Cannelli	232
Cappelletti	232
Caramel pudding	262
Cardons à la crème	186
à la moëlle	184
au jus	186
Cardoons	184
tinned	186
Carrots	191
Cases, how to make paper	117
Cassolettes de pommes de terre	112
de riz	112
Cauliflower	187
au gratin	188
Celery	186
fritters	82
in salad	214
Chapelure	67, 101
Charlotte de pommes	260
russe	260
Chaud-froid	158
Chaud-froid of fowl	159
Cheese, to cook	254
Chestnut soufflé	267
stuffing	143
Chives in salad	214
Chocolate soufflé	269
Cleanliness	18
Codfish au gratin	67
Coffee soufflé	268
Conserva di pomi d'oro	197
Consommé à la royale	43

Consommé aux chouxfleurs	page 40
aux haricots verts	40
aux pâtes d'Italie	40
aux pointes d'asperges	40
aux quenelles	40
au riz	40
de soles	38
de volaille	39, 41
aux pois	40
Cos lettuce	212
Court bouillon	62
Cream salad-dressing	224
Creams, to colour	259
Croci di Malta	233
Croquettes	114
de homard	66
de saumon	66
fish	64
Croustades	112
Croûte au pot	44
Croûtes	258
Cucumber	195
Cup custard in salad-dressing	225
Currant fritters	81
Cutlets à la Maintenon	103
mutton	99, 100
breaded	100
Dandelion	214
Dried beans	205
Drink, a new	272
Duchesses	165
Egg snow pudding	270
Eggs	244
hard boiled	253
to fry	245
to poach	43
scrambled	246
stewed	252

Eggs with a purée	page 245
Endive	178, 189
Entremets sucrés	258
Epigrams	104
mutton	104
veal	106
Farinaceous food	230
Fécule de pommes de terre	239
Fedelini	232
Fettuccie	232
Fidelini	231, 237
Fillet of beef à la Française	150
Fish au gratin	67
aux fines herbes	67
croquettes	64
quenelles	64
reliefs of	63
to cook	62
Flour, On a pinch of	49
Fondue	254, 265
Fowls, how to bone	133
cut up	136
old French way of boiling	92
roasting	152
trussing	126
for boiling	130
French beans	176
to cook	177
Fravaglie	72
Fritters	80
apple	80
apricot	81
celery	82
currant	81
flower	88
greengage	81
lemon	81
nectarine	81
orange	81

INDEX.

Fritters, peach . . . . *page* 81
    pear 81
    pineapple 82
    plum 81
    raspberry 81
    rhubarb 82
    strawberry 81
    vegetable 87
Friture 74
Fruit soufflés 268
Frying 72

Game, to roast 152
Garnishing 21
Girasole 34
Gnioccoli 233
Greengage fritters 81
Greens 167
    on toast 172

Ham, boiling a 93
Hare, roasting a 154
Haricot beans 178
    dried 206
        varieties 206
Horseradish sauce 123

Indian corn 237

Jelly, aspic 155
    to clarify 156
Jerusalem artichoke 34
Julienne 41

Kidney, omelet 250
    taste of 124
Kromeskys 85

Laitue pommée 213
    romaine 213

Lamps	page 6
Lasagne	231, 232
Lasagnette	231
Lasagnoni	232
Lemon fritters	81
Lentils	206
à la reine	206
Lettuce	189
Liaison	189
Lobster cutlets	64
soup	30
Maccaroncini	231
Maccaroni, to cook	233
Neapolitan way	234
au gratin	235
pie	236
soufflé	267
with tomatoes	234
with raù	235
di Zita	232
varieties of	230
Maccheroni grandi	231
piccoli	231
rigati	232
Maccheroncini	232
Marinade	70, 123, 150, &c.
Matelotte	68
d'anguilles	68
Mats	10
Mayonnaise	221, 226
various recipes	222
Meat salads	225, 226
Menus	10
Mince	110
of foies gras	118
of liver	118
vol-au-vent	111
Mostacciuoli	232
Moutarde de Maille	219

Moutarde, to imitate	page 219
Mushrooms	200
Mushrooms à la provençale	202
broiled	200
in cases	201
stewed	201
Mustard	219
Mustard and cress	213
Mutton, cold	107
chops	99
cutlets	99
hashed	108
leg of	107
loin of, en papillote	151
mince	110
Names, on	53
Navets glacés	191
Nasturtium flowers	214
Nectarine fritters	81
Nivernaise	43
Occhi di pernice	233
Œufs à la neige	269
au beurre noir	245
au fromage	245
au gratin	252
au miroir	245
brouillés	246
farçis	253
sur le plat	245
Oil	216
Olives in salad	226
Omelet	247
of fish	251
of kidney	250
of oyster	251
Omelette à l'Espagnole	249
au jambon	248
au lard	249

INDEX. 297

Omelette au parmesan	page 249
au Thon	251
au rhum	263
aux champignons	249
aux confitures	263
aux fines herbes	248
aux pois	250
aux pointes d'asperges	250
aux tomates	249
aux truffes	249
soufflée	264
sucrée	263
Onions	192
small white	192
in salad	214
Spanish	193, 194
Orange fritters	81
Oranges au riz meringuées	262
Ornamentation of salads	227
Oysters fried	87
in omelette	251
Croustades of	251
Palestine soup	34
Pancakes	83
Paper cases	116
Parsnips	192
Paternostri	232
Pâtes d'Italie	230
Peach fritters	81
Pear fritters	81
Peas	179, 206
dried green	206
Spanish	206, 209
Penne	232
Peperini	233
Pesci	233
Pineapple fritters	82
Plum fritters	81
Poached eggs in soup	43

Polenta	page 233
Milanese	239
Pommes au riz meringuées	261
charlotte de	260
de terre, cassolettes de	112
fécule de	239
gateau de	267
à la Lyonnaise	163
Pork, cold, to dress	110
Pot au feu	25
Potage à la bonne femme	36
à la Condé	205
à la Conti	205, 206
à la Crécy	52
à la crème d'orge	35
à la jardinière	41
à la purée de legumes	34
à la printanière	42
à la Reine	31
printanier	42
Potato chips	166
snow	164
soufflé	267
Potatoes	162
à la maître d'hôtel	163
à la Lyonnaise	163
à la J'aidit	165
to boil	162
baked	164
duchesses	165
fried	165
mashed	164, 166
sautées	163
Punte d'aghe	233
Purée, artichoke	175
endive	173
chestnut	175
mushroom	175
potage à la	174
spinach	173

Purée, sorrel	page 172
turnip tops	172
Purées	174
Purpe	72
Quenelles de veau	40
fish	64
Ramequins	257
Ramakins	257
Raspberry fritters	81
Raù	235
Recch'i prevete	232
Rhubarb fritters	82
Rice, border of	242
cassolettes	112
soufflé	266
pudding	243
how to boil	240
Risotto	241
Rissoles	113
Riz à l'Impératrice	243
à la Turque	241
Roasting	147
Gallic mode	150
game	153
poultry	152
venison	153
time required	149
Rognons au vin de Champagne	250
omelette aux	250
Rôtissoire	153
Rougets en papillote	71
Russe, dinner à la	4, 5
demi	11
Salad dressing	215, 220
Salade de homard en aspic	228
Russe	229
Salad of Australian beef	97

300 INDEX.

Salads	page 210
a profession to make	211
bacon and ham	224
eggs in	219
Salads of cooked vegetables	215
without oil	224
Salmon cutlets	66
aux concombi	66
Salpicon	85
Sauce à la maître d'hôtel	54
à la poulette	56
à l'Italienne	58
à la Périgueux	59, 145
à la tartare	57, 223
à la Provençale	59
Allemande	60
au pauvre homme	56
aux champignons	56
aux câpres	54
aux cornichons	54
Béchamel	60
bigarade	61
blanche	51
blonde	54
brown	59
Espagnole	59
Hollandaise	55
horseradish	123
Lady Peg's	61
liver	61
Mirepoix	60
piquante	57, 58
poivrade	57, 224
ravigotte	57, 223
remoulade	57, 223
Robert	57
Soubise	54, 146
suprême	60
tomato	196, 198
velouté	60

INDEX.

Sauce, white . . . . *page* 60
Savoy 167
Scarlet runners 176
Scotch kale 171
Scorze di nocelle 233
Seakale 181, 186
Selleri 232
Semenze di cicoria 233
    di mellone 233
    di peperoli 233
Semolina 237
Sippets 23
Soles en caisses 119
Sorrel 172
Soufflé 264
    apple 267
    chestnut 267
    chocolate 269
    coffee 268
    fruit 268
    maccaroni 267
    potato 267
    rice 266
    tea 269
Soupe à l'oignon 36
    à la Cussy 192
    aux choux 37
Soups, ancient 30
    au gras 34
    au maigre 34
    clear 39
    thick white 33
Spaghetti 231, 232, 237
Spinach 173
    greening 173
Sponge cake 259
Steaks and a pie 121
Stelle 233
Stelloni 232
Steps in cookery 17

Stivaletti	page 233
Stock	25
vegetable	34
Strawberry fritters	81
Stuffing, chestnut	143
truffle	143
various	144
Stuffing of vegetables	194, 199
Suc colorant	26
Sweet capsicum	229
Sweets, simple	258
Tagliarini	231
Tagliarelle	231
Talmouses à la St. Denis	257
Tea soufflé	269
Tomato sauce	196, 198
Tomatoes stuffed	199
(Italian)	200
Truffes	202
à l'Italienne	203
à la serviette	202
à la Périgueux	203
au vin de Champagne	203
sautées	202
a classical recipe for	203
Truffle stuffing	143
Trussing	116, 126
fowls	126
for boiling	130
for braising	130
for roasting	126
Tunny fish	251
Turkey	142
to braise	144
to boil	145
to garnish	145
to roast	144, 152
to stuff	143, 144
Turnip tops	172

Veal, cold, to dress . . . . *page*	110
mince	113
Veal, quenelles	40
Vegetable stock	34
marrow 189,	190
to stuff	195
Vegetables	161
to steam	162
to stuff 194,	199
Vermicelli	231
Vinaigrette sauce	193
Vinegar	216
to clarify	217
to make	216
to flavour	217
tarragon	218
aux fines herbes	218
Waiting at table	15
Wine	13

www.ingramcontent.com/pod-product-compliance
Lightning Source LLC
Chambersburg PA
CBHW022054230426
43672CB00008B/1165